STEALTH INVASION

STEALTH

INVASION

MUSLIM CONQUEST THROUGH IMMIGRATION AND RESETTLEMENT JIHAD

LEO HOHMANN

 WND Books

STEALTH INVASION

Published by WND Books, Washington, D.C. WND Books is a registered trademark of WorldNetDaily.com, Inc. ("WND")

Book designed by Mark Karis

WND Books are available at special discounts for bulk purchases. WND Books also publishes books in electronic formats. For more information call (541) 474-1776, e-mail orders@wndbooks.com or visit www.wndbooks.com.

Hardcover ISBN: 978-1-944229-58-0
eBook ISBN: 978-1-944229-59-7

Library of Congress Cataloging-in-Publication Data
Names: Hohmann, Leo, author
Title: Stealth invasion : Muslim conquest through immigration and the
    resettlement Jihad / Leo Hohmann.
Description: Washington, D.C. : WND Books, 2017. | Includes bibliographical
    references and index.
Identifiers: LCCN 2016035955 (print) | LCCN 2016050434 (ebook) | ISBN
    9781944229580 (hardcover) | ISBN 9781944229597 (ebook) | ISBN
    9781944229597 (e-book)
Subjects: LCSH: Muslims--United States. | Islamic countries--Emigration and
    immigration. | United States--Emigration and immigration. | Islamic
    countries--Emigration and immigration--Religious aspects. |
    Refugees--United States. | Refugees--Islamic countries.
Classification: LCC E184.M88 H64 2017 (print) | LCC E184.M88 (ebook) | DDC
    305.6/970973--dc23
LC record available at https://lccn.loc.gov/2016035955

Printed in the United States of America
17 18 19 20 21 LBM 9 8 7 6 5 4 3 2

CONTENTS

PREFACE

WORLD WAR III HAS BEGUN.

The one defining, devastating facet of this war is that only one side is engaged. Only one side is on high alert, filing into the trenches and preparing themselves psychologically for the next battle. Most Americans are still under the false impression that we are at peace with the world. Europe may be in crash-and-burn mode, but life in the United States is still business as usual. Oh, we have our problems, but they are nothing a new resident in the White House can't fix.

I can't blame them. This world war bears little resemblance to the first two, which were fought with massive armies gathered on a single battlefield. The enemy in World War III is stealthy, blending in with the rest of us "normal" folks and operating on several fronts with an emphasis on patience and psychological tactics. It's difficult for most Americans to recognize these intermittent battles as one coherent war, and they definitely don't know where or when to expect the next attack. It could erupt in their city, their neighborhood mall, their favorite restaurant or bar, but usually it's in someone else's. They see only bits and pieces of this war, skirmishes here and there. It's hard to connect the dots.

The enemy's attacks come in fits and spurts, but when they come they are devastating to the national psyche. As time wears on and the war progresses, the attacks will get closer together, closer to home, and more horrific. The reason they are so devastating is because they come against soft targets—people eating in restaurants, partying at nightclubs, riding trains, catching a sporting event, or out celebrating a national holiday.

World War III is being fought for a singular prize—Western civilization and who gets to run the world.

With such huge stakes, it's remarkable that so few Americans are aware of what's happening. Most of us are lost in our diversions—sports, music, movies, work, and families who need our attention. The buzz of everyday life, filled with mindless media offerings, is too noisy for reality to penetrate. So we continue life in the matrix with a false view of reality.

Meanwhile the foot soldiers in this new war have been filing into position since the early 1980s, spreading out across our country, first into our big cities but increasingly into small-town America. The vast majority of them are not sneaking across the Rio Grande to cross our southern border. They don't speak Spanish or work on construction sites.

As a journalist for more than twenty-five years I'd covered my share of immigration issues. But, like most Americans, my view of this issue came from the narrow lens of "illegal" immigration and how it affects schools, courts, jails, and job markets. In the summer of 2014, I received an e-mail from an anonymous reader who challenged me to look at one of America's most sacred political cows—legal immigration. Who was getting the majority of the coveted green cards? Where were many of our "refugees" and asylum seekers coming from? And, perhaps most important, who was getting paid by the government to "resettle" them in such nondescript American cities as Bowling Green, Kentucky; High Point, North Carolina; St. Cloud, Willmar and Owatonna, Minnesota; and Twin Falls, Idaho?

I had no inkling how to answer this reader's questions. So, I got busy. Real busy. Over the course of two years I researched and wrote more than one hundred articles on immigration for WND, focusing mostly on Muslim immigration, a subject no journalist had really explored because it goes against the political correctness movement that is sweeping our country and capturing media companies big and small. Little did I know in the summer of 2014 that, one year later, the issue of refugees—specifically Islamic refugees from Syria, Iraq, Afghanistan and elsewhere in the Middle East and North Africa—would become the story of the century.

Promises to build a wall and deal with illegal immigration, while a step in the right direction, won't solve this problem. That's because our government is busy rubber-stamping visas and welcoming into the country a mortal enemy who subscribes to an ideology based on hate and intolerance, everything our liberal Democrat friends say they stand against. We are bringing this enemy here on air-conditioned planes as legal refugees, legal guest workers, legal green-card holders, legal students, legal entrepreneurs, and legal professors and preachers.

It's happening not only in America but in Canada and Western Europe, all of which are governed by the same globalist elites. While these ruling elites may call themselves Democrats or Republicans, Tories, Christian Democrats, or Social Democrats, they share one unifying trait. They work to implement secret trade deals and mass immigration policies that inevitably erode national sovereignty, divide national populations against each other, and cause civil strife. Open borders are part of a political philosophy they espouse with religious fervor. The enemy is taking full advantage, building the ranks of its army a little more every day, every week, and every year. They're preparing the battlefield.

Only when they have sufficient strength will they start to unleash the full force of their attacks. They are now ready, especially in Europe, to move to the next phase of the war, the more violent phase. They're getting close in America, too.

Former FBI counterterrorism specialist John Guandolo, author of the book *Raising a Jihadi Generation*, said the United States is probably ten to fifteen years behind Europe in terms of the advancement of Islam and the eventual subjugation of its non-Muslim population.

"You have a different situation here. We're much larger than any of the countries in Europe, and we have some significant cultural differences. But we are making the same mistakes," Guandolo told me. "We have Jewish and Christian leaders falling over themselves to kiss the asses of Muslims, and they clearly have no clue to what Islam teaches—what

Muslims are teaching one another—nor do they understand the jihadi network here and that almost all the major U.S. Muslim organizations are dominated by the Muslim Brotherhood."[1]

If you want to understand Islam, he said, pay attention to what Muslim leaders are saying to other Muslims rather than what they are saying to non-Muslims, for that's where you'll find the truth.

Guandolo, who advises several states and their law enforcement agencies on security issues related to Islamic terrorism, told me in a series of interviews that our nation is woefully unprepared for what is coming. "I do get a lot of these questions from state leaders, and I tell them, 'You're going to see individual acts of jihad,' but you should think in terms of one precipitating event," he said.

On April 16, 2013, a group of terrorists, still unknown as of this writing, entered a power grid station in northern California, sliced AT&T telephone fibers cutting off phone service to nearby cities and fired more than one hundred rounds of .30-caliber ammunition into the radiators of seventeen transformers. Engineers were able to reroute power but it was a struggle to keep the power on during the attack.[2]

"If they had not been able to shut that down quickly, you would have had a large portion of California without power for up to a year," Guandolo told me. "We still don't know who did that, but it was a handful of individuals armed with weapons and wire cutters, and that could have been a huge precipitating event followed by riots and shootings. You just can't make this stuff up. They are preparing the battlefield in every way, and we are asleep at the wheel."

The city of Nice, on the French Riviera, was asleep on July 14, 2016. It was filled with more than forty thousand people watching a fireworks show in honor of Bastille Day. A legal Muslim immigrant from Tunisia arrived in a nineteen-ton truck, got past security by saying he was delivering ice cream and proceeded to ram the heavy truck into the crowd, killing eighty-four and wounding more than three hundred. The promenade became a bloody crime scene of severed body parts, and people running frantically in the opposite direction of the truck.

Happy chatter turned into screams of pain and horror. Among the dead were more than a dozen children. All this carnage wrought by one man behind the wheel of a truck.[3]

Three days later the promenade was reopened. Families were back out enjoying the southern France sunshine, tourists were again seen smiling and taking pictures. The grisly war zone was quickly transformed into a tranquil scene of "normal" French life. To those living in the matrix of ignorant bliss, it was almost as if the attack had never happened. Or if it did happen it did so in isolation and was unrelated to the pattern of previous jihadist attacks on France and Europe.

Less than a week later, on July 18, a small city in southern Germany was asleep. On that day, a seventeen-year-old Muslim "refugee" from Afghanistan pulled an ax out of a bag and started hacking train passengers, severely wounding five Germans.[4] The trains rolled again the next day, no worse for wear. Did it really happen?

The mayhem continued in the winter, spring, and into summer of 2016 with a bombing at the airport in Istanbul, Turkey, killing 45; an attack on the airport in Brussels, Belgium, that killed 32; a hostage-taking in Bangladesh that killed 22; a mass shooting against the Charlie Hebdo magazine office and a kosher store in Paris that killed 12; the attacks on Paris nightclubs and national soccer stadium that killed 130 and injured more than 350.

This is what the battlefield looks like in World War III—quick, surgical attacks designed to terrify the populace. Normal one day, bloody and horrific the next, then quickly scrubbed and returned to normal. The authorities, the media, all do their best to downplay the motives behind the attack. Could they be mentally ill? Perhaps a disgruntled worker or student acting out? Often it is said that life as normal should resume so the terrorists would not feel that they had won. But hadn't they?

Only one side is prepared for battle in World War III. Only one side typically has any weapons. The attackers are almost always Muslim immigrants or children of immigrants and the victims are usually unarmed civilians. The attacker is almost always shot and killed by police, leaving only a social media account and a cellphone behind as evidence of his "radicalization."

And there have been plenty of warning signs that America's Muslim population is getting restless, similar to Europe's.

Attacks carried out by Muslims in 2015–16 in the United States included the murders of five unarmed U.S. servicemen in Chattanooga, Tennessee; an attack against an office Christmas party in San Bernardino, California, killing fourteen; a knife attack that wounded four in a Columbus, Ohio, restaurant; and another knife attack by a Muslim student at University of California–Merced that wounded five.

Then on June 12, 2016, at a gay nightclub in Orlando, Florida, a Muslim-American born of immigrant parents from Afghanistan entered and began methodically mowing down patrons with a semi-automatic rifle and a pistol. He killed forty-nine and wounded dozens more in the worst terrorist attack on U.S. soil since the September 11, 2001, airplane attacks that killed more than twenty-nine hundred people.

The European Union cataloged a record number of terrorist attacks in 2015, and 2016 was on pace to surpass that record. Attacks on American soil also reached post-9/11 highs. Though the media have duly reported on many of the events I have described, most attacks never get reported in the news, especially if the attacks were against Jewish targets. Anti-Semitic attacks have skyrocketed to post–World War II highs in many of the European countries receiving the most Muslim migrants—France, Belgium, Germany, Sweden, the UK, and the Netherlands.

After nearly every one of the attacks that did get major coverage, President Barack Obama went on TV and said these attacks had nothing to do with Islam. Hillary Clinton said the same while running for president.

"Muslims are peaceful and tolerant people and have nothing whatsoever to do with terrorism," Mrs. Clinton famously said with a stern face in a November 2015 speech before the globalist Council on Foreign

Relations.[5] That statement was bizarre given the facts that have unfolded in 2015 and 2016. It certainly fails to square with the broad sweep of history dating back to the brutal Ottoman (Turkish) Empire and the hundreds of jihads launched across the Middle East before the Turks became the torchbearers for Islam.

President Obama has repeatedly given the same lip service saying ISIL, also called ISIS or the Islamic State, is not Islamic and that Islam is a religion of peace and tolerance.[6]

President George W. Bush, after the devastating terror attacks on September 11, 2001, also repeated the lie that Islam is a religion of peace, despite the fact that all of the hijackers were Muslim, that many Muslim scholars justified the attacks, and many average Muslims celebrated the attacks across the globe.

The purpose of this book is not to condemn all Muslims, but it will indict Islam, a religion of intolerance that does indeed breed violence, the worst kind of violence, against women and children, against unarmed soft targets, against the fabric of Western civilization itself.

The major media have also done their best to whitewash and obfuscate the truth about who is behind these attacks. They refuse to name the enemy: Islam. Not "radical" Islam, but regular, mainstream Islam—the kind that teaches jihad and sharia as spelled out in the Quran and the hadith. It is true that only certain Muslims take the principles of jihad seriously enough to attack us, but let's not kid ourselves and say Islam is a religion of peace and tolerance.

And make no mistake. The pace of these jihadist attacks will only increase as the U.S. government continues its suicidal policy of importing Muslim refugees and immigrants from sharia-compliant countries.

Islam has invaded America largely over a period of the last thirty years, taking advantage of liberal immigration laws. Islam has infiltrated Western democratic nations to the extent that it can now launch attacks with impunity, turning up the heat in World War III. In essence the same type of guerrilla war that has been waged against Israel for decades has now taken root and metastasized in Europe. It is about to do the same in the United States.

The only difference is Israelis realize they are in a war. Americans do not. Most Europeans are also living in denial, although they are starting to wake up. The question is, will it be too late to save their countries? While it may be too late for Germany, Belgium, and France, America is still in play.

This Islamic invasion is no accident of history. It's a well-planned attack being waged by the Muslim Brotherhood, aided by treasonous Western politicians who will lie with impunity in the faces of their constituents. They work for the globalists in America's largest corporations, banks, the United Nations, and prestigious nongovernmental organizations with lofty-sounding names like the Council on Foreign Relations. The United States is currently importing more than five thousand Muslim migrants monthly from the Middle East, Africa, and Asia, and Hillary Clinton campaigned on the promise to increase the number of Muslims coming from jihadist-infested Syria by 550 percent.

These Muslims are being brought to America with no real screening. They are questioned on whether they might have any connections to known terrorist organizations, such as ISIS or al-Qaeda. They are not asked about their beliefs in sharia or jihad. That would be profiling and is considered unconstitutional by our politically correct politicians, even though foreign nationals have no claim whatsoever to any rights under the U.S. Constitution.

Even if we did screen our Muslim immigrants properly and ask them about their allegiance to jihad and sharia, it's not a guarantee that we would filter out all of the bad apples. Not when the enemy is awake and we are asleep. The awakened enemy is constantly recruiting new adherents. A peacefully vetted refugee one day can turn into a radicalized killer the next. All it takes is an imam preaching jihad in a mosque or on a YouTube video, a willing ear, and a change of heart. Bingo: The peaceful Muslim who passed through America's vaunted screening process now becomes radicalized.

Is every Muslim a terrorist? Certainly, the majority are not. But, due to the nature of Islam, it's very difficult, often impossible, to sniff out a radicalized Muslim before he strikes. Terrorism experts tell us the process of radicalization can happen within a matter of weeks.

The players in this war have been preparing the battlefield for fifty years, secretly importing thousands of sharia-compliant Muslims into Europe, Canada, and the United States—the free world, as it is known.

And Barack Obama was the perfect president to finish the job. Obama grew up learning the principles of Islam in madrassas in Indonesia. During his eight years in office he routinely criticized Christians as intolerant bigots who cling to guns and Bibles, while he steadfastly defended Islam as a religion of peace at every opportunity. He said the sound of the Muslim call to prayer was "one of the prettiest sounds on Earth."[7] He oversaw the insertion of Islamic teachings into the school curricula associated with Common Core. He tried to strip Christians in the military of their rights even as Muslims were allowed to expand theirs. He put up barriers to true refugees, such as the persecuted Christians of Syria and Iraq, while welcoming thousands of Muslim refugees selected for permanent resettlement in the West.

Obama's policies were not merely naïve or ill-informed but intentionally destructive. We read about refugees and watch stories on the nightly news and our hearts are broken for the millions of people displaced by what seems like never-ending wars in Syria, Somalia, Afghanistan, and Iraq. But the humanitarian face of the refugee movement is not what it seems. Behind that veneer, in which some very needy people are brought to America, is what actually amounts to an invasion of sharia-adherent Muslims who have absolutely no intention of assimilating into our society and respecting American values of individual freedom, equality of women, tolerance of homosexuals, freedom of speech, and freedom of religion. They believe in an ideology that places Islam above the rest of the world, a world that was created by Allah to be subjugated by Islam. That singular goal lies at the heart of Islamic law. While many Muslims may not support violent jihad, we will explore how there are actually two forms of jihad, one of which is not violent in the traditional sense of the word. We will compare these two forms of jihad and show how they differ only in means. They work toward the same end: subjugation. Immigration at current rates will eventually lead to Muslim majorities in many Western nations and the world has no example of a Muslim-majority nation that lives under anything remotely resembling the U.S. Constitution and its Bill of Rights. The ideas of limited government, separation of powers, freedom of speech, freedom of religion, and the right to bear arms are nonexistent in Muslim-majority countries. If they do exist at all they are roundly relegated to the sidelines of society and portrayed as foreign, even dangerous, concepts propagated by the West.

So, because of the lies repeated over and over by our most prominent politicians, the Clintons, Bushes, and Obamas, along with congressmen such as House Speaker Paul Ryan and governors including Jeb Bush of Florida, John Kasich of Ohio, and Mark Dayton of Minnesota—Americans continue to live in a state of numbness. They are impervious to reality and deceived into thinking America is forever entrenched on top of the world, even as its only real source of strength is being eaten away, hollowed out from within.

When Ryan, a notorious globalist who never met an open-borders plan he did not like, was running in 2016 for reelection in Wisconsin's first district GOP primary, he sent out mailers in which he described himself as a border hawk, someone who is concerned about illegal immigration. Ryan also spoke loudly in interviews with major media outlets against Obama's plans to bring ten thousand Syrian refugees to America in 2016. Then he turned around and orchestrated a vote that fully funded the importation of all of Obama's refugees, not only from Syria but from Somalia, Sudan, Afghanistan, Iraq, Burma, and practically every other jihadist hotbed in the world.[8]

Americans want to know why. Why do establishment politicians on both the left and the right—Ryan, Bush, Obama, Kasich and Clinton—continue to place us on a path toward national suicide? Why do they continue to negotiate the same sort of secret trade deals and disastrous immigration policies that have eroded our middle class, all while telling us they are for the middle class?

Keep reading. We will answer those questions and explain how the establishment politicians, despite their rhetoric, don't really work for you, the voters and taxpayers. They work for globalist elites who fund their campaigns. The goal of these elites is global governance with the ultimate endgame being a borderless world controlled by unelected technocrats at the helm of a centrally planned global economy. But before they can implement their utopian vision of a unified socialist system under the control of a few, they must tear down what is left of the old world order—an order based on Judeo-Christian values. Islam just happens to be the perfect tool, a battering ram, for that brutal task. With each new terrorist attack, launched by people who never should have been allowed to enter the United States in the first place, we lose more of our individual freedoms. Politicians rush to enact new "security" measures, pass new gun laws, and require every American to share more of their personal data to get a driver's license, pay their bills, and hold a job.

These establishment politicians have their message reinforced by the establishment media, which never holds them accountable for their lies and half-truths. This all but guarantees the vast majority of Americans will remain ill-informed and ill-prepared for the world war that is just beginning. Middle-class Americans may sense they are under attack, but they don't understand the nature of the war.

It's time to wake up to the stealth invasion.

1

A TROJAN HORSE IN THE MAKING

The United States is under siege from within by growing armies of imported Muslims and illegals being brought here to wreck the lives of U.S. citizens by those guilty of high crimes and treason within our own government.

—WILLIAM GHEEN

ON A COOL EVENING IN EARLY MAY 2015, a sleek touring-style bus with its windows covered pulled slowly into a Shell station in Victorville, California. Under cover of darkness, the bus made a routine pit stop for fuel, snacks and cold drinks. Few people would have noticed anything out of the ordinary about this bus. What—or rather who—was inside the bus would never have been known had the driver not encountered a curious thirty-something Hispanic mother of four with a cellphone camera. She and her husband noticed something about the bus that stood out—it sported decals on both sides reading "Department of Homeland Security."[1]

As the agent responsible for the bus got out to fuel up, Anita Fuentes and her husband, a local pastor, approached him.

When Fuentes asked the driver if he was transporting illegal immigrants, he responded with the calm professionalism typical of a federal agent. "No, we ended up taking some people to a detention facility. Somalis and all the Africans," he said in a conversational tone, all caught on video and posted to YouTube.

"A detention center over here?" Fuentes asked.

"Yeah," he said.

Victorville is about 161 miles from the Mexican border.

"Is that because they're crossing the border?" Fuentes asked.

"Well they're coming in asking for asylum," he said.

"That's what it is, that special key word, huh? That's a password now?" Fuentes said, referring to the word "asylum."

The federal agent nodded. "That's what the password is now."

But when Fuentes asked about the presence of ISIS near the border, a story watchdog agency Judicial Watch had reported a month earlier in April 2015,[2] the agent's friendly tone suddenly changed.

"I'm not going to talk to you when you're recording me, ma'am," the agent said. "Any information you want, ma'am, go ahead and look it up online."

It was a dramatic case of blatant lawlessness being carried out by our own government, importing asylum seekers from a watch list country. That country, Somalia, has a place on the State Department watch list for good reason—it is known for its vitriolic hatred of America and Americans as vividly portrayed in the 2001 movie *Black Hawk Down*. The bus incident and the importation of Somalis is a slap in the face to the families who lost sons in the dusty ghettos of Mogadishu, Somalia, where they went to perform a humanitarian feeding mission but found themselves in the middle of a fierce Somali ambush. Eighteen American soldiers lost their lives that day in October 1993. Their bodies were paraded through the streets of Mogadishu and spat upon amid shouts of "Allahu Akbar!"[3]

After viewing the video from Mrs. Fuentes, I spoke with an immigration lawyer about the busload of Somali asylum seekers who were being taken to a detention center. He told me the standard procedure would be for them to be processed, given physicals, assigned to an asylum hearing and allowed to go free into the American city of their choice. The overwhelming majority will never show up for their asylum hearings. Few if any will get deported.

In fact, at least 80 percent of foreign nationals apprehended at the U.S.–Mexico border are set free and never deported back to their home countries, according to congressional testimony by Brandon Judd, president of the National Border Patrol Council. They qualify for President Obama's "catch and release" program. Others are temporarily detained but then released. Only a small percentage ever get deported.[4]

According to official Department of Homeland Security data, 688 Somalis entered the United States between 2004 and 2013 by sneaking across the border.[5] They show up at the border and claim to be asylum seekers. This after they make the grueling trip across the Horn of Africa, stow away in a commercial ship that takes them across the Atlantic Ocean and then make the long trek up through South and Central America to the U.S.–Mexican border.

While most of us have been focused on Hispanics pouring across the border, the number of non-Mexicans crossing our southern border has been growing over the years.[6] And the number of people coming to the U.S.–Mexican border from African nations with large Muslim populations has also been increasing. According to DHS data, 139 Libyans crossed into the United States between 2011 and 2013, while only twenty had made the risky journey between 2004 and 2010, when dictator Mu'ammar Gadhafi was in power. The number of asylum seekers from Eritrea and Ethiopia is also growing: 1,495 came from Eritrea between 2004 and 2013, and 5,863 came from Ethiopia. All of these nations have high rates of violence against women and homosexuals under the dictates of sharia law, and many also perform the horrific cultural practice of female genital mutilation.[7]

Contrast the treatment of the busload of Somali Muslims with another group of asylum seekers who tried to cross the U.S.-Mexico border at about the same time, in April and May 2015. A group of 27 Chaldean Christians from Iraq set out to cross the border and were detained and held for six months; five of them were charged criminally with falsifying their asylum applications and the rest were promptly deported by the Obama administration.

"This is extremely disturbing and wrong," Jim Jacobson, president of Christian Freedom International, told FoxNews.com in a September 30, 2015, report on the twenty-seven Chaldean Christians. "I've never seen anything like this and I've been doing this work for more than 20 years. Western governments should allow persecuted minority Christians asylum within their borders. This should be a priority over other asylum seekers."[8]

Those twenty-seven Iraqi Christians, unless they managed to gain asylum in Europe, were likely returned to the very place they had fled from their jihadist persecutors. One can only hope that, by the grace of God, they may have found refuge in a church building or a safe house run by other Christians. Even the United Nations–run refugee camps in the Middle East are considered extremely unsafe for Christians because of the large number of Sunni Muslims in these camps, many of them working in positions of authority.

As for the Somalis, who were almost certainly released, most will end up melting into one of America's growing Muslim enclaves, perhaps in Minneapolis, Minnesota; Columbus, Ohio; Seattle, Washington; Lewiston, Maine; Atlanta, Georgia; or sunny Southern California. All of these areas have growing Somali communities where they will be taught at their local mosques not to assimilate into American society and to disdain American concepts of individual freedom, tolerance, and democracy.

THE REFUGEE RESETTLEMENT PROGRAM

Despite all the attention grabbed by my article on the busload of Somalis sneaking across the border and being bussed into the nation's interior by DHS vehicles, there is another avenue by which sharia-compliant Muslims from Africa, the Middle East, and Asia are entering the United States. This avenue is much wider, allowing larger numbers of Islamic migrants to come, but not on foot across the treacherous border after an arduous trek and dangerous sea voyage. No, in this case, they are flown on air-conditioned airplanes straight into U.S. cities—and it's all perfectly legal, compliments of the United Nations and the U.S. government.

More than 240,000 migrants from Muslim-dominated countries find their way to the United States every year and about half of them will come on green cards, which allow them "lawful permanent residency." The United States issues approximately 1 million green cards every year, and more than 120,000 of them go to individuals from Muslim-majority countries. The average under President Obama has been 138,669 per year, according to the Senate Subcommittee on Immigration and the National Interest.[9] The green card is highly coveted because it not only gives permanent residency and work authorization but it offers the foreign national a fast track toward full U.S. citizenship, including voting rights.

In a six-year stretch under President Obama, from 2009 to 2014, the United States issued 832,014 green cards to foreign nationals from Muslim-majority countries and the administration was on pace to issue at least 1.1 million green cards to persons from these countries on the president's watch, according to a news release from Sen. Jeff Sessions on June 17, 2016.[10]

So we see that since the devastating attacks of September 11, 2001, on New York and Washington, D.C., when it would have made sense to reevaluate the country's immigration policy and scale back the numbers flooding in from the Middle East and North Africa, the United States has done just the opposite. Because of the way U.S. immigration law has been designed since 1965, those "new Americans" with green-card status will in turn be given the opportunity to bring their families into the United States.

Muslims not only come to the United States as permanently resettled refugees or employees of U.S. corporations on green cards. They also come as temporary guest workers, skilled and unskilled on the H1-B and H2-B visas, and as students at American universities. Others come from Pakistan, India, and a host of other countries to run hotels and convenience stores on the so-called entrepreneur visa. If you don't fit the bill for any of these programs, perhaps you'll get lucky in the annual

"Diversity Visa Lottery," which selects about fifty thousand foreigners annually to come to America simply because they are from a country that doesn't otherwise send many immigrants to the United States.

If you live in a Muslim country and want to come to America, do not despair. The U.S. State Department likely has a visa program under which you can migrate to the USA. Statistics show these programs have resulted in a rising percentage of overall immigrants coming from Africa, Asia, and the Middle East in recent years and a declining number from Europe and the West.[11]

ORIGINAL INTENT CORRUPTED

Refugees are different from asylum seekers, who show up uninvited at the border. Refugees, by contrast, enter the United States through a legal process that has been in effect since Congress passed the Refugee Act of 1980. The current refugee resettlement process traces its roots to the late 1970s and a tug-at-your-heartstrings piece of legislation authored by the late senator Teddy Kennedy and former senator Joe Biden.

The original intent of America's refugee program was to provide a safe haven for people fleeing communism in Southeast Asia and other parts of the Soviet bloc. Tens of thousands of Vietnamese children, many of them fathered by American GIs, found safety in the United States. Many Russians came to the United States as refugees in the 1990s.[12] But since that time the refugee program has evolved into an entirely different beast, and it has flown under the radar of the American public for thirty years.

The results have been catastrophic. We've created an emerging fifth column of Muslim migrants, transforming American culture and values, and essentially changing America by changing its people.

According to the State Department, more than one million Muslims have been legally transplanted into more than three hundred American cities and towns through the Refugee Resettlement Admissions program since the Refugee Act of 1980 was passed by Congress and signed by President Jimmy Carter. By the early 1990s America's refugee program had been hijacked by the United Nations High Commissioner for Refugees, who now hand-selects about 95 percent of all international refugees coming to the United States. You read that correctly: The United Nations chooses who comes to live within our borders. Is it any wonder that nearly half of them come from countries with active jihadist movements hostile to the United States—like Somalia, Afghanistan, Iraq, Burma, and Syria?[13]

It should be no surprise, then, that Muslims made up the single largest religious affiliation of the nearly one hundred thousand refugees sent in 2016 to American cities, according to the State Department's Refugee Processing Center database.[14] Left behind in the Middle East are the persecuted Christian and Yazidi minorities. They have been hunted down like dogs by the Sunni Muslim population—crucified, beheaded, shot, and burned alive throughout Syria and Iraq. Christians are also severely persecuted by Muslim majorities in Libya, Pakistan, Indonesia, parts of Thailand, northern Nigeria, Egypt, and Sudan, yet we don't see any monumental effort on the part of ruling Western elites to bring these persecuted Christians into safe havens or resettle them in America.

According to the 1951 Geneva Convention, a "refugee" is a person displaced by a "well-founded fear of persecution" due to their religious, political, or ethnic affiliation.[15] Under this time-honored definition, migrants seeking economic opportunity or even those fleeing wars had no standing as refugees eligible for permanent resettlement in far-off countries. There is perhaps no class of people who would fit the 1951 definition of a refugee better than the persecuted Christian minorities in today's Middle East.

Yet, instead of bringing Middle Eastern Christians to America, the Obama administration focused on bringing their persecutors—the Sunni Muslims—to the United States. In some cases, such as in Sterling Heights, Michigan, the very same vulnerable Iraqi Christian communities that did find refuge in the United States were later surprised to learn that their Muslim persecutors were now being imported into nearby neighborhoods where they are proposing to build a mega-mosque, the *Detroit Free Press* reports.[16]

The Refugee Act of 1980 gives the federal government almost exclusive authority over the nation's refugee admissions program with the president controlling the administration and Congress providing the funding. Once the UN determines which refugees to send to the United States, the executive branch takes over the vetting and placement process. In the wake of the Syrian civil war, which has created a refugee crisis of epic proportions, more than two dozen U.S. governors sent notice to President Obama that they did not trust the government's vetting process and did not wish to receive any Syrian refugees in their states. It didn't matter. Secretary of State John Kerry cited the Refugee Act in declaring that he could send the refugees wherever the feds saw fit over the objections of any mayor or governor.

The legislative foundation for the current migration mess was established long before 1980, however. The Immigration and Naturalization Act of 1965 changed the basic premise of American immigration law from a per-country quota system to one based on family reunification. Again we find a familiar figure behind this legislation. Senate Immigration Subcommittee chairman Edward "Teddy" Kennedy reassured his colleagues and the nation in 1965:

> First, our cities will not be flooded with a million immigrants annually. Under the proposed bill, the present level of immigration remains substantially the same . . . Secondly, the ethnic mix of this country will not be upset . . . Contrary to the charges in some quarters, [the bill] will not inundate America with immigrants from any one country or area, or the most populated and deprived nations of Africa and Asia . . . In the final analysis, the ethnic pattern of immigration under the proposed measure is not expected to change as sharply as the critics seem to think.[17]

Everything the good senator from Massachusetts assured us would not happen is exactly what happened. Kennedy concluded his speech with more assurances that now read like prophecies in reverse: "The bill will not flood our cities with immigrants. It will not upset the ethnic mix of our society. It will not relax the standards of admission. It will not cause American workers to lose their jobs."[18]

In 1965, Attorney General Nicholas Katzenbach also testified, "This bill is not designed to increase or accelerate the numbers of newcomers permitted to come to America. Indeed, this measure provides for an increase of only a small fraction in permissible immigration."[19]

So it can be argued that two pieces of legislation, pushed and sponsored by Teddy Kennedy, paved the way for a historic transfer of population from the Islamic Middle East, Asia, and North Africa to America, all directed by the UN and the White House. Congress, whether controlled by Democrats or Republicans, has done nothing to stem the tide.

NINE PRIVATE AGENCIES SERVE AS FRONTS FOR U.S. GOVERNMENT

The U.S. government contracts with nine volunteer agencies or VOLAGs to permanently resettle refugees into more than three hundred U.S. cities and towns. These nonprofits include:

- the U.S. Conference of Catholic Bishops
- Lutheran Immigration and Refugee Services
- Episcopal Migration Ministries
- World Relief Corp. (an arm of the National Association of Evangelicals)
- Church World Services (part of the World Council of Churches)
- the U.S. Committee for Refugees and Immigrants
- the Ethiopian Community Development Council
- the Hebrew Immigrant Aid Society
- the International Rescue Committee

These nine refugee VOLAGs have offices in more than two hundred U.S. cities and are essentially working as government contractors. They work with more than 350 subcontractors and receive government cash in return for secretly placing ever-increasing numbers of refugees throughout the United States, without the knowledge or consent of local citizens. By contracting out this resettlement work, the federal government can evade many of the state open-records laws and the federal Freedom of Information Act and conduct the nefarious colonization of American cities largely under cover of darkness.

Local newspapers typically cover the refugee issue from a flowery feature-story point of view, focusing on the refugees' tumultuous lives in their homeland and the opportunities for a "fresh start" in America. Any activists or journalists who look to give a more balanced, serious look at the refugee resettlement program are marginalized and labeled as "anti-Muslim," "Islamophobic," and even "racist" by resettlement advocates.

The federal government pays these nine primary contractors by the head—$2,025, for every refugee they resettle in the United States.[20] In return these agencies, six of which are religiously affiliated with Christian or Jewish groups, must agree not to proselytize the refugees. Yes, you read that right. Christians affiliated with the Catholic, Lutheran, Episcopalian, and evangelical church groups agree to hide the gospel from spiritually hungry Muslims.

When the federal grant monies run out, local communities are left to deal with these needy refugee populations. The Office of Refugee Resettlement reports welfare usage rates wildly out of proportion to their numbers. Even after five years, refugee welfare use is exponentially greater than that of U.S. citizens. For example, 60.2 percent of refugees still use food stamps after five years, while the rate for native-born citizens is 15.1 percent—a rate that has soared under President Obama to its highest level in history. In their first year, refugees use food stamps at a rate of 75.9 percent (90 percent for Middle Eastern refugees) and cash assistance at a rate of 46.9 percent (Americans use cash assistance at a rate of 5.3 percent). Medicaid is used by 60 percent of refugees and by 75 percent of those from the Middle East and Africa.[21]

"We are $20 trillion in debt, and cannot afford to expand our burgeoning welfare state further with populations of people supported by welfare," says James Simpson, author of *The Red-Green Axis: Refugees, Immigration and the Agenda to Erase America.*[22]

The Obama administration puts the costs of the refugee program at a little over $1.2 billion per year, but that is not a reliable figure as it does not include federal welfare benefits or the cost of educating refugee students at the state and local level. According to Robert Rector at the Heritage Foundation, the additional ten thousand refugees that Obama brought from Syria in fiscal 2016 will cost U.S. taxpayers $6.5 billion over the course of the refugees' lifetimes.[23] Sen. Jeff Sessions (R-Ala.), chairman of the Senate Subcommittee on Immigration and the National Interest, warned his colleagues in the Senate that funding for the refugee program could easily surpass $55 billion in 2016.[24]

THE ROLE OF U.S. FOREIGN POLICY IN CREATING "REFUGEES"

It could be argued that the world is awash in refugees because of the foreign policy directives of Obama and previous U.S. administrations, which helped to create the global refugee crisis in the Middle East in the first place. It was the policy of Obama and then-secretary of state Hillary Clinton that encouraged uprisings against Westernized, secular dictators in Syria, Egypt, and Libya and empowered Sunni radicals in those countries.

In Iraq, the U.S. took out the secular dictator, Saddam Hussein. Though Muslim, Saddam protected the Christian community from jihadist attacks. That singular act of regime change by President George W. Bush opened up hell's fury on Iraq's ancient Christian community, exposing more than 1.5 million Iraqi Christians to vicious attacks by both Sunni and Shiite Muslims. Pastors were abducted and killed, churches were burned, and fear struck the hearts of Iraq's Christian community starting right after Saddam's removal in 2003. This is a story the U.S. media never reported to the American people. Bush's war also led to a flood of 135,000 Iraqi refugees into the United States.[25]

By the time the last U.S. troops left Iraq under Barack Obama, there were fewer than 150,000 Christians left in the country, according to a *Wall Street Journal* report. More than 800,000 had either been killed, forced to convert, or compelled to flee the country. About 300,000 fled to Syria but then came under new attacks when the U.S.-instigated uprising against Syrian dictator Bashar al-Assad again unleashed the Sunni militants on Christians in that country.

By this time, the Christians were running out of places to hide. In the spring of 2016, the European Union (EU) conceded that a genocide against Christians was in progress in the Middle East. But did that change U.S. policy? Not one iota.

In fact, Mr. Obama doubled down and brought thousands more Syrian Sunni Muslims to America and punished a Chicago immigration lawyer who had been successful in getting Chaldean Iraqi Christians asylum in the United States. Robert DeKalaita, the hero of Iraq's Chaldean Catholics for his exemplary work in gaining them asylum in the United States since the 1990s and the first Bush war on Iraq, was convicted of "falsifying" and "embellishing" asylum applications to make it appear the Iraqi Christians' situations were worse than they actually were, according to the government. Perhaps DeKalaita, if he truly did embellish the applications, knew what was coming. It was not long after his alleged embellishments occurred that the monstrous Islamic State rose to power, sweeping across large portions of Iraq and Syria in murderous fashion. The number-one target in the crosshairs of the Islamic State is Christians.

The EU and US genocide declarations should have helped DeKalaita's case and led to the dismissal of all charges against him, but the Obama Justice Department ignored it and pressed ahead for his conviction, sending a message in the process – no migration of Christian refugees will be tolerated outside of the very few who get approved by the United Nations. Meanwhile, the UN sends more Muslim refugees to America every year and DeKalaita faces up to thirty-five years in federal prison.

George W. Bush's war on Afghanistan also unleashed a flurry of refugees into the U.S. from that hardline, sharia-compliant country, a stream that continues to this day with a fifteen-year total of just under twelve thousand, according to State Department figures. And his father's first Iraq war, code-named Desert Storm, led to about sixteen thousand Iraqi refugees coming to America.

Even President Ronald Reagan cannot be let off the hook on this issue. He supported the Afghan hard-line Islamists known as the Mujahideen, calling the militantly sharia-adherent soldiers "freedom fighters" simply because they were fighting the Russians.[26] Among the ranks of Reagan's freedom fighters was none other than Osama bin Laden, who was in the early stages of unleashing a shadowy new organization on the world. That organization was al-Qaeda, which claimed responsibility for the September 11, 2001, terror attacks on New York and Washington, D.C. As part of the Reagan CIA's "Operation Cyclone," the United States would arm and train these "freedom fighters" in their war against the Russian communists. When the Russians pulled out and the freedom fighters claimed Afghanistan for Allah, the war did not end completely. Reagan brought several thousand of his freedom fighters to the United States as refugees.

Hollywood did its part to make Americans believe that Reagan's freedom fighters were good guys who deserved a nice, comfortable life in America. The Afghans were portrayed as American-loving, freedom-pursuing superheroes in the movie *Rambo III* starring Sylvester Stallone. They joined with Rambo to help him free his old Vietnam superior officer from an evil Russian torture master. These were comrades in arms who hated communists and were willing to kill them by any means available. What's not to love about that? Why, nothing, of course, unless you consider that they were just using the Americans, thousands of whom they would attack and kill after they were rid of the Russians.

The pattern is now clear. In each of the countries where Bush,

Obama, Clinton, and Reagan supported the overthrow of secular dic-tators—especially Iraq, Libya, and Syria—the floodgates of Muslim refugees, many of whom are sharia-compliant, were opened to the West. As I will show in later chapters, sharia, or Islamic law, is in no way preferable to communist law. If only Reagan had been as aware of the dangers of sharia as he was of the threat of communism.

The annals of history reveal an ugly truth: nearly every Middle East war in which the United States has engaged has led to more Muslims migrating to the America. That's the dirty little secret of U.S. foreign policy. Go in, do a regime change, and welcome thousands of the native population to America, despite clear evidence that they will come without any intention of assimilating into American culture. To the contrary, most will come with an open hostility toward the Judeo-Christian values enshrined in the U.S. Constitution.

This, of course, plays right into the hands of the globalists at the United Nations and its supporters, who have for years seen America as a roadblock to global governance with its pesky Declaration of Independence and Bill of Rights guaranteeing certain unalienable rights "endowed by our Creator" that no government can take away. Free speech, freedom to exercise one's religion or no religion at all, freedom of the press, freedom to own firearms—none of these rights exist under Islamic law as interpreted and practiced over the last fourteen hundred years, and are in fact antithetical to it.

William Gheen, president of Americans for Legal Immigration PAC (ALIPAC), told me in a personal interview that the record immigration rates of the last forty-five years will play heavy in helping Democrats and liberal Republicans clear the last hurdle in their attempt to turn the United States into their version of a borderless utopia—something akin to the European Union.

"Obama is breaking many laws and destroying the U.S. Constitution to import as many people as possible who can be counted on to vote Democrat, oppress Americans loyal to the Constitution, and insti-tute their radical agenda for full gun confiscation," Gheen told me.

Confiscating American guns and violating the freedoms enshrined in the Bill of Rights is a job most Americans won't do. "But Obama's imported illegal aliens and Muslim refugees will," he said. "The United States is under siege from within by growing armies of imported Muslims and illegals being brought here to wreck the lives of U.S. citizens by those guilty of high crimes and treason within our own government."

While I share some of Gheen's concerns about illegals coming from Mexico and Central America, especially in the realm of jobs and the economy, at least we don't have to worry about these mostly Catholic men and women trying to implement sharia law, waging jihad on our soil, or sending their remittance checks back home to terrorists overseas.

LEAVING THE PERSECUTED BEHIND

The story of American refugee resettlement demands an examination of exactly whom the U.S. is "rescuing" from persecution. There is a class of people, the Christian minority of the Middle East, who have lived under threat of extermination for more than a century. As stated earlier, if any group fits the bill of a "refugee" as defined by the 1951 Geneva Convention—remember the key is a "well-founded fear" of persecution due to one's religious or political beliefs—it's the Christians. These minority communities are being obliterated by ISIS and other Sunni Muslim groups. The Sunnis, which represent the religious sect of Saudi Arabia, Osama bin Laden's al-Qaeda, ISIS, the al-Nusra Front, Boko Haram in Nigeria, al-Shabab in Somalia, Turkey's Islamist regime, and most of the world's most radical Muslim groups, make up the overwhelming majority of every Arab nation.

More than 13,000 Syrian refugees were sent to the United States for permanent resettlement between March 2011, when that country's civil war broke out, and October 1, 2016. At least 98 percent have been Sunni Muslim, while a paltry 0.5 percent have been Christian, according to the U.S. State Department's Refugee Processing Center database. The Christians made up 10 percent of Syria's overall population before the war started, yet they account for less than 1 percent of those Syrians being sent by the UN to the United States and many other Western democracies.

Among Iraqi refugees, nearly 70 percent of those permanently reset-tled in the United States since the second Iraq War have been Muslim.

In Somalia, more than 99 percent of the refugees escaping to America and other Western nations have been Sunni Muslim and the percentage is similar from Afghanistan.

Persecuted Christians are being left behind, their stories largely untold. I gained great insight into the plight of Christians in the Middle East when I met at the Atlanta airport with Sister Hatune Dogan, a brave little Orthodox Christian nun, a few days before Christmas in 2014.[27] Sister Hatune arrived in Atlanta for a stopover on her way back to Germany. She was dressed in traditional black garments, a habit covering her dark hair. She wore a simple wooden crucifix around her neck and carried with her a well-worn copy of the Quran, which has become her constant companion wherever she goes to teach about the current situation in the Middle East. She believes Christians in the West should learn what is written in the Muslim holy book. If they did, they would realize that the Islamic State, also called ISIS, is not doing anything that hasn't been done in the past by devout Muslims who have conquered a people they see as "infidels."

Sister Hatune's native Turkey was once almost all Christian, and by 1914 about 20 percent of the country still claimed that religious affiliation. But today, after numerous jihads and the 1915 genocide of Armenian Christians, followers of Jesus account for less than 0.2 per-cent of Turkey's population. Iraq had nearly 2 million Christians under Saddam Hussein, but now only about 150,000 remain.[28]

"Where are all these Christians? Where are these people? Just ask yourself," said the fearless nun. Born in 1970 the middle daughter of ten children, Sister Hatune learned to speak thirteen languages, but none make her more proud than her native Aramaic. "This is the language of Jesus," she told me as we sipped coffee in an Atlanta café.

The Sister Hatune Foundation works in thirty-five countries with Matthew 25:34-40 as its mission statement[29]—feeding, clothing, sheltering, and providing medical care to the poor and persecuted. She has been making regular trips to the Middle East since 2005, and ISIS presents a new challenge: trying to rescue orphaned children from its clutches. Sister Hatune regularly visits refugee camps in Iraq, Jordan, Lebanon, and Turkey. She has also sneaked into Syria to meet with Christians there.

"They need your support. Without your support they can't continue," she said. "They live like animals. Starving. No food. Unsanitary. No one should have to live like this."

It's a plight with which she is all too familiar. Her question "What happened to all the Christians?" is purely rhetorical and completely personal. Her family lived through the genocide of 1915 in Turkey, the country from which her parents fled in 1985. Her great-aunt Sarah lived through the 1915 atrocities in Zaz, a small village in southeastern Turkey. "She was eighteen years old, very beautiful," Sister Hatune recounted. "One of the Muslim men saw her and said, 'She is beautiful. She belongs to me.'"

Sarah had four brothers, a mother and father, several cousins, aunts and uncles living in the village. "Twelve in all in October 1915; they killed them in front of her eyes," Sister Hatune said with a thick accent, motioning with her hands. "Shot them in front of her eyes."

The operation was carried out by Islamic jihadists, both Turks and Kurds, with the blessing of the Turkish army. In all, 365 members of her family's church, St. Demetrios, were murdered, representing about half of the village's population. "First they shot them. More than half were still alive so they burned them alive in the church in 1915 in my village," she said, as a tear rolled down her cheek. In 1921, her great-grandmother was forced to beg her Muslim masters to let her keep one of her two children and raise him as a Christian.

This history of what it was like to live as a Christian or any non-Muslim under the Ottoman Empire is not taught to school children in America. It should be. The Ottoman Empire was the last great example of an Islamic caliphate that was allowed to expand outside the boundaries of its own nation. Until today. Now we have the Islamic State—ISIS. It is not nearly as large as the Ottoman Empire but has been allowed by the West to take large swaths of territory in Iraq and Syria and has attracted other Islamic extremist networks, such as Boko Haram in Nigeria, to pledge their allegiance to the ISIS caliphate. The Middle East was more than 95 percent Christian at the turn of the eighth century. Sadly, the Christian population has dwindled to less than 6 percent in the region today and is quickly being emptied of its remaining Christian minorities through endless jihads that have been conducted, on and off, since the time of Muhammad.[30]

The same brutal treatment that Sister Hatune's family experienced in Turkey two generations ago is now playing out under ISIS in Iraq and Syria. "The most beautiful ones they take for their wives and say 'now you have to be Muslim,'" she told me. The others are forced to convert or die. Many have been slaughtered in front of their parents. She showed me a video smuggled out of Iraq that shows three young boys, around five or six years old, being psychologically tormented by their eventual killer.

"Tell me which one should I cut first," the ISIS thug asks the Christian boys in Arabic. A long butcher knife sits on a table beside him. "Come put your head here," he says, as the boys scream in terror.

They take a step back, but the confines of the small room leave nowhere to run. When neither boy steps forward to volunteer his neck, the man yells, "Come, all of you! Come, all of you!" He grabs one of the boys. The boy screams and the other two cry.

"Are you ISIS?" the man yells over the screaming boy. "Are you ISIS?"

"No!" the boy answers through his tears.

All three were beheaded. The nun said she received the video from a relative of the boys.

In another video three Christian priests with their hands bound are shown being led out into a field. A Muslim man wrestles one priest to the ground and slices his head off. As the blood flows out of the priest's body, several hundred Muslim men can be heard yelling "Allahu Akbar!

Allahu Akbar! Allahu Akbar!"

Despite the emotional pain Sister Hatune's family has suffered at the hands of Islam, she has written more than a dozen books, which she says are fact-based from studying the Quran and the other Islamic texts. "I not write from my head. All facts," she said. "Muhammad came and he brought killing, beheading, pedophilia. He slept with a nine-year-old girl who he married when she was six years old. We know because she says it herself in the hadith. In Yemen today, where sharia is the law, they have to marry the girl before her first menstruation, maximum of age thirteen, because it is written."

Sister Hatune thumbed through her Quran and found a verse that she said leads Muslims to murder Christians in the places where Islam dominates. "Twenty-five times in Quran it says to kill Christians because we are involved in polytheism," she said, explaining that Muslims do not understand the concept of the Holy Trinity. "Also it says to not make friends with Christians."

Europe is on its way to becoming the next battleground for Islam, especially Belgium and France, where Muslims make up 6 to 10 percent of the population. Sister Hatune's adopted country of Germany is 5 percent Muslim and has more than four thousand mosques. "A mosque is not just for prayer," the nun informed me. "It is to prepare to kill the unbeliever and control the world."

There are ninety-seven verses in the Quran against the unbeliever. "And there are verses against the Christians who say God is Father, Son and Holy Spirit, or that Jesus is the Son of God. They have to be beheaded, the head cut off from the neck, or crucified. This is what the Muslims are doing. Normal Muslims, who are really Muslims, have to follow this rule," she said. "There will never be peace on Earth if these verses of the Quran are not stopped. It is in the Quran, hadith and sunna 36,800 times, the words 'cut,' 'kill' or 'attack.' How can there be peace on Earth?"

The Quran also gives Muslim men permission to rape non-Muslim girls and women who are held captive as slaves (Sura 23:5–6). In conquered cities, ISIS has marked the homes of Christians with a red symbol of the Nazarene. They are then visited by ISIS militants who bring unspeakable horrors upon the families. Sister Hatune says it is justified under Sura 5:33 in the Quran, which states: "Indeed, the penalty for those who wage war against Allah and His Messenger and strive upon earth [to cause] corruption is none but that they be killed or crucified or that their hands and feet be cut off from opposite sides or that they be exiled from the land."

Muslim apologists in the West say the verse is taken out of context by "Islamophobes," but Sister Hatune knows otherwise. "Those of us Christians from Middle East. We know them. We know their rules," she said.

Today there are fifty-seven Islamic countries represented at the United Nations by the influential Organization of Islamic Cooperation. Almost every one of these nations is sending refugees, guest workers, students, entrepreneurs, and other types of immigrants to the United States and the federal government is secretly making them your new next-door neighbors. Not only is our government resettling Muslims from hard-line sharia-adherent nations into U.S. cities and towns, but it's being done on the backs of the hardworking American taxpayers.

REFUGEES: A PROTECTED CLASS OF SUPER-AMERICANS?

The green card entitles foreign nationals to "lawful permanent residence" in the U.S. and gives them access to federal benefits, lifetime residency, work authorization, and a direct route to becoming U.S. citizens with full voting rights. It also affords them the opportunity to have their family members abroad join them here in America.

Refugees must apply for the green card one year after they are admitted into the Unites States but, unlike most other immigrants, they have instant access to a full plate of federal welfare benefits, including Temporary Assistance to Needy Families, or TANF; food stamps; the supplemental nutrition program for women, infants and children or WIC; and Medicaid. The most recent report from the U.S. Office of

Refugee Resettlement shows that 39 percent of Mideast refugees use TANF, 76 percent use Medicaid, and 90 percent use food stamps.[31]

Perhaps most infuriating to the hardworking U.S. taxpayer, refugees who come to America at age 65 or older immediately qualify for Social Security benefits.

According to a statement from the office of Sen. Jeff Sessions (R-AL), who chairs the Senate Subcommittee on Immigration and the National Interest, Census Bureau data indicate that migration to the United States from Muslim-majority countries is one of the fastest-growing group of immigrants.[32] If left in place, Obama's refugee plan would substantially boost the annual number of migrants admitted to the United States from this region. They, in turn, would be qualified to petition for their relatives to migrate to the United States. Refugee and asylee admissions from Iraq, Somalia, and Iran alone contributed 124,000 new green-card recipients from 2009 to 2013.[33]

The foreign-born population in the United States now stands at a record 41.3 million, according to analysis by the Center for Immigration Studies.[34] One-quarter of the U.S. population is now either foreign-born or has foreign-born parents, Sessions's committee reported. The Census Bureau projects the percentage of the population born outside the country will soon pass the highest percentage ever recorded and continue rising to new all-time records never before witnessed—unless Congress passes a law to reduce green card allotments.

Polling data collected by Pew Research Center show that 83 percent of the public (across all parties) "opposes this baseline and believes the level of immigration should either be frozen or reduced," Sessions reported. "By a nearly 10-1 margin, Americans of all backgrounds are united in their shared belief that companies with positions to fill should raise wages instead of bringing in new lower-wage labor from abroad."

Yet, meatpacking companies JBS Swift, Cargill, and Hormel; yogurt-maker Chobani; window maker Amesbury/Truth; and many others have for years been filling a large percentage of their job openings with refugee and immigrant labor. Small towns such as Willmar, Austin,

St. Cloud and Owatonna, Minnesota; Bowling Green, Kentucky; and Twin Falls, Idaho, are being transformed by the federal government working in concert with the United Nations and "faith-based" organizations including Lutheran Social Services and Catholic Charities.

Chobani is a textbook example of a high-profile company that moved into a town with a glitzy economic development announcement, saying it would invest more than $430 million in a new one-million-square-foot plant in Twin Falls, in 2011. The "world's largest yogurt plant" would employ six hundred people, almost all of them local, officials with the chamber of commerce and other local agencies chirped as they basked in the positive local media attention. What actually happened was that a steady stream of refugees was resettled in Twin Falls from more than a dozen different countries, filling nearly one-third of the six hundred jobs at the yogurt factory. Twin Falls has received nearly twenty-four hundred refugees since 2002.[35]

Which takes us back to the busload of Somalis at the beginning of this chapter. Clearly, one busload was not enough. Since 1983 the United States has imported 132,332 Sunni Muslims from Somalia alone. They have been secretly planted in dozens of communities. The largest number are in the Minneapolis–St. Paul region of Minnesota, followed by Columbus, Ohio; San Diego; Seattle; and Atlanta. Smaller but still significant numbers of Somalis have been distributed to cities in Maine, North Dakota, Idaho, Florida, Kentucky, Michigan, New York, New Jersey, Pennsylvania, New Hampshire, Texas, Tennessee, Oregon, Virginia, and Alaska.

The Cedar Riverside area of Minneapolis is home to the largest community of Somali refugees in America, the vast majority of whom did not illegally cross U.S. borders but were sent here legally through the United Nations refugee program supported by the White House and Congress and paid for by U.S. taxpayers. More than forty young Somali Americans have been investigated since 2007 for trying to leave the United States and join foreign terrorist organizations, including al-Qaeda–linked al-Shabab in Somalia and ISIS in Syria and Iraq.[36]

Dozens of others have been tried and convicted of providing material support to overseas terror organizations.

The situation grew so acute in April 2015, after six more Somali men were arrested for repeatedly trying to board planes for the Middle East to join ISIS, that U.S. attorney for Minnesota Andrew Luger stated publicly at a press conference that "Minnesota has a terror recruitment problem."[37] What Luger failed to say is that it's a problem of America's own making. The word *refugee* never came out of his mouth during that press conference, as that would have tipped off the public that its own government was responsible for importing this recruitment problem.

Then, on the night of September 17, 2016, just before 8 p.m, fear struck the heart of a crowded mall in the city of St. Cloud, one of the many Somali refugee distribution points in Minnesota. Twenty-two-year-old Dahir Aden, a Muslim dressed as a security guard, went on a stabbing spree, injuring ten people before he was shot dead by an off-duty police officer. He shouted references to Allah as he attacked shoppers at several locations throughout the mall, including the food court, as terrified customers ran for their lives. Aden was also heard asking people if they were Muslim before he stabbed them. It was the latest slap in the face to a state that has bent over backwards to help Somali refugees, offering them all of the goodies of life in the West, including a free education for their children, free healthcare, subsidized housing, and other benefits. Astonishingly, the *Washington Post*, reporting on the incident two days after it happened, was still withholding from its readers the fact that Aden was a refugee, reporting merely that he "moved to the United States from Kenya at age 2."[38] The United Nations runs the world's largest refugee camp in Dadaab, Kenya, housing nearly 350,000 Somalis before sending them to a multitude of Western democracies including the United States, Canada, and Europe.

On the same day, September 17, Ahmad Khan Rahami, a twenty-eight-year-old immigrant born in Afghanistan, was being sought for his alleged involvement in multiple pipe bomb attacks including one in New York's Chelsea neighborhood that injured twenty-nine people, another in Seaside Park, and a foiled bomb attack the next day near a train station in Elizabeth, New Jersey.[39]

The state of Minnesota and the federal government have gone to bizarre lengths to try to convince Somali youth not to become radicalized and succumb to the temptation to join terrorist organizations. One program, developed under Luger's leadership, attempts to buy off the Somalis' loyalty to America by providing expanded social services to the community.[40]

Another program sent more than $300,000 in federal grant money to six nonprofit organizations that work with Somali youth in Minnesota as part of a federal pilot project designed to combat violent extremism. The grant recipients include a youth sports group, a program that "empowers" Somali parents, an organization that plans to enhance youth employment opportunities, and a group that addresses mental health issues for refugees, the *Twin Cities Pioneer Press* reported. "An additional $100,000 has been set aside to help with technical assistance, professional development and other resources with the goal of keeping the programs going on their own in the future."[41]

Boston and Los Angeles are also participating in the federal pilot project, which the Obama administration launched in late 2014 to stamp out "violent extremism," a term Obama invented to blur the reality that most violent extremists are Islamic jihadists. The United States imports more than 120,000 migrants from sharia-compliant nations every year, and our politicians wonder why we have a problem with terror recruitment![42]

It seems the federal government is willing to spend all manner of taxpayer money on new social programs aimed at containing the admitted problem of radicalized Somali youth. But there is one solution—the most obvious solution—that the elite political class will not consider. They will never turn off the spigot of refugees that flows from the United Nations, to the tune of more than seven hundred Muslim refugees flowing into the United States every month from Somalia alone.

Ami Horowitz, a documentary filmmaker with the David Horowitz

Freedom Center in New York, took his cameras into the streets of Minneapolis's Cedar Riverside community in the spring of 2015 and began interviewing random Somalis—young, middle-aged, male, and female. The attitudes he found to be prevalent among so many of the Somalis would be seen by the average American as insulting and ungrateful, especially in light of congressional research that shows 90 percent of Muslim refugees in America are on food stamps and 76 percent receive Medicaid, their children are educated for free, and many of them live in subsidized housing.[43]

All but one of the twelve Somalis Horowitz interviewed on the streets of Minneapolis said they preferred sharia or Islamic law over U.S. law and the Constitution. The same number said it should be a crime to speak unfavorably about the Muslim prophet Muhammad.

You might ask, does the wider Muslim population in the United States have the same disturbing views? A 2015 study commissioned by the Center for Security Policy found that 51 percent of American Muslims preferred to live under sharia law as opposed to laws governed by the U.S. Constitution.[44] Among American Muslims under age thirty, 60 percent said they preferred to live under sharia.[45]

So, why don't American Muslims return to their native countries in the Middle East and Africa if they prefer to live under sharia? The answer can only be found by taking a look at the Muslim holy book, the Quran, along with the hadith, a compilation of the sayings of the "prophet" Muhammad. We will crack open these texts, and we will also consult the teachings of devout Muslim scholars, former Muslims, and leaders in Islamic thought.

We'll pay particular attention to a little-known Islamic concept called the *hijra*. Many Americans have heard of sharia and jihad, but few know about *hijra*, an Arab word that means "journey" or "migration." If you take away nothing else from this book, the hijra is key to understanding the mind-set of Muslim leaders when it comes to conquering new territories for Allah.

In the simplest terms, the hijra is a modern-day Trojan horse.

According to Greek legend, the ancient Greeks were at war with Troy but found they could not defeat the rival Trojans in a conventional war. So they pulled out of Troy and returned home. Later the Greeks sent an ambassador to Troy with the gift of a giant wooden horse. The Greek ambassador convinced the Trojans that this man-made horse was an offering to Athena, the goddess of war, and would make the city impregnable. After the horse was wheeled inside the city gates of Troy and welcomed by naive Trojans as something that would protect them from outside invasion, hundreds of Greeks poured out of the horse and opened the city gates for the waiting Greek army. It was a brilliant ruse that allowed the Greeks to destroy Troy from within.

In the United States today, the *hijra* is being carried out with aid from our refugee resettlement program—the horse—and our nation is being transformed from within, one city at a time. The results, as in the case of the citizens of Troy, have been disastrous and have the potential to forever change our country.

2

A MASTER PLAN

The Ikhwan [Muslim brothers] must understand that their work in America is a kind of grand jihad in eliminating and destroying the Western civilization from within and sabotaging its miserable house by their hands, and the hands of the believers, so that it is eliminated and Allah's religion is made victorious over all other religions.

—MOHAMED AKRAM, THE MUSLIM BROTHERHOOD IN NORTH AMERICA

PEOPLE OFTEN SAY there are many good Muslims, and certainly that is true. But how do you separate the good from the bad when they are coming in such large numbers from jihadist strongholds in Syria, Iraq, Afghanistan, Burma, Bosnia, Sudan, Uzbekistan, and Somalia? Some of these countries, such as Syria and Somalia, don't have reliable data for U.S. law enforcement to inspect in the vetting process.

As Robert Spencer, author of the *Jihad Watch* blog and many books about Islam, stated during a conference in California in the spring of 2016, "If I give you thirty pieces of candy and tell you ten of them are poisonous, will you eat them all?"

Brigitte Gabriel, founder of ACT for America! explored the same issue in her speech before the Family Research Council's Watchmen on the Wall Conference in June 2015. She cogently drew a parallel between the "good Muslims" and the "good Germans" during the 1930s and the "Good Russians" in the 1920s. The "good" made up the majority of their respective nations. But, as it turned out, "the peaceful majority were irrelevant."[1] The minority with the power, financing, media backers, and weapons are able to drive both the propaganda narrative and the terrorist strategy. In the case of Islam, that would include violent and nonviolent jihad against the West.

Even if we could fully vet the refugees, is past behavior an accurate predictor of future radicalization? The facts tell us it is not. As Islamic attacks proliferate in this country and around the world, the Left in America is serving up a false narrative that the answer to the problem lies in taking away the weapons of law-abiding citizens. Logic be damned.

Germany, Russia, and almost every other nation that fell to totalitarianism had to first disarm the population so a small minority of revolutionaries were the only remaining armed force. In the leftist mind-set, might makes right, and he who has the guns has the power.

Some critics say the West should not take in male Muslim immigrants of fighting age because this demographic carries the highest risk for violent jihad. They say we should accept only families. This might be helpful in the short term. But even families can turn out to be dangerous, as we will see later in this chapter with the cases of Muhammad Youssef Abdulazeez of Chattanooga, Tennessee, and Hoda Muthana of Birmingham, Alabama. Both were products of what appeared to be fully assimilated American Muslim families living in middle-class American neighborhoods. The same could be said for Omar Mateen, the son of Afghan Muslim immigrants, who carried out the Orlando, Florida, massacre of forty-nine Americans at a gay nightclub. Perhaps, then, the problem isn't that these individuals aren't Americanized enough. Maybe the problem lies in Islam itself.

I am often asked why I am so passionate in my efforts to educate Americans about the tenets of Islam. Why not just relax and welcome the needy Muslim refugees who are simply coming to Europe and America in search of a better life for themselves and their children? They come from Somalia, Syria, Afghanistan, and Iraq, just as my Catholic ancestors came to America in the 1920s from Italy and Germany.

"Aren't you being a little selfish and anti-American?" my critics say.

And what's all this stuff about sharia law?

"It's easier to get a Muslim to slander their prophet than to get an American to live under sharia," one reader told me after reading my article reporting that 51 percent of American Muslims prefer some form of sharia over U.S. law.[2] "They are fighting a battle they can't possibly win," the reader said. "Their armies are as weak as their ideology. All of the Muslim armies combined could not defeat the American military on its weakest day."

I would be the first to concede that if we look only at military capacity, there is no comparison. America wins, hands down. But what if that's the wrong comparison? One of the problems in our modern Western culture, dominated by political correctness, is that we often ask the wrong questions.

What if the question of who wins World War III has nothing to do with military might? What if Islam has another agenda, another plan, to bypass armies and navies, and what if I could prove that such a plan exists with actual documents seized by our government in raids on Muslim Brotherhood safe houses just outside of Washington, D.C.? As I will demonstrate, that's exactly what happened. The United States government is in possession of documents that are so incriminating that if average Americans read them, they would be scratching their heads, asking why every Muslim Brotherhood operative in the country is not locked up and the organization banned.

DESTROYING WESTERN SOCIETIES "FROM WITHIN"

The Muslim Brotherhood was founded in 1928 in Egypt with plans to turn that country away from the West and steer it into a system based on sharia law. By 1970 the Brotherhood had transitioned from a primarily nationalist Islamist organization to an international one with a strong plan for the world. Rather than defeat the West, it planned to infiltrate it and change it from within. This secret plan was revealed in a document, which received almost no coverage in the national media, explaining the practice of what the Muslim Brotherhood calls "civilization jihad." Unlike the violent jihad we see in daily acts of terror around the world, civilization jihad is stealthy and less obvious. It uses migration (al-hijra), high birthrates, and lack of assimilation to build a parallel society—a society within a society—in unsuspecting Western democracies where knowledge of Islam's major tenets of sharia and jihad remain abysmally thin. This strategy will allow for the taking of America without firing a shot, just like that Trojan horse mentioned earlier, by eating away at our freedoms, one bite at a time. It may take fifty or even a hundred years to complete the takeover, but that's okay. Islam is in this fight for the long term and can patiently wait for the attainment of its ultimate goal, which is nothing less than the replacement of the U.S. Constitution and the subjugation of the people it governs.

If this sounds conspiratorial, it is. Allow me to let the documents speak for themselves.

"An Explanatory Memorandum: On the General Strategic Goal for the Group in North America" was written by Mohamed Akram and published on May 2, 1991. It was seized in 2004 by FBI agents during a raid on a Muslim Brotherhood safe house in northern Virginia and presented as evidence in the Holy Land Foundation trial of 2007 in Dallas, Texas. This was the largest terror-financing trial ever conducted on U.S. soil and led to the conviction of five American Muslims caught sending money and aid to Hamas, a group of anti-Israel, anti-Christian militants recognized by the U.S. State Department as an international terrorist organization.

The "Explanatory Memorandum" has a lot to say about Muslim settlements planted in the United States, but its author could not have envisioned in the late 1980s the level to which the U.S. government would help the Brotherhood accomplish its goals:

> The process of settlement is a "civilization jihadist process" with all the word means," according to this document. "The brothers must understand that their work in America is a kind of grand jihad in eliminating and destroying the Western civilization from within and

sabotaging its miserable house by their hands, and the hands of the believers, so that it is eliminated and Allah's religion is made victorious over all other religions.[3]

Discover the Networks, a website that tracks leftist and Islamist organizations, has stated that Akram's document, at its heart, "details a plan to conquer and Islamize the United States—not as an ultimate objective, but merely as a stepping stone toward the larger goal of one day creating 'the global Islamic state.'" To accomplish this goal, Akram and the Brotherhood resolved to "settle" Islam and the Islamic movement within the United States so the Muslim religion could be enabled within the "souls, minds and the lives of the people of the country."[4]

The Network added:

> Akram explained that this could be accomplished "through the establishment of firmly-rooted organizations on whose bases civilization, structure and testimony are built." He urged Muslim leaders to make "a shift from the collision mentality to the absorption mentality," meaning that they should abandon any tactics involving defiance or confrontation, and seek instead to implant into the larger society a host of *seemingly benign* Islamic groups with *ostensibly unobjectionable motives*; once those groups had gained a measure of public acceptance, they would be in a position to more effectively promote *societal transformation* by the old Communist technique of boring from within.[5]

"The heart and the core' of this strategy," said Akram, "was contingent upon these groups' ability to develop 'a mastery of the art of "coalitions."'"[6] In short, by working closely with various non-Muslim allies on the left, they could gain far more influence and accomplish far more of their agenda than if they worked alone. Enter the VOLAGs we discussed in chapter 1—Christian, Jewish and secular agencies that work to resettle refugees into U.S. cities and towns.

Muslim Brotherhood front groups, such as the Islamic Society of North America and the Islamic Circle of North America, work hard to establish interfaith relationships with well-meaning but blind Christian and Jewish groups in almost every community that has a sizable Muslim community. If you can head off the Christians and Jews, who are Islam's natural spiritual enemies, then you hold the upper hand in that community, even if you represent only a tiny minority. We'll explore further in chapter 5 the interfaith strategy and how devastating it can be for Christian communities.

On the last page of the "Explanatory Memorandum" is a list of twenty-nine organizations established within the United States with the specific goal of destroying our country from within.[7] Number one on the list is the Islamic Society of North America, or ISNA, several officers of which became advisers to President Obama. Not surprising, then, is Obama's determination to resettle record numbers of Muslims in the United States and his refusal to point to Islam as a motivating factor in terrorist attacks. "We not only have the fox watching the henhouse," said Gabriel in regard to ISNA, "we have the fox inside the White House dictating policy."[8]

Number two on the list is the Muslim Student Association.[9] The MSA has more chapters on U.S. college campuses than the Democrat and Republican parties combined. Established in 1963 at the University of Illinois by the Muslim Brotherhood, today MSA chapters cover the map. The organization was listed by the NYPD in 2007 as a "radicalization incubator."[10] And if the group's "pledge of allegiance" is any indicator of the spirit of the group, then I suspect they are correct. It says, "Allah is our objective. The Prophet is our leader. Quran is our law. Jihad is our way. Dying in the way of Allah is our highest hope." Is it any wonder that American universities have become infestations of anti-Israel hatred, where naive American teenagers walk in with no opinions about the Israeli-Palestinian conflict and walk out a few years later as activists in the cause of Hamas and the Muslim Brotherhood?

Another Muslim Brotherhood front group is the Council on American-Islamic Relations, or CAIR, which focuses on Muslim civil liberties, using America's freedoms spelled out in the Bill of Rights against us in an effort to get schools, police, businesses, and local governments to bow to Muslim demands. Whenever a Muslim is suspected of terrorist activity, CAIR can usually be found defending them, lamenting the violation of their "rights" and promising us that if it was a terrorist attack, it had nothing to do with Islam.

Another prominent Muslim group set up by the Muslim Brotherhood is the Islamic Circle of North America, which gets involved in interfaith movements, playing on the good faith of Christians seeking to reach out to their fellow Muslim citizens and spreading the damaging lie that Christians and Jews worship the "same god" as Muslims.

The North American Islamic Trust (NAIT) also was noted in the list of organizations working to subvert the United States from within. NAIT holds the deed to roughly 25 percent of the mosques in North America.[11]

The apparatus is in place in the United States, as established by the Muslim Brotherhood, and the process of civilization jihad is well under way. All that is needed is to build up the Muslim population to a more formidable level.

THE HIJRA (MIGRATION) TO EUROPE AND AMERICA

As hundreds of thousands of Muslim refugees flooded into Europe in the summer of 2015, one had to ask, why there? Why would a devout Muslim pick up and travel to an infidel nation such as Germany, Sweden, Belgium, France, or England, and on to the United States, where alcohol flows freely, pornography is found in corner stores, and where women have rights equal to men? Remember: only about 50 percent of those migrants showing up in Europe in 2015 came from war-torn Syria.[12] Others came from Afghanistan, Iraq, Pakistan, Somalia, and other nations throughout North Africa and the Middle East.

Why did none of them try to storm the borders of Iran, Pakistan, Saudi Arabia, or the wealthy Gulf States? Those countries were certainly closer and would have made for a far less treacherous journey. Wouldn't it make sense that a Muslim would want to live in a Muslim country under Islamic law? And if the Somalis interviewed by Ami Horowitz in his video documentary are so unhappy with life in America, why do they stay? Why do their compatriots from Somalia keep coming to join them in America at a rate of five thousand to ten thousand per year?

Dr. Mark Christian is a former Sunni Muslim who grew up in Egypt the son of a Muslim Brotherhood father and became a child imam after memorizing two-thirds of the Quran by age fourteen. He says the answer to these questions lies in the Quran: "Whoever emigrates for the cause of Allah will find on the earth many locations and abundance," it says. "And whoever leaves his home as an emigrant to Allah and His Messenger and then death overtakes him, his reward has already become incumbent upon Allah. And Allah is ever Forgiving and Merciful" (Quran 4:100).

"Why did the Muslims move, as refugees, north and northwest instead of south (toward Saudi Arabia) and west (into North Africa)? Because those lands are already Islamic and do not need to be conquered," said Dr. Christian, who changed his name from Muhammad Abdullah and converted to Christianity in his late twenties. "They also know that the cradle to grave benefits are in Europe and in America; therefore, their incomes would increase, sometimes by a factor of ten, and they have to do nothing to receive and keep those benefits."[13]

The Muslim doctrine of migration isn't a modern concept. It stems from the idea that Muhammad himself made the hijra from Mecca to Medina in the seventh century. It proved highly successful in spreading the "religion of peace," as Muhammad found vulnerable tribes he could attack and conquer, claiming their treasures, land, and women as booty, then move on in a stronger position than before. Muhammad personally beheaded between six hundred and nine hundred Jewish men and boys at the Battle of the Trench outside Medina in AD 627.

"And this is how he became victorious and after the migration this is when he became more successful," Christian said. Muhammad's example is clear—make hijra and achieve success for Islam.[14]

HIJRA SECOND ONLY TO JIHAD IN ISLAM

Hijra is looked upon very highly in Islam, Dr. Christian explains. "Dying in jihad is number one in terms of the merit it will gain a believer after death, but hijra is right there next to it, very, very close to jihad." As a matter of fact, the doctrine, as interpreted by Muslim scholars, says that if the person dies while he is away from his hometown, he is considered a martyr. "He doesn't have to blow himself up," says Dr. Christian. "If he dies in London, he is going to heaven."[15]

That's because Islam, unlike Christianity and Judaism, is not merely a religious system. About 80 percent of the Quran speaks of political and civil empowerment of Muslims, and only 20 percent about religious concepts. Most of what Muhammad said and modeled for his followers was about conquest and growing the base.

"Islam as a political movement looks for expansion," Christian said. "First and foremost it's a political ideology and, number-two, it's expansionist. It's about how to establish your leadership in a region and very important how to expand, pushing those borders a little bit every day."[16]

Americans tend to view the world from their own narrow scope, believing that other cultures are like their own, undergirded by tolerance and pluralism. This is simply not the case with Islam, which sees itself as superior in every way to Western culture, which must be subjugated and brought under the umbrella of Islam. If it can't be done militarily, it will be done demographically through civilization jihad.

"America is unique in this way: it's the biggest, most successful nation and yet it doesn't measure its success in taking over other nations but by liberating other nations," Christian says. "America is very different in that way, so Americans have difficulty understanding Islamic ideology. Islam is an ever-expanding political empire that is to continue expanding until it controls every corner of the earth. That's why any Muslim on *hijra* is praised because he is bringing the word of Allah into a place where it did not exist before."[17]

Which brings us right back to Muslim resettlement in the United States. *Hijra* explains in no uncertain terms why Somali refugees, who are acclimated to a hot desert climate, are willing to go to Anchorage, Alaska, to start a colony there for Allah. The U.S. State Department has sent so many Muslims from Somalia and other Middle Eastern nations to Alaska that there are now enough to support a large mosque in Anchorage. And that's why the Saudi royal family is happy to fork over thousands of dollars every time a new mosque is needed in America. This is not like a Christian family sending money to an overseas mission for a church planting. This is about taking a long-term view toward political domination.

"You move to Alaska, and you are building a mosque in Alaska where there was no mosque before; you are bringing the word of Allah to Alaska, a place that it did not exist before," Christian said.[18]

POLITICAL CORRECTNESS RUN AMOK

Presidential candidate Dr. Ben Carson's comment in September 2015 that he would not support a sharia-compliant Muslim for president because Islamic law is incompatible with the U.S. Constitution led to the former brain surgeon's roasting among media pundits and politicians of all stripes.

He was excoriated by CAIR, a spinoff from the extremist Muslim Brotherhood, and other American Muslim groups as "anti-Muslim," "bigoted," even "anti-American." In short, he was unfit for office, they said. Any candidate who would place the long-term interests of American citizens before those of the global Muslim Brotherhood and its radical front groups must be destroyed, and the liberal U.S. media was more than happy to assist in the assault on Carson. When he made those comments, Carson was consistently polling among the top tier of two or three GOP front-runners in the race for the GOP nomination. But within a few weeks, he would be a political has-been, unable to survive the barrage of negative media.

"For any candidate to suggest that someone should not be elected president because of what he or she may believe is nothing short of religious bigotry," said Rep. Andre Carson (D-IN), one of two Muslim congressmen in the U.S. House of Representatives.[19]

BUT WHAT DO AMERICAN MUSLIMS BELIEVE?

CAIR, which was most vocal in its calls for Carson's withdrawal from the GOP presidential race, claims to speak for American Muslims. The organization has a long history of ties to terrorists, as documented by WND's "Rogues gallery of terror-tied leaders," but it is still treated by most U.S. media as the Muslim equivalent of the American Civil Liberties Union. According to a local newspaper report, Omar Ahmad, a CAIR founder, told a conference hall packed with California Muslims in July 1998 that Islam isn't in America to be equal to any other faith, but to become dominant. The reporter paraphrased Ahmad, saying, "The Quran . . . should be the highest authority in America, and Islam the only accepted religion on earth."[20]

When CAIR issued a statement in 2003 denying that Ahmad made the remarks and claiming the paper had issued a retraction, WND news editor Art Moore talked to the reporter and two of her editors and found that they stood by the story. Moore then spoke with CAIR national spokesman Ibrahim Hooper, who repeated the claim that the paper had issued a retraction. When Moore informed Hooper that the reporter and the editors stood by the story, the CAIR communications director abruptly ended the call. But he called back a few minutes later saying he wanted to amend CAIR's statement to say the Muslim organization was seeking a retraction.[21] Three years later, however, when the issue came up again, CAIR still had not contacted the paper.[22]

On April 4, 1993, Hooper told a reporter for the Minneapolis *StarTribune*: "I wouldn't want to create the impression that I wouldn't like the government of the United States to be Islamic sometime in the future."[23] Hooper appeared on Michael Medved's radio show in October 2003 and said: "If Muslims ever become a majority in the United States, it would be safe to assume that they would want to replace the U.S. Constitution with Islamic law, as most Muslims believe that God's law is superior to man-made law."

Other CAIR leaders also "express their contempt for the United States," reports Middle East scholar Daniel Pipes. Ihsan Bagby of CAIR's

Washington office said Muslims "can never be full citizens of this country," referring to the United States, "because there is no way we can be fully committed to the institutions and ideologies of this country," Pipes reported in his 2006 article, "CAIR Islamists Fooling the Government."

Pipes also noted that Parvez Ahmed, who followed Ahmad as CAIR chairman, touted the virtues of Islamic democracy in 2004 by portraying the Afghan constitutional process as superior to the U.S. Constitution. Ahmed was quoted in the *Orlando Sentinel* as saying: "The new Afghan constitution shows that the constitution of a Muslim nation can be democratic and yet not contradict the essence of Islam."

I REPEAT: 51 PERCENT OF U.S. MUSLIMS PREFER SHARIA!

There are now an estimated 3.3 million Muslims residing in the United States as citizens or with permanent legal status,[24] and more than 240,000 new Muslim residents per year enter our country as refugees, on green cards, temporary work visas, and student-based visas. Unfortunately, as noted earlier, 51 percent of American Muslims would prefer to have their own sharia courts outside of the legal system ruled by the U.S. Constitution. Worse, nearly a quarter believe the use of violent jihad is justified in establishing sharia.[25]

"That would translate into roughly 300,000 Muslims living in the United States who believe that Sharia is 'The Muslim God Allah's law that Muslims must follow and impose worldwide by Jihad,'" wrote Frank Gaffney Jr., president of the Center for Security Policy, who served under President Reagan as assistant secretary of defense for international security affairs.[26] A study by the nonpartisan Pew Research Center also found about the same number of European Muslims prefer some form of sharia law over the laws of their host nation.[27]

All of these statements by prominent Muslim groups in the United States seem to support, rather than contradict, Dr. Carson's statements about sharia and the Constitution. Nevertheless, the American public is being told there is nothing to be concerned about with regard to the increasing Muslim presence in the United States.

SPLC SAYS, "NO WORRIES"

Along with CAIR, the Southern Poverty Law Center takes great strides to assure the American people that concerns about Islamic law, or sharia, is a fiction being peddled by unreliable "conspiracy theorists." On its Teaching Tolerance website, it quotes from an Islam-loving document titled "What Is the Truth About American Muslims? Questions and Answers." This document says sharia is essentially no different from any other religious code of conduct and compares it favorably to Judaism.[28]

The SPLC asks, "Do American Muslims want to replace the U.S. Constitution with Sharia?" It then provides the following answer:

> No. American Muslims overwhelmingly support the U.S. Constitution and do not seek to replace it with Sharia or Islamic law. The vast majority of American Muslims understand Sharia as a personal, religious obligation governing the practice of their faith, not as something American governments should enforce.[29]

The facts, however, reveal that Islamic tribunals are already allowed in matters of family law, with eighty-five of them operating in the UK offering binding arbitration. An attempt to set up the first sharia court in the United States, in Irvine, Texas, was blocked by alert and courageous Mayor Beth Van Duyne and the Irvine City Council.[30]

These sharia tribunals serve as a parallel legal system within Western democracies for Muslims and are especially destructive for Muslim women, many of whom fled the Middle East hoping to get away from these barbaric, seventh-century dictates. Followers of Islam "see Sharia as the law of God, revealed through divine revelation," according to the *Stanford Journal of International Relations*. "They view Sharia as the embodiment of social justice—the only body of law under which civil and personal matters should be adjudicated."

Since 2007, the journal reports, sharia courts in Britain "have issued hundreds of rulings . . . concerning marriage and divorce, finances, inheritances and domestic abuse criminal proceedings."[31]

The *Stanford Journal*, hardly a bastion of right-wing "Islamophobia," after examining the issue of whether Western democracies should enter-tain sharia courts, concluded that "Sharia is a dangerous doctrine of civil arbitration, and [we] advocate for its rejection from binding arbitration."[32]

But the hard-core Left, as reflected by the SPLC, is not to be swayed by history or scholarly research. They maintain that if a Roman Catholic or an Orthodox Jewish family or business is allowed to work out dif-ferences among themselves according to their own religious laws, as a form of private arbitration, then Muslims in America should have the same rights. Roman Catholics and Jews, however, don't believe, as do sharia-compliant Muslims, that it's okay to beat one's wife if she refuses to have sex. Nor do Catholics or Jews believe that slandering Jesus or Moses makes one worthy of extreme punishment up to and including death. A sharia-compliant Muslim absolutely believes that death is a just penalty for blaspheming Allah or his prophet, Muhammad.

The *American Catholic* magazine delved into the issue in 2010 when it asked, "Is Sharia compatible with the U.S. Constitution?"

"The simple answer is of course, 'no,'" the magazine concluded and then listed thirteen reasons why. Number four on the list read, "Instead of precedents and codes, Sharia relies on medieval jurist's manuals and collections of non-binding legal opinions, or fatwas, issued by religious scholars (*ulama*, particularly a mufti); these can be made binding for a particular case at the discretion of a judge."

But let's turn to Muslim leaders themselves to see what they say. While speaking at an "Islamophobia" panel discussion hosted by Florida Atlantic University's Muslim Student Association—which is a front for the Muslim Brotherhood—in May 2016, Dr. Bassem Al-Halabi, a professor of computer and electrical engineering at the university, openly stated his preference for sharia law in the United States. In making his case for sharia, incredibly, he stated:

> Where there is no Sharia, Islamic Sharia, [people] die in dozens and
> hundreds every day because of organized crime. People kill people,
> other people, or steal pizza for ten dollars, and so—so when Islamic
> Sharia is saying about capital punishment—so even though it sounds

like it is severe, but if that is the solution to prevent any crimes, then it still has a lot of rules and regulations. I will just mention one and stop here, which is, let's say, cutting off the hands of a person if they steal. It sounds very severe. It sounds very barbaric, I know. But if it takes one or two people to have their hands cut off, and then there's no more stealing and there's no more stealing in the whole nation—that's a much better resolution than having hundreds of people die every day.[33]

Amazingly, Halabi suffered no consequences for his statement and still holds his job at Florida Atlantic as of this writing. Imagine if a Jewish or Christian professor had advocated a return to strict Mosaic law and the stoning of adulterers. Somehow, I don't believe he or she would still be employed at Florida Atlantic University.

WHAT DO MUSLIM SCHOLARS SAY ABOUT WESTERN DEMOCRACY?

Yusuf al-Qaradawi, a Sunni Muslim cleric and head of the European Council for Fatwa and Research, is quoted in "The Islamization of the West" by Patrick Sookhdeo, as saying: "Islam entered Europe twice and left it. . . . Perhaps the next conquest, Allah willing, will be by means of preaching and ideology. The conquest need not necessarily be by the sword. . . . Perhaps we will conquer these lands without armies. We want an army of preachers and teachers who will present Islam in all languages and in all dialects."[34]

Well-known British Islamist Anjem Choudary spoke similarly in a February 2010 interview with Iran's Press TV. "Our objectives," he said, are "to invite the societies in which we live to think about Islam as an alternative way of life . . . and ultimately, as well, to establish the Sharia on state level."[35]

That hardly sounds like a man teaching Islam solely as a "personal, religious obligation," as the SPLC assures us.

In December 2015, prominent Canadian imam Mazin Abdul-Adhim urged Muslims everywhere to help fund Syrian refugees on their hijra to the West. He also said that the only way to prevent another refugee crisis like the one in Syria is to build a worldwide Islamic caliphate. In a fiery sermon at an Islamic conference on the grounds of Mohawk College in Hamilton, Ontario, Abdul-Adhim alleged that Western powers have caused all the bloodshed in the Middle East and will not relent in their assault against the *ummah*, or global Islamic community, until the *Khilafa*, or caliphate, is implemented.

"The problem is that we don't understand our own system—the Khilafa (caliphate)," he said. "And therefore, how do we support the people of Syria? We must send money and help the refugees that are coming here in every way that we can. . . . So we are calling, as an ummah, the people of Syria and everywhere around the world . . . for the best system that exists on earth from the designer of the universe."[36] That "best system," of course, is sharia.

While calling for the full implementation of a global caliphate, the Canadian imam made it clear that ISIS was *not* the caliphate he envisioned. Rather, he sees a legitimate caliphate spreading through ideas. (His beef with ISIS seemed to boil down to tactics, not its strategic goal of the entire globe under the control of Islamic law.)

Abdul-Adhim, a native of Iraq, now lives and preaches in London, Ontario, about an hour's drive from the U.S.–Canadian border at Michigan. The zealous imam, who could pass for a Baptist youth minister in his Western attire and stylish haircut, has an active YouTube channel with more than a thousand subscribers.[37] He is also approaching two thousand followers on his Facebook page,[38] where he recently posted a link to a video denying that the Holocaust ever took place.[39]

"[According to Abdul-Adhim], helping Syrian refugees coming to Canada and building an Islamic caliphate are part of the same cause," the *Toronto Sun* reported.[40]

"You look at the justice of the ruling system . . . and the removal of racism that the unity of Islam brings, the economic justice, the land laws and the releasing of the monopolies and the hoarding, and a more just currency system, and the public property laws of Islam that released all this oil wealth and so forth that is being locked to a few individuals," he went on while standing beside the flag and banner of Hizb ut-Tahrir, a global organization that promotes the unification of all Muslim countries as one caliphate. "It brings justice to the world. And you compare this to what the colonialists are constantly trying to push on us," he continued. "Look at what they have. They have how many single mothers?"

Abdul-Adhim derided those Westerners who criticize Muslim women for wearing the *hijab*, or female head covering. "So they talk about hijab. How are their women treated in society other than an object to be looked at, and to be used and abused?" he asked. "Look at the alcohol. The amount of alcohol that is being drunk. . . . Is this what we want to bring to Islamic lands? The depression. Right now eighty people own as much wealth as 3.5 billion on earth. Is this the economy we want? Would anybody in their right mind, Muslim or non-Muslim, want this system to replace a significantly superior system?"

He continued his diatribe against "colonial powers," accusing them of killing half a million children in Iraq, destroying Iraq and Afghanistan, and now destroying Syria. "Name it. Name one place they didn't turn into a prostitution center," he told his audience, concluding that the Islamic doctrine of hijra could cure the West of all these ills.

Not surprisingly, Mohawk College, the scene of this tirade, has since distanced itself from Abdul-Adhim.

ESTABLISHING THE CALIPHATE THROUGH MIGRATION

In his presentation at Mohawk, Abdul-Adhim condemned modern Muslims for talking about the hijra as though it were "some spiritual journey or moving from oppression to justice." He wants Muslims to stop spiritualizing Islamic concepts such as hijra and to, instead, take them literally. Properly understood, he said, the hijra should be seen as nothing short of "the symbol of the establishment of the political authority of Islam." After all, Muhammad went from "having no political authority to being a ruler," thanks to his migration to Medina, said Abdul-Adhim. "From having no army to having established the military protection for Islam. That's what the hijra is. But how did he achieve it? He achieved it by spreading ideas."

These ideas can be spread peacefully through civilization jihad, also called "stealth" jihad, as described in the Muslim Brotherhood's "Explanatory Memorandum," discussed earlier, which explains how the Brotherhood intends to infiltrate and destroy the United States from within. How? By using liberal immigration laws and the country's own tradition of tolerance and civil rights.

According to Abdul-Adhim, Muhammad spent two years teaching Islamic ideas to the people of Medina. "It's a major component. One of the last steps in how to establish a (Islamic) state, and it's established by spreading ideas," he said. "If the ummah understands what is required of us as Muslims, what does a caliphate look like? What a system of Islam looks like, and how to re-establish caliphate, according to the method of (Muhammad), the ummah will rise up and know exactly what we have to do.

"That's the cause of the whole problem," he continued. "It's a lack of understanding. It's not a lack of military power—we have more military power than anyone else in the whole world. It's not a lack of resources or wealth; we have the youngest and strongest demographic in the world. That's not our problem. The problem is we don't understand our own system, the caliphate."

With the help of leaders like Abdul-Adhim, more and more Muslims are waking up to the calling of Islam as originally expressed by the prophet Muhammad in the Quran.

William Wagner, writing for the Family Research Council, noted that

> with the patient planting of new enclaves, the process of establishing the parallel society and political system has begun. Those behind this process seem willing to master an understanding of the occupied country's government and legal system, systematically dismantling it while building the framework for an Islamic theocracy as its replacement. Such a replacement, when complete, dogmatically declares a different kind of absolute than the self-evident Truths, which undergird the American Constitution.[41]

John Guandolo, a former Marine officer who served in the first Iraq war and later became a counterterrorism expert for the FBI, also warns that it's not just the threat of terrorism that the U.S. government should be concerned about from the growing Muslim enclaves in American cities.

Guandolo reports that another one of the "gems" discovered in the 2004 FBI raid of the Brotherhood's safe house in Annandale, Virginia, was a recording of a senior Brotherhood leader speaking to a group of Muslim Brothers in Missouri. That recording revealed the Brotherhood has "numerous training camps inside America and conducted regular firearms training," according to Guandolo.[42]

"To be clear, they are not planning on conducting violent actions in the immediate future, but are planning for 'Zero Hour'—their term for when the violent jihad will begin when the time is right," Guandolo writes on his website, Understanding the Threat. "They may wait until an outside influence from a foreign power or a major event initiates conflict, and then the Islamic Movement can begin the jihad and act independently or as an ally for a hostile foreign power such as Iran or China."[43]

Guandolo further notes that the Muslim Brotherhood's five-phase "World Underground Movement Plan"[44]—discovered in the 2004 FBI raid—states that in phase two they focus on "Establishing a shadow government (secret) within the government."

The purpose is to have operatives on the inside of our government who will serve as the leadership for the Islamic Movement when they seize power in the United States, according to Guandolo. "Until then, their role is to (1) gather intelligence and (2) conduct influence operations at all levels of the society, especially within the decision-making process. This is much more a counterintelligence and espionage issue than it is a 'terrorism' matter. The enemy is preparing the battlefield now for the eventual battle to come."[45]

MUSLIM BROTHERHOOD GROUPS CRAFT THE DIALOGUE

The power and influence of American Muslim organizations such as CAIR, MSA, and ISNA have never been more obvious.

After the December 2, 2015, terror attack by Illinois native Syed Farook and his jihadist, Pakistani wife, Tashfeen Malik, which killed fourteen people at a Christmas party in San Bernardino, CAIR staged a bizarre nationally televised press conference. Within a few hours of the attack and before the FBI had even declared it an act of terrorism, CAIR trotted out Farook's brother-in-law, who said he was sorry for the tragic deaths. CAIR's California chapter president then said the attacks were work-related and had nothing to do with Islam, a fact that was quickly debunked by FBI investigators, who found the couple had been in touch with terrorist networks and had spent more than a year planning for the attack. Farook had brought his wife to the United States from Saudi Arabia on a fiancée visa. Ironically, despite her obvious adherence to sharia and radical Salafist Sunni Islam, evident from the burqa she wore in her official passport photo, she passed unnoticed through the U.S. State Department's vaunted background screening process.

CAIR is further crafting their false narrative by working with the military and law enforcement agencies to make sure Muslims are granted certain privileges, whether it be in the way police are allowed to investigate Muslim suspects or concessions for Muslim members of the military. The group went so far as to file a civil suit against the New York Police Department because a Muslim officer was not allowed to grow out his beard, as it was a violation of department policy.[46]

In the case of the deadly Fort Hood, Texas, attack by Army Maj. Nidal Hasan, who in 2009 gunned down thirteen of his fellow soldiers, the Obama administration directed that the case be investigated, not as an act of terrorism, but as workplace violence.[47]

Countless private businesses in the United States have been sued for not allowing Muslim employees to have time off for Muslim holidays and daily prayer times or for not allowing Muslim women to wear the hijab at work.

In 2011, the FBI, at CAIR's insistence, scrubbed all of its training manuals of all references to Islam that were deemed offensive to Muslims. The list goes on for examples of CAIR's influence and power in the United States.

BRINGING THE TERROR TO OUR STREETS

Despite the indisputable reality that a growing number of American Muslims are awakening to the possibilities of jihad, our government and the major media outlets appear blind to the risks of importing ever-larger numbers of un-vetted (and un-vettable) Muslims into the country. Let's take a look at just a few of the cases in which this liberal immigration policy has backfired on the United States, where Muslim immigrants or sons and daughters of immigrants, turned into terrorists.

The 2013 Boston Marathon bombers, Tamerlan and Dzhokhar Tsarnaev, were natives of Dagestan whose father came to the United States as a tourist in 2002 and was later granted political asylum by the U.S. government. They attended the Islamic Society of Boston, a notoriously radical mosque under the influence of the Muslim Brotherhood, where they met fellow Muslims who preached hatred for America.

Muhammad Abdulazeez, the Chattanooga shooter, emigrated to the United States from Kuwait at the age of six and was one of his high school's most popular students. He earned an engineering degree from the University of Tennessee at Chattanooga and by all appearances was one of the success stories of assimilated U.S. Muslim immigrants—until he started attending mosque more regularly, grew out his beard, and began studying the Quran. In May 2015 he pulled up to a strip mall and started firing at a military recruitment center, then moved on to the Navy installation nearby and shot more. He gunned down four Marines and a sailor that day, all unarmed, like sitting ducks, before he was shot dead by police.

Six Somali college students in Minnesota, where terror recruitment is now a troubling issue, were arrested in April 2015 after they used student loan money to pay for flights to Turkey so they could join ISIS. All six students were from refugee families.

Hoda Muthana, twenty, lived with her parents in a middle-class suburb of Hoover, Alabama, a suburban community outside of Birmingham that has seen a significant number of Muslim immigrants over the years and now has three mosques. Her parents came to the

United States in 1992 from Yemen. Hoda, an attractive, bright teenager, graduated with honors from Hoover High School in 2013 and enrolled as a business student at the University of Alabama at Birmingham. She slipped out of the country in November 2014 to become an ISIS bride and never returned.

In May 2015, two jihadists, one the son of a Pakistani immigrant father, attacked attendees standing outside of a "Draw Muhammad" cartoon contest in Garland, Texas, with assault rifles and knives, planning to kill as many participants as possible and behead the event organizer, Pamela Geller. Fortunately, the attack was foiled by a policeman who shot and killed the attackers before they could enter the auditorium.

As 2015 drew to a close, there were other attacks by Muslims with knives and machetes. On the campus of University of California–Merced in November, an eighteen-year-old student named Faisal Mohammad attacked fellow students and an instructor with a military-style knife, injuring four before he was confronted by a brave construction worker and eventually shot dead by a policeman. Less than a month later we saw the San Bernardino attack.

Shortly after the turn of the new year, in February 2016, thirty-year-old Muslim migrant Mohamed Berry slashed and injured several people, one critically, at a café in Columbus, Ohio. Then came yet another devastating attack, on June 12, 2016, by twenty-nine-year-old Omar Mateen, mentioned earlier. He was born in New York, the son of immigrants from Afghanistan, more than likely refugees or asylum seekers allowed into the United States during President Reagan's adoption of the Afghan freedom fighters.

Mateen's father had made it abundantly clear, in videos he had posted to YouTube before his son carried out the attack, that he supported the Taliban. Yet after the attack he tried to say that neither he nor his son was anti-American. Sorry. You can't have it both ways.

The truth is, Mateen's coworkers had turned him in to the FBI for threatening them and making "inflammatory and contradictory statements" expressing virulently anti-American views.

The FBI investigated Mateen for ten months after his coworkers' complaint, beginning in May 2013. Agents interviewed him twice, and he admitted to making the comments, but said he'd only done so because his coworkers were racist and making fun of him because he was Muslim. The case was dropped.

"Islamophobia, a club Muslims wield to silence critics of Islam and stymie law enforcement," stated outspoken anti-sharia activist Pamela Geller, reacting on her blog to Mateen's unfruitful vetting by the FBI.[48]

While the Obama administration seemed conflicted about Mateen's motives and elected to make gun control the focus of its response to the Orlando attack, any reasonable person or honest investigator could have easily concluded from whence his motive came. Mateen had called 911 minutes into the attack and given a lengthy diatribe about his allegiance to ISIS commander Abu Bakr al-Baghdadi.[49] He'd also posted on Facebook his anti-American rantings and dedication to Islam and Allah. But Obama's FBI didn't want the American public to know the true motive for the attack, and scrubbed the 9-1-1 tape of all references to Islam and ISIS. Members of Congress, including House Speaker Paul Ryan, called on Obama to make all of Mateen's words public.[50]

Yet, it is patriots such as Geller whom the U.S. media paint as the extremists. In the wake of the Garland attack, she was asked repeatedly by CNN, Fox, and other news outlets whether her style was too provocative. She is convinced it is not. Why? Because "ISIS is here," in America, she told me after the attack. "The war is here."[51] One cannot be too bold in challenging this threat.

Both of the Garland attackers attended the Islamic Center of North Phoenix, which has ties to the Muslim Brotherhood and is known for its radical teachings. Around the time Nadir Soofi and Elton Simpson launched their attack, one of the two men posted on a Twitter account with the hashtag "#texasattack."[52] Groups such as ISIS picked up on the hashtag and posted messages of support for the two gunmen.

The same Somali-American refugee, a young man named Mohamed Hassan, apparently played a key role in inspiring both the Garland,

Texas, and the San Bernardino attacks. Hassan came to the United States as a child refugee from Somalia and attended Roosevelt High School in Minneapolis. During his senior year at Roosevelt in 2008, he disappeared, later turning up in Somalia as a fighter for al-Shabab, an al-Qaeda affiliate.

Hassan, as reported by WND, had contact through Twitter with Elton Simpson just ten days before the Garland attack when he congratulated the "brothers" in Paris for launching the deadly attack on the *Charlie Hebdo* magazine office and suggested the "brothers in the U.S." should now do the same. He followed up that tweet with another giving a link to Geller's event in Garland, Texas. Hassan was also in contact with Farook before the San Bernardino attack, the FBI told Fox News.[53]

Many U.S. media pundits blamed Geller for deliberately provoking Muslim anger and therefore inviting the attack while others vigorously defended her right to hold the cartoon contest on First Amendment grounds. Ralph Sidway, author of the *Facing Islam* blog, put the debate in perspective in his May 15, 2015, article "Freedom Provocation and Targets: No Cartoons Required." "For Americans and Western Europeans," he wrote, "cartoons of Muhammad seem to have become the flashpoint of the 'clash of civilizations.' But for Christians living in the Islamic world, their very being is all the provocation Muslims need."

He provided the following examples:

- 'Arab Spring' Muslim gangs go through buses in Cairo, Egypt, checking the wrists of the passengers. Those with the cross tattooed on their wrists—a Coptic tradition—are summarily killed;

- 21 Coptic Christians in Libya are beheaded because they refuse to deny Jesus Christ and convert to Islam, or to pay the jizya [head tax];

- 30 Ethiopian Christians are shot or beheaded for refusing to deny Jesus Christ;

- The Grand Mufti of Saudi Arabia declares that all Christians must be expelled from the Arabian Peninsula and all churches destroyed;

- 100 years after the Armenian Genocide (which taken in the larger context of Ottoman persecution saw 4 million Christians killed by their Muslim overlords and neighbors between 1894 and 1922) we are witnessing yet another Muslim genocide against Christians.[54]

We could provide countless other examples of similar persecution, such as the April 2015 slaughter of 147 Christian students at Garissa University in Kenya. A group of Somali Muslims with the al-Shabab terrorist organization burst in with machine guns and sorted the students by religion, asking which ones were Christian and which were Muslim. Those who claimed to be Muslim were asked to recite familiar verses from the Quran. Those placed in the Christian group were summarily executed.[55]

"Christians themselves in the Islamic world are—by their very being, by their very presence—all the provocation Muslims need to slaughter them. No cartoons required," Sidway wrote. He further pointed out that "Christians in the Islamic world cannot openly wear or make the Sign of the Cross without it provoking Muslims. They don't even have to do that much, they just have to be breathing. And now with Muslim desecration of Christian grave sites,[56] they don't even have to be doing that."[57]

The longer one studies these Muslim attacks against non-Muslims, the clearer it becomes that the term "provocation" is inaccurate and unsuitable to the true cause. Sidway believes there is a better word to describe the Muslim pathology: "predisposition."

"The extent to which a Muslim grows in devout observance of Islam is the extent to which he/she is likely to follow more and more literally the commands in the Koran and the example of Muhammad," he wrote. "Devout observance leads to the predisposition to take action against non-Muslim targets which the Muslim believes offends his religion.

"In Muslim majority nations," he continued, "this predisposition becomes so intense that the mere presence of Christians or other non-Muslims cannot be tolerated at all. This very principle is clearly expressed in the Quran: 'And *fight them* until there is no more fitnah (persecution and oppression: *i.e. worshipping others besides* Allah) and the religion (worship) will all be for Allah Alone.'—Sura 8.39."[58]

Most Westerners have a hard time understanding this. They cannot accept that the more devout a Muslim becomes, the likelier he is to become a jihadi. Sidway says:

> It would seem that God is not without a sense of irony, for in the Islamic world, as we have seen this tsunami of Muslim genocidal persecution of Christians, we have also seen immensely powerful examples of heightened Christian faith. Rather than leading Christians to fear, hatred and retaliation (though one can find some examples of those humanly understandable reactions also), the Muslim slaughter of Christians has provoked (there's that word again) responses of absolutely Christ-like behavior, with Coptic, Iraqi, Nigerian and Niger Christians forgiving and praying for the Muslims who are killing their families. These examples are the very definition of true freedom: freedom from hatred, fear, and even death itself. Meanwhile, the Muslim jihadis are slaves of rage, bloodlust, and the example of their warlord prophet.

"For the devout jihadi, the entire world is filled with targets," he concluded. "No cartoons are needed."[59]

"THE WAR IS HERE"

"The left, the RINOs and the Islamic apologists say I am 'provocative' for standing against sharia," wrote Pamela Geller on her blog. In response to that charge, she asks:

> Were the [three] Jewish children murdered in cold blood [along with a rabbi] by a devout Muslim at a Jewish Day School in France [in 2012] "provocative"?

Was Daniel Pearl [the *Wall Street Journal* reporter beheaded in Pakistan] "provocative"?

Were [Americans] James Foley, Steve Sotloff, Alan Henning, et al "provocative"?

Were the [Jewish shoppers] killed [in January 2015] at the [Paris] kosher deli, Hyper Cacher, "provocative"?

Are the Yazidi and non-Muslim girls gang-raped and sold into slavery 'provocative"?

Is the existence of Israel "provocative?"

Are the millions of non-Muslims being ethnically cleansed across the Middle East "provocative"?

Were the World Trade Center towers "provocative"?

Were the [thirteen] soldiers killed [in November 2009 by Maj. Nidal Hasan] in Fort Hood Texas "provocative"?

Was beheading victim Colleen Hufford in Oklahoma [in September 2014], "provocative?"[60]

Further, were the twenty-one Coptic Christian men beheaded by ISIS on a Libyan beach in February 2015 "provocative"?[61]
And the list goes on.

3

CULTURE CLASH

Muslims in the United States are about 5,000 percent more likely to commit terrorist attacks than non-Muslims.
—MARK KRIKORIAN, EXECUTIVE DIRECTOR, CENTER FOR IMMIGRATION STUDIES

PRESIDENT OBAMA SAID during his first term in office that America is "no longer a Christian nation," and there is much truth to that statement.[1] So, if we're not Christian, what are we? People are inherently religious. But if Christianity is no longer the dominant religious system undergirding our democracy, then what other, outside system is positioning itself to fill the spiritual void left by the dwindling number of committed Christians?

Islam, as we have seen, is the fastest-growing movement in the world, and its influence in America is expanding rapidly, thanks in no small part to the massive influx of refugees and immigrants from Islamic nations. The transformation from a Christian nation into an Islamic one is well under way. That transformation may be further along in Western Europe than in America, but America has been firmly set on the same path by its political leaders, and most of our Christian pastors and teachers have barely taken notice. They're not guarding the flock from invasive false doctrines as required by their holy book, the Bible.

A THREE-PRONGED STRATEGY FOR CONQUEST

The Muslim Brotherhood's strategy to undermine Christianity and thereby bring down Western civilization is three-pronged, says Dr. Mark Christian, who was introduced in chapter 2.[2] It uses its front group CAIR to influence the government and military life, while ISNA works to foster "interfaith" dialogue with major Christian denominations and Jewish organizations. A third front group, the Muslim Student Association, or MSA, focuses on influencing K–12 and university education. It is through these three groups that the Brotherhood wages "cultural jihad," or what Dr. Christian calls "stealth jihad." The Brotherhood itself calls this strategy "civilization jihad" against the West.

"They want to influence the whole United States," Christian told me. "They see the U.S. as three things—it's a government, it's a religious institution and it is the education system; so we have three organizations and all are designated to each one of those things."

ISNA concentrates mostly on outreach to Christian and Jewish religious groups. "They say they are 'building bridges,' but in reality they are building death tracks for these churches, watering down their theology, trying to influence the Christian teachings of the Bible and trying to find common ground with Islamic teachings," Christian said. "Basically they are trying to find common ground with Christianity so they can kill it."

According to Dr. Christian, the Shoulder-to-Shoulder movement is one of ISNA's crowning achievements. Shoulder-to-Shoulder is a coalition of twenty religious groups that include many of the major Christian denominations. Members include the U.S. Conference of Catholic Bishops, the Evangelical Lutheran Church of America, the United Church of Christ, the Episcopal Church in the USA, the Presbyterian Church USA, the Reform Judaism movement, and left-wing organizations such as *Sojourners* magazine, operated by noted American Marxist Jim Wallis. Their stated goal is to fight "anti-Muslim bigotry," but that's just the window dressing, Christian said.

When a similar interfaith movement started in his own community of Omaha, Dr. Christian began working through an organization he formed, the Global Faith Institute (http://globalfaithinstitute.org/), to help get accurate information about Islam to the churches. Christian's organization sought to stop the Muslim Brotherhood's "Tri-Faith Initiative," which calls for the construction of a Jewish synagogue, Christian church, and Muslim mosque on the same campus in Omaha. Dr. Christian said the Brotherhood front groups prefer to work with the large denominations and rarely pay attention to small churches.

CHURCHES ARE FAILING TO REACH MUSLIMS WITH THE GOSPEL

Shahram Hadian, a native of Iran who defected to the United States, converted to Christianity, and now pastors the Truth in Love Christian Fellowship in eastern Washington, believes the continued influx of Muslim migrants, if not tempered soon, will have disastrous results for America. He doesn't believe the American church is prepared to handle this mass migration in a biblically responsible way.

Most of the Christian charities that help resettle refugees, contracting with the government or one of the nine major resettlement agencies, do not share the gospel with Muslims or consider this a part of their work. "Most of those that even claim to be Christian are usually of the interfaith variety and are not very big on evangelism," Hadian told me. "Their whole thing is, be nice and do good works."

After Hadian gave a presentation on Islam in Boise, Idaho, a woman from the audience approached and made a comment about refugees coming from Iraq and how they're so open to Jesus.

"So you guys had an opportunity to share the gospel?" Hadian asked.

"No," she said. "They asked, 'If we come into the church, what benefits will we get?'"

Hadian believes that providing aid is not the best way for churches to interact with Muslims, unless the aid being provided also comes with a clear gospel message.

"I said, 'You guys are bringing these refugees in, you're giving them free housing and things, and so now even if they think they want to become a Christian, it's seen as a monetary gain,'" he told me. "Is this what we're doing to the gospel now—accept Jesus and we'll give you free things? If they could be bold with the gospel, yes, but I don't see any evidence of that. They usually want to say, 'Let's be friends with them; let's have a Ramadan meal with them,' and this is why I say we should have a moratorium on Muslim immigration."

SHAPING MINDS, POISONING SOULS: ISLAM IN THE SCHOOLS
According to Dr. Christian, MSA has a chapter in almost every American college and university, no matter how small. "They try to change the mindset of the kids and college students and they're very active," he said. "Their job is to degrade America, degrade Israel, and then degrade Christianity."[3]

Every country is different and is treated as such. In the West, the Brotherhood loves to promote women into high-profile positions to put up a façade of equal treatment for females. This is a strategic tactic, Dr. Christian said, used to convince the world that their Muslim women are not oppressed. "The best thing a jihadist can do is marry an educated white woman from a Western country, convert her to Islam, and then use her as a spokesperson for Islam."

Many women are targeted at European, Canadian, and U.S. universities for exactly that purpose. Our publicly funded universities, no matter how large or small, have all been importing growing numbers of Muslim students since the September 11, 2001, terror attacks, even though several of the jihadists in that devastating attack were here on student visas. The reason for the upsurge is simple: Foreign students, especially those from wealthy oil states, such as Saudi Arabia, Kuwait, Oman, Qatar, and the UAE, represent cash cows for the universities. They often pay the full tuition rate, unlike American students who attend these same public institutions and need financial aid or discounted in-state tuition rates. The problem is, these foreign students are screened even less closely than refugees, and then we have to worry about them targeting our female students for romantic relationships.

Not only do romantic relationships with Western women further the goal of propagandizing the Western world; they can also come in handy for gaining U.S. green cards and eventual citizenship.

Muslim Brotherhood front organizations such as MSA have also worked to influence the content of American school textbooks, increasing the favorable references to Islam and its prophet, Muhammad, Dr. Christian told me. Many of these textbooks "talk about him like he's a Robin Hood character," he said. "He's this amazing guy whose message was spread around the world, and he wanted to take from the rich and give to the poor. Very few details are given of any of his conquests, the beheadings, the taking of female sex slaves, nothing."

Islam is now being taught in the public schools throughout the country, from large cities to the smallest hamlets. Since Obama's Department of Education launched the Connect All Schools initiative in 2009 with funding from the Muslim Brotherhood–linked Qatar Foundation International, school districts began dishing out basic Islamic teachings such as the five pillars, Muslim dietary laws, and reasons that women wear the headscarf or hijab.[4]

When the National Governors Association Center for Best Practices and the Council of Chief State School Officers launched Common Core State Standards into the states in 2010 and 2011, more schools started incorporating the Islamic lesson plans. As in England, it is not uncommon now for an American middle school classroom to go on a field trip to a local mosque. The students are taught to dutifully remove their shoes, and in some cases the girls wear head coverings. And textbooks are being rewritten to reflect long passages on Islam as "the religion of peace."

In June 2014, about fifty teachers and administrators from the Lebanon, Pennsylvania, school district attended a training session on Islam and Arabic culture held at a local mosque— at taxpayer expense. The workshop was led by former district Arabic translator Mohamed Omar, who "took time off from his new job as a case worker for the Department of Human Services in Philadelphia to share his knowledge of Islam with the staff," which included superintendent Marianne Bartley, the *Lebanon Daily News* reported.

"I think this is the first time ever in the United States that a school district goes to a mosque," mosque founder Hamid Housni told the *Daily News*. "Usually a representative of a mosque goes somewhere. We don't have words to explain to you how we appreciate that. This is very, very special."[5]

He is correct. Usually, the mosque comes to the school. I have learned of many incidents across the United States in which an imam or other representative of a local mosque has been invited into a public school to give a presentation to students about their religion.

When I inquired of the principal at Cartersville Middle School in Cartersville, Georgia, about a Muslim woman's presentation at his school, he said, "What's fair is fair," adding that he would be happy to have a Christian, Hindu, and Jewish presentation as well. He said the presentations were to be kept on a strictly historical basis and would not include any religious indoctrination. I give him credit for that. Most educators have been less careful in controlling these types of outside instructors. However, even from a historical perspective, the Cartersville project would come up short as a practice in academic integrity.

I asked the principal if the Muslim presenter included anything about Islam's history of spreading its faith by the sword. No, she left that part out, he admitted. She focused instead on the fallacy that Muhammad was a great man of peace, presenting him as a modern-day version of Dr. Martin Luther King. The truth about Islamic jihads being waged against non-Muslims was conveniently omitted. In other words, children were being fed a warped view of history and a false narrative about Islam.

New York City schools now close for the Muslim holiday of Eid al-Adha,[6] while Christmas and Easter—both Christian holidays—have been merged into generic "winter recess" and "spring break." Meanwhile, ritual footbaths and prayer rooms have been installed in Minnesota high schools and colleges to accommodate Muslim prayer times, which occur five times a day.[7] The University of Michigan and many other major college campuses have done the same.[8] This seems like an over-the-top accommodation for an increasingly secular nation in which Muslims account for only 1 to 2 percent of the overall population.

Even some Catholic universities are accommodating Muslim students. For example, University of St. Thomas in St. Paul/Minneapolis opened Islamic prayer rooms and ritual washing stations for observant Muslims in September 2013 in response to a surging enrollment of Middle Eastern students. "Yes, we are a Catholic school," Karen Lange, dean of students, told the Minneapolis *Star Tribune*. "But I think this shows we're also a diverse place, and we're welcoming of students from all faiths."

The *Star Tribune* asked Saudi student Afnan Alowayyid if she could imagine a Saudi university doing the same for visiting Christians. Her response? "Not in your wildest dreams. Sorry to say, but that's the truth. That's reality. There is no other faith, other than Islam, that's practiced in Saudi Arabia."[9]

In New Jersey, Muslim parents became militant when the school board voted to reject school closures for Eid al-Adha. Muslims stormed the board meeting and forced a debate that became so contentious that one school board official instructed security guards to "take charge" of the situation.

"We're no longer the minority," said one female Muslim parent to the school board. "That's clear from tonight. We're going to be the majority soon."[10]

Middle schoolers across the country are now taught the Shahada, which is the Muslim prayer of conversion—"There is no God but Allah and Muhammad is his messenger"—and the five pillars of Islam. But the Ten Commandments and the Lord's Prayer remain strictly off-limits. It seems separation of church and state applies only to Christianity.

Freshmen at Hendersonville High School in Tennessee were taken on a field trip to the Islamic Center of Nashville, where they heard Islamic prayers and were given copies of the Quran. Jessica Connor, a student who opted out of the trip, was given a worksheet stating that Muslims treated their conquered people better than the United States treated minorities.

The students were in an honors world studies class, and the field trips to the mosque and to a Hindu temple, where they were taught to meditate, were part of a three-week course on world religions.

Some parents questioned why the school would tour a mosque and a Hindu temple but not a Christian church or a Jewish synagogue. "If you can't go to all five, why are you going to any?" parent Mike Conner told Fox News. "We sent the principal an e-mail and voiced our concerns. She sent back a reply and told us they could not afford to go to all five."

When Conner's daughter declined to attend the field trip, she was assigned to write an essay comparing Christianity, Hinduism, and Islam. The material she was given for the assignment, she noted, contained just one page on the sayings of Jesus, two-thirds of a page on the sayings of Gandhi, but five pages on Muhammed. When she refused to complete the assignment, saying that she had not been provided enough information about Jesus Christ and Mahatma Gandhi to make an informed, accurate comparison, she was given a zero by her teacher.[11]

WHAT DO U.S. MUSLIMS BELIEVE?

According to Pew Research Center, Islam is the fastest-growing religion in the world, and 53 percent of the world's 1.6 billion Muslims believe some form of sharia should be the law of the land. Yet, after the 2015 San Bernardino attack, the establishment media did its best to cover for the American Muslim community.[12]

CNN posted a story titled, "The Truth about Muslims in America," which made a clear attempt to put the U.S. Muslim population's best foot forward, while downplaying its darker side. The news agency cited a Pew Research study estimating the nation's Muslim population at a "minuscule" 1 percent, and said roughly the same number of deadly terror attacks were committed by non-Muslims as Muslims between September 11, 2001, and the end of 2014.[13]

The *New York Times* published a similar story about U.S. Muslims, saying that Muslim-inspired terror attacks have killed forty-five people since September 11, 2001, while "racist" or "anti-government" whites killed forty-eight over the same time frame.[14] But if the *Times* had really stopped to think about what it was reporting, it may not have been so quick to tout those two figures.

According to an article in *National Review* by Mark Krikorian, executive director of the Center for Immigration Studies, what the *Times*-cited study shows is that U.S. Muslims, with a paltry 1 percent of the population, managed to account for *half of all the terror attacks* over a thirteen-year period! "That means Muslims in the United States are about 5,000 percent more likely to commit terrorist attacks than non-Muslims," Krikorian wrote.[15] And this doesn't even take into account the massive attack on September 11, 2001, that killed nearly three thousand people in New York's World Trade Center Towers, at the Pentagon in Washington, and on a flight that crashed into a field in Pennsylvania.

Meanwhile, the long-term demographic trends strongly favor Islam over Christianity in many Western nations—mainly due to mass immigration of Muslims and high birth rates by Muslim families as compared to Christian and nonreligious families.

Unfortunately, there are no *official* statistics on the number of Muslims living in America today. The U.S. Census does not track religious affiliations of residents. All we have are various estimates. The Pew Research Center conducted the last major study of Muslim population in 2015 and found 3.3 million living in America.[16]

As of mid-2015, there were 3,186 mosques in the United States. A new mosque opens every week, and every state has at least one. Texas has 302 mosques, California has 525, Illinois has 200, Pennsylvania has more than 100, Michigan has 139, New York has more than 500— even Alaska has a couple.

In Europe the conversion of dormant churches into mosques is endemic. But it's only starting here in America.[17] In 2010 the U.S. Conference of Catholic Bishops and the Syracuse Landmark Preservation Board approved a plan to convert the landmark Holy Trinity Catholic Church in Syracuse, New York, into a mosque. To add insult to injury, the project was funded by U.S. tax dollars.

"In addition to being yet another violation of the establishment of religion clause in the First Amendment under the Obama administration, this is an ominous sign of our times, a sign of the spread of Islam in America, and the collapse of Christianity," wrote Ralph Sidway on *Jihad Watch*.[18]

Every time a mosque takes over the space of a former church, the Muslims hold a "breaking of crosses" ceremony. Muslims cut down or painted over thousands of crosses to convert the Catholic church in Syracuse to a mosque.[19]

Mosques are traditionally not only the center of religious worship but the soul from which political Islam gets its message of militant supremacy out to the rank-and-file Muslims. In Germany, police raids near a mosque in 2016 uncovered large weapons caches—news that was of course never reported in the American media.

In the Middle East, jihads have relentlessly been launched through the mosques, notes former Marine officer and FBI counterterrorism specialist Guandolo, whom we introduced in the previous chapter. One hundred years ago during the Armenian Genocide of 1915-1917, the Ottoman Turks used the mosques to convey hatred against Armenian Christians, whipping otherwise decent Muslim people into a frenzy of bloodlust against their Christian neighbors.

This historical evidence suggests the Muslim Brotherhood Islamic Centers and mosques are the places to watch in the United States in the years ahead as the Muslim population continues to swell and these mosques become more influential.

"All of the mosques our military entered during the wars in Afghanistan and Iraq and mosques that European authorities have raided in the last two years have had weapons in them," Guandolo writes. "The purpose of a mosque is what Mohammad used a mosque for, and the launch point for jihad is one of those purposes."[20]

MUSLIM PROPHECY FULFILLED?

For observant Muslims, the conversions of churches into mosques is seen as early fulfillment of one of Muhammad's prophecies about the end-times, when, Muslims believe, Jesus will return to "break the crosses." As Sidway noted, "Isa (the Muslim Jesus) will return and 'fight the people for the cause of Islam. He will *break the cross*, kill the swine and abolish jizya' and establish the rule of Allah throughout the world *(Hadith from Sunan Abu Dawud, Book of Battles, 37:4310).*"[21]

The Islamic State, al-Qaeda, and other jihad groups hold to this apocalyptic scenario. Ryan Mauro, national security analyst for the Clarion Project, has noted that

> [their] offensiveness at the sight of a cross comes from these teachings [about the cross] about *Sharia*. Since they believe Jesus finds it so offensive that he will one day break the crosses, these Islamists believe they are commanded to likewise be offended by Christianity and the symbol of the cross in particular.
>
> . . . Islamist terrorists like Al-Qaeda can cite authoritative *Sharia* rulings to show that attacks on Christianity are permitted before Jesus' descent from heaven.[22]

According to Sidway, when Islamists destroy crosses or talk of destroying the cross, they are emulating the anger they believe Jesus Himself has toward the cross.[23]

THE DECLINE OF WESTERN CHRISTIANITY

Pew estimates that approximately 64 percent of all U.S. Muslims are foreign-born immigrants and another 17 percent are second-generation. Meanwhile, Christians will decline from more than three-quarters of the population in 2010 to two-thirds in 2050, and Judaism will no longer be the largest non-Christian religion. If current immigration trends continue, Muslims will be more numerous in the United States within twenty years than people who identify as Jewish on the basis of religion.[24]

By 2050 several major centers of Christianity will lose their Christian majorities, including France, the United Kingdom, the Netherlands, and New Zealand, according to Pew projections based on current growth. If influxes of Muslim migrants out of the Middle East and Africa and into Europe continue at an accelerated rate such as that seen in 2015 and 2016, these forecast models are likely to be shattered.[25]

Among American Muslims, the level of commitment to their faith also seems stronger than among many Western Christians and Jews. According to Pew data, of those who consider themselves culturally part of the Muslim community, 84 percent said they were "absolutely certain" about their belief in God and another 12 percent were "fairly certain." Only 1 percent didn't believe in God and another 1 percent "didn't know" what they felt about God. The study further showed that 64 percent considered religion "very important" to their lives, while 24 percent said it was "somewhat important" and 8 percent "not too important." Only 2 percent said it was "not at all important" and 1 percent "don't know."[26]

That compares to only 58 percent of Catholics and 53 percent of mainline Protestants who, in the same survey, said they considered religion as being "very important."[27]

When it comes to politics, Pew found that 70 percent of Muslims in the United States vote Democratic, while only 11 percent vote Republican. When Pew asked about attitudes toward government, 73 percent of U.S. Muslims said they wanted "bigger government, more services" while only 23 percent said "smaller government, fewer services." Concerning the environment, 67 percent of U.S. Muslims said "stricter environmental laws and regulations are worth the cost."[28]

SHARIA-BASED CRIME PROBLEMS (HONOR VIOLENCE)

As the Muslim population grows, inherently Islamic problems will grow with it. Rape, female genital mutilation, and honor violence have been skyrocketing for years in Sweden, Norway, the Netherlands, Britain, Belgium, France, and other countries that have imported large Muslim populations. As Muslim populations increase in American cities, communities will be forced to deal with issues common to Islamic culture, such as arranged marriages forced upon teenage girls, the grisly procedure of female genital mutilation embraced by many Muslims from Africa and the Middle East, forced veilings, and spousal abuse.

In April 2015, a case of a forced marriage exploded into domestic violence in Phoenix, Arizona. The case involved thirty-year-old Mohamed Abdullahi, a Muslim refugee from Somalia brought here by the UN and resettled by the U.S. Conference of Catholic Bishops. He entered into a "nikah," which is an arranged Islamic marriage, with the parents of an eighteen-year-old Muslim woman.

Phoenix police arrested him April 22 on charges of kidnapping and sexual assault. The *Arizona Republic* reported that his bride-to-be was brought to his apartment that day by her parents, against her will. According to court records, the woman's parents arranged the marriage with Abdullahi and their daughter in November without her knowledge. When the woman learned of the marriage, she fled the state but returned fifteen days later to finish high school, police told the *Arizona Republic*.

The woman's parents drove her to Abdullahi's apartment. Once she was inside, Abdullahi punched her in the left eye, a blow that sent her tumbling helpless to the floor, according to court records. Abdullahi then allegedly grabbed his future bride around the throat and began strangling her while she was on the floor. At that point, Abdullahi dragged the woman into the bedroom and proceeded to rape her, police said.

Daniel Akbari, a former top defense lawyer who argued death-penalty cases in Iran's sharia courts before defecting to the United States in 2007, said spousal abuse is expressly allowed by the Quran. "Chapter 4, verse 34, of the Quran expressly says if a woman does not comply with her husband's command he has the right to beat her up, and that is what you see happening here and what has happened over 1,400 years," said Akbari, who now lives in Texas. "What is going on here in Phoenix is totally Islamic, under sharia. Everyone in that Muslim community will agree with that except the girl here." The hadiths, he said, are just as strict on this matter as the Quran.

According to well-regarded historic Islamic scholar Ibn Majah, a woman must comply with her husband's demand for sex even while on the back of the camel. He cited volume 3, book 9, hadith 1852 (English reference), which states, "No woman can fulfill her duty towards Allah until she fulfills her duty towards her husband. If he asks her (for intimacy) even if she is on her camel saddle, she should not refuse."

The Council on American-Islamic Relations predictably told Fox News that such violence has "no basis in the Islamic faith." Yet Sura 4:34 in the Quran says, "Men have authority over women because God has made the one superior to the other, and because they spend their wealth to maintain them. Good women are obedient. They guard their unseen parts because God has guarded them. As for those from whom you fear disobedience, *admonish them and forsake them in beds apart, and beat them.* Then if they obey you, take no further action against them" (emphasis added).

Akbari said it's time U.S. media stopped swallowing the "explain it away" propaganda that is spoon-fed to them by CAIR.

Honor violence is not the only problem being imported with African immigrants.[29] The number of women and girls at risk for female genital mutilation (FGM) in the United States more than doubled between 2005 and early 2015.

More than half a million women and girls in the United States are at risk or have already been subjected to FGM. The skyrocketing numbers are directly attributed to increased immigration from countries in the Middle East and North Africa, where the practice is common.[30]

CULTURE CHANGE IS MAKING AN IMPACT

The changing culture is beginning to take its toll on society, forever changing cities and towns in the United States. Dr. Christian, the former imam with direct family ties to the Muslim Brotherhood in Egypt, is talking a lot these days about "stealth jihad," the Brotherhood's way of exploiting liberal immigration policies while working relentlessly through various Islamic front groups to pressure government, education, and religious institutions to make concessions to Islam.

Christian said the violent jihadists' job is to spread fear, while those practicing the finer art of stealth jihad are expert at presenting Islam as a religion of peace that is being oppressed and punished simply because a few bad apples have hijacked the faith. These are the exact talking points being persistently pushed out through the media by President Obama and Hillary Clinton.

The net effect of this strategy is that the more Islam goes on the offensive and launches violent jihadist attacks, the more it opens itself up to public criticism, but anyone who publicly criticizes Islam is immediately branded a racist and an "Islamophobe." So the more fearful and justified Americans become in their criticism of Islam, the more they are cast as the oppressors and the actual "cause" of the violence being perpetrated against them, Christian explained.

"Their plan here is to use the influence of the U.S. government to further their own agenda. It has been going on for quite some time," said Christian, who broke with the Islamic faith in 2003, converted to Christianity, and came to America two years later. He changed his name from Muhammad to Mark and settled in Nebraska, only to be threatened and harassed by Muslims, including some from his own family.

"The Muslim Brotherhood is so big right now and so influential and so wealthy that they can do things on their own," he said. "The only thing that is missing is the power of the U.S. military to be on their side."

He went on to explain that the Brotherhood's goal is "to restart the Islamic empire," which officially died with the end of the Ottoman Empire in 1923. "They think if they can restart it again, they can reconquer the whole earth." Their plan starts with immigration and stealth jihad.

Dr. Christian is intimately familiar with the Muslim Brotherhood's strategies. His great-uncle was one of the cofounders of the Muslim Brotherhood and shared an Egyptian jail cell in the 1960s with Sayyid Qutb, whom many, including Osama bin Laden, have revered as the doctrinal godfather of the Brotherhood. Christian's father is still an influential member of the Brotherhood in Cairo, Egypt.

Upon his defection from Islam, Dr. Christian and his wife settled in Omaha, which he thought would be a safe haven. "I chose Nebraska because it's not that popular and nobody knows about Nebraska in the Middle East, because I had a very bad experience with the Muslims in England," he told me. "I was new in my faith and trying to learn more about Christianity. After I moved to Omaha, some of the guys learned about me converting and going to church, and they started threatening and harassing me, calling my wife."

Dr. Christian has a dire warning for Americans: they should not be deceived by the fact that, despite increasing immigration, the Muslim population is estimated at only 1 to 2 percent. He told me that the Muslim Brotherhood strategy from 1966 forward has been to avoid confrontations with American power. Instead, he said, the Brotherhood attempts to coax the U.S. government into using its power for the Brotherhood's own benefit. "Their influence is huge."

Americans, if not armed with the truth, will not know how to react to the onslaught of Islam and take action to protect their cities and states. They will not be informed enough to elect the right leaders. They will end up succumbing to jihad, whether violent or nonviolent. One way or the other, their children or grandchildren will end up subjugated.

"They say, 'Oh we all worship the same God and we need to find common ground,'" Christian said. "It's all about 'respecting women, Islam is great, Islam is peaceful' and it's all a bunch of lies. Whenever you find those kinds of movements within a church, you always find a watered down, very liberal theology that is anti-Semitic and anti-Zionist. But there is money involved and influence involved."

Yes, there is certainly money involved. And lots of it. Let's follow the money.

4

OBAMA'S "FORCED" WELCOMING PARTY

This is a takeover, a socialist overthrow of the United States.

—WILLIAM GHEEN, AMERICANS FOR LESS IMMIGRATION

TO GET TO THE ROOT of who is driving the open-borders plan for America, one must look beyond Congress, the courts, or even the White House. The leadership of both parties in Congress and most of the occupants of the White House since World War II have been completely captured by a globalist agenda that has existed since the beginning of time, but really found its footing with the birth of the United Nations.

By "globalist" I am referring to the idea that the world's problems could be solved if the world just came together, erasing borders between nations, making every nation and people group an interdependent part of the whole. National sovereignty is considered an impediment to the creation of a global superstate run mostly by unelected bureaucrats. Think of it as collectivism, which is socialism, only on a global basis.

The men and women who backed the United Nations have from the beginning harbored utopian dreams of a new international paradigm. Some refer to it as a one-world order that transcends national boundaries and neutralizes the sovereignty of these pesky nation-states, which they blame for all the world's problems. Truly independent nations run by democratically elected leaders are anathema to the global elites in charge of most Western nations.

But there has always been one bulwark that these elites brush up against—traditional Christianity and its adherence to Judeo-Christian values. This is the value system upon which all of Western civilization has been based for more than a thousand years. It is the system that led to equal rights for women, freed the slaves of Europe and America, and brought prosperity to many of the previously downtrodden peasants of Europe and America with the advent of the Industrial Revolution.

While there is nothing wrong with peaceful and free trading among nations, the idea that somehow war and poverty can be eliminated by global governance is a proven failure. Jesus said the poor will always be with us (Matthew 26:11), and while we are to help them out of the goodness of our hearts, the forced redistribution of wealth will do nothing but cause division and more war. We see that happening now in Europe, where socialism has reigned for five decades. In the elites' drive toward greater inclusiveness and open borders, they have actually created more divisions within their societies, to the point that they now have uncontrolled terrorism in France and Belgium and rampant sexual assaults against women in Germany and Sweden. The inevitable back-lash is now starting to occur. In the first eight months of 2015, at least 200 attacks had been carried out against asylum centers in Germany.[1] In Britain, voters chose to exit the European Union, largely due to fears about uncontrolled immigration of Muslim migrants.

America has been led by the same elite globalists in the form of the Clintons, the Bushes, and Obama. Their plan is to corral the United States into a North American Union with Canada and Mexico, mod-eled after the very European Union that the citizens of Europe are now desperately trying to dismantle because it's a total failure.

Yet every president since George H. W. Bush has referred to a new world order, which should send up red flags to any freedom-loving American. President Obama, in his last speech to NATO leaders in Europe on July 8, 2016, said "globalism is here to stay."[2]

While many critics believe Obama is an Islamist at his core, I would argue that he is first and foremost a globalist. The rationale for almost every policy coming out of his administration can be found in the documents of sustainability and global wealth redistribution found at the United Nations. Whether it be Common Core, with its intense data collection and focus on creating a dumbed-down workforce-training curricula for the vast majority of students; his health care policy, with its invasive digital record keeping on every American; his antigun agenda; his efforts to create a global police force through the Strong Cities Network; or his open-borders amnesty policy, they all have their roots in the United Nations documents on sustainability, as well as other documents, such as the UN Small Arms Treaty.

So let's start to peel back the layers and find out exactly where this globalist, elitist agenda is coming from, and where it would like to take us.

The refugee movement is but one weapon in the United Nations's arsenal that is meant to wear down nations and the distinct cultural norms that make up a country's national identity. By shifting people around the globe as refugees, as low-skilled guest workers, students, and highly educated technicians, the elites are able to gradually homogenize the world over time. Germany will look less like Germany, France less like France, and Morocco less like Morocco. Just as every new sedan coming out of Detroit or every new strip mall along our cities' main boulevards looks basically the same, every country will look basically the same if the globalists have their way. Nations across the globe will have the same interchangeable workforces, the same Common Core–based educational systems, the same unarmed populations, and the same multicultural diversity. The uniqueness of each nation will be destroyed over time in favor of a boiler-plate template that suits the financial interests of the globalists.

As keynote speaker during the commencement exercises for Northeastern University in Boston in May 2016, Secretary of State John Kerry told the students to prepare for a "borderless world."[3]

In his address, Kerry mocked the views of candidate Donald Trump, who pinned his campaign on the promise to build a wall along the U.S.–Mexico border and bring a temporary halt to Muslim immigration. This stems from old-fashioned and narrow-minded thinking, Kerry told the students. He said 9/11 should have taught the United States a lesson. I would agree, but Kerry draws a very different lesson than do those of us who seek to protect America from the terrorists.

"There are no walls big enough to stop people from anywhere, tens of thousands of miles away, who are determined to take their own lives while they target others," he said. Kerry conveniently left out the fact that most of the 9/11 hijackers were in the United States on student and tourist visas from Saudi Arabia and Pakistan, two countries filled with radical Muslims who hate America. Yet they were *allowed* to come here, which is a privilege, not a right, and take advantage of our country's educational system without being vetted for adherence to the principles of sharia and jihad.

He also failed to tell the students that the Boston Marathon attack that killed three and maimed dozens in 2013 was carried out by two Muslim asylum seekers from Dagestan, and that the Chattanooga attack that killed five U.S. servicemen in 2015 was perpetrated by an immigrant from Kuwait. He must have also forgotten that the San Bernardino attack was carried out by the son of immigrants from Pakistan, and a Pakistani woman who entered the United States on a fiancée visa from Saudi Arabia. These were people who supposedly passed through a screening process and were given visas by the U.S. government. All of them came from Islamic countries filled with people who hate America, yet each was screened as if he or she had come from Australia or Britain. Even the 9/11 attackers could have been stopped by a federal government that took its primary role of protecting its people seriously—a government that took its borders seriously. But under globalism, safety must be subservient to the free flow of money and people un-vetted across open borders.

Rather than screen out bad apples, the U.S. strategy since 1965 has been to welcome the world and hope they embrace the Western principles of freedom and democracy. While that strategy may have worked well in welcoming the waves of immigrants from peace-loving countries, it should never have been applied to those from countries harboring terrorists.

President Obama's dedication to a borderless world was nowhere more prescient than in the creation of his White House Task Force on New Americans.[4] He unveiled this group's plans in April 2015, saying it embodied a national strategy to "integrate" millions of new immigrants and refugees into "welcoming communities" across the United States.[5] The cochair of the task force, Obama's domestic policy adviser Cecilia Muñoz, said her focus would be on making sure Obama's historic immigration policies get "institutionalized" so they will live on long after she and her boss are gone from the White House.

Obama created the task force November 21, 2014, when he announced his plan to unilaterally grant amnesty to more than 5 million illegal immigrants and child migrants. His administration brought in 85,000 to 110,000 refugees per year from some of the world's most dangerous countries—Iraq, Afghanistan, Somalia, Burma, Sudan, and Syria.

The April 2015 conference was titled "The New National Integration Plan: Making the Most of a Historic Opportunity." It was an opportunity all right—an opportunity to transform the demographics of city after city across America by infusing Middle-Eastern refugees with radically different values than those who have lived and worked in many of these towns for generations.

Muñoz, a former executive with the radical socialist National Council of La Raza, said it was her job "to make sure we build this really into the DNA across the federal bureaucracy, at a leadership level, but much more importantly to make sure that when political appointees like me are no longer here this (immigration strategy) is built into what those agencies do and think about every day."

Muñoz said it was important for the federal government to standardize, set benchmarks, and use data to "measure successes," ensuring that states and localities create the desired "welcoming communities" for immigrants and refugees. This obsession with standardization and using data to measure and enforce a global template on every nation and every community within each nation comes straight out of the technocracy movement that is embedded in the United Nations sustainability principles. Obama also rewrote the Fair Housing Act of 1965, renaming it the Affirmatively Furthering Fair Housing Plan.[6] It uses the same data-driven tactics to force local communities that accept federal block grants to measure the amount of low-income housing opportunities in their cities for people of various racial backgrounds. If an area is "too white," Obama's U.S. Department of Housing and Urban Development can now force the city to rewrite its zoning laws to allow more low-income housing projects to rise in the midst of affluent suburban neighborhoods.

The Obama immigration agenda has also included the encouragement of so-called sanctuary cities, where local police refuse to turn immigrant criminals over to federal immigration officials for deportation. The sanctuary policies also pressure police not to ask the immigration status of crime suspects. The United States now has more than three hundred sanctuary cities, and the Obama administration was unleashing a plan that would encourage and threaten more cities to join the fray of lawlessness.[7] He would use both the carrot and the stick to make sure almost every major city's police department refused to cooperate with federal immigration officials. Cities such as New Orleans and Ferguson, Missouri, were threatened with loss of grant monies if they did not implement sanctuary policies.

Eva Millona, cochair of National Partnership for New Americans, a coalition of thirty-four organizations involved in everything from protecting immigrant rights to providing social services, echoed the call for a strong federal role in protecting immigrants from deportation and integrating them into the civil fabric of every city and state. This includes immigrants who have been convicted of crimes, from drunken driving to sexual assaults and even murder. "We have been pushing to really have a centralized leadership in terms of implementation of this report," Millona said. "We are happy that the report has called for a centralized entity to really move it forward."

Centralized. That's a key word. It's always part of the globalist mind-set. At a time when the people of the world are yearning for freedom and more local control, the globalists are seeking to lock down the world into centrally planned socialist unions, such as the European Union, which are run by elitist technocrats with very little accountability to voters. Politicians may be elected, but they are being increasingly relegated to figurehead status. The real power rests in bureaucratic appointees at the regional, national and international levels.

"And let me make a pitch for philanthropy," Millona said. "There's a huge opportunity for them to have their voice and their say and many of our friends and funders are involved."

She spoke of "diverse needs" of the immigrants and making sure those needs were met, stressing that it is critical "to have a very strong and centralized entity to make things happen."

In April 2015, Millona said the thirty-four organizations affiliated with the National Partnership for New Americans already had "boots on the ground" in twenty-nine states, including all manner of service providers, immigrant rights attorneys, interpreters, and advocates "to make sure immigrants have what they need."

The title of the White House task force's report was revealing: Strengthening Communities by Welcoming All Residents: A Federal Strategic Action Plan on Immigrant and Refugee Integration.[8]

"INTEGRATION" INSTEAD OF "ASSIMILATION"

The 2015 White House conference and task force report were also notable for what was not addressed. Hot-button issues of assimilation and protecting national security never came up during the ninety-minute conference at the Migration Policy Institute in Washington.

The poor record of assimilation into American society by refugees from Somalia and other Muslim countries never got mentioned and has, in fact, been largely ignored by the media. Dozens of Somalis living in Minnesota and other states have been arrested on charges of providing material support to Islamic terrorist groups al-Shabab, al-Qaeda, and ISIS. The FBI's newest most-wanted terrorist in early 2015 was Liban

Haji Mohamed, a Somali American cab driver in northern Virginia who entered the country as a refugee.[9] Two Iraqi refugees living in Kentucky were also arrested in 2011 and charged with sending support to al-Qaeda. An Uzbek refugee living in Boise, Idaho, was convicted in August 2015 of conspiring to blow up U.S. military installations and was making homemade explosives in his apartment while recruiting others to his cause.

Six Bosnian natives who immigrated to the United States were indicted in February 2015 in New York for allegedly sending money and military equipment to al-Qaeda in Iraq and to the ISIS terror group.[10] In April 2015, another Somali American, twenty-three-year-old Abdirahman Sheik Mohamud of Columbus, Ohio, was indicted on charges that he provided a computer and other support to terrorists during a trip to the Middle East. He came to the United States from Somalia as a young child refugee.[11]

Since the September 11, 2001, mega terror attacks, a whopping 580 people have been convicted on terrorism-related charges in the United States—and an astonishing 380 of them were foreign-born, according to Fox News.[12]

But rather than addressing the obvious assimilation and national-security problems related to our nation's immigration system, Obama's task force focused on making sure the new immigrants had their needs met by government and that they were being adequately "integrated" into our cities. "Integration" is the bureaucratic buzzword for planting diverse, multicultural communities within communities, nurturing them and coddling them with government programs, then watching them grow and take over their host communities. Obama, in a November 21, 2014, memo, challenged sixteen federal agencies to get involved in the effort of creating welcoming communities. As Muñoz had said, the focus should be three-pronged—economic, linguistic, and civic.[13]

What was meant by "civic" was never explained, but some observers see it as preparing the new migrants to be registered voters and activist citizens who will engage in political issues favorable to open borders and easy pathways to citizenship for new generations of migrant workers and refugees.

A woman representing the National Council of La Raza said at the conference, "Our affiliates are ready to help local partners on the ground . . . to pull together civic, economic and linguistic resources in an integration zone."[14]

Global integration zones are seen as the new economic unit, transcending national borders and linking specialized economic functions such as transportation, low-income migrant housing, work-training centers, and so forth. Workers freely cross in and out of a country to work in the zone.

Kevin Appleby, director of immigration and migration services for the U.S. Conference of Catholic Bishops, stood up at the 2015 conference and urged Obama's team to include faith-based organizations in its integration plans. That was an odd comment that seemed staged. Appleby knows full well that his employers, the Catholic Bishops, are already up to their ears in migrant aid efforts and profit greatly from their status as one of nine primary government contractors in the resettlement business. The Lutherans, Episcopalians, evangelicals, and Reform Jewish groups are also running resettlement agencies funded largely by our federal tax dollars.

"The local church is often the second place, after the family, the immigrants go to and the role of faith-based groups is often overlooked," Appleby opined. ". . . So as we go forward look at the ways the government and faith-based groups can work together. Where do they meet and how can they meet?"[15]

It would be hard to imagine these faith-based groups being any more intertwined with the federal government than they already are, but Appleby apparently thinks that would be a good idea.

PLANTING "SEEDLINGS"
In a broadcast on February 26, 2015, radio host Mark Levin interviewed Susan Payne, a Baltimore, Maryland, talk-show host, who infiltrated

a series of three telephone conference calls with more than a dozen members of Obama's White House Task Force on New Americans. The teleconference was hosted by Muñoz and included sixteen White House officials and representatives from open-borders groups.

Payne told Levin that by listening in on the calls, she learned that the participants planned to plant "seedlings" of immigrant populations into "receiving communities" that would be cultivated into fertile "soil."[16]

The idea was that the seedlings would sprout and grow into communities within communities. This is integration. The soil, meaning the community, needed to be changed to accommodate the needs of the seedlings, rather than the other way around. Eventually, the mature seedlings would grow up and come out of the shadows, ready to overtake the host community.

As the "New Americans" fully blossom, the citizens of the receiving communities will then be pushed into the shadows.

One member of the task force said these immigrants and refugees will be forming a "country within a country."

At the meetings, it was said that "immigrants need to be aware of benefits they are entitled to."

The participants in the meeting also discussed the fact that these immigrants would not be interested in assimilating. They would "navigate, not assimilate."

Obama's plan was to treat the "new Americans" as refugees as soon as amnesty is pushed through, whether that happened in his administration or under Hillary Clinton, whom he anointed as his successor. Refugees are given a cash allowance, subsidized housing, food stamps, medical care, free education, and an immediate pathway to citizenship.

White House Task Force leaders said at their April 2015 conference that they held three national outreaches involving three thousand so-called stakeholders, which included people from government agencies, NGOs, and immigrant advocacy groups as well as local elected officials. The tax-paying public who will be forced to pay for the immigrants' needs in these receiving communities were apparently not considered important enough to be included in the stakeholder meetings.

WAGING A PROPAGANDA WAR ON "RECEIVING COMMUNITIES"

Preparing the receiving communities requires agitators on the ground at the local level. Their role is to combat any pushback or resistance that might be encountered from local taxpaying residents. One big player in this propaganda war is Welcoming America, which was started with seed money from atheist, far-left, anti-American billionaire George Soros. The stated mission of this organization is to work at the grassroots level, setting up "welcoming communities" in cities and counties across the United States. It was started in 2010 with $150,000 in seed money from Soros's Open Society Institute.

A press release posted on the Welcoming America website describes the nonprofit as a "collaborative that promotes mutual respect and cooperation between foreign-born and U.S.-born Americans. Through a countrywide network of member organizations and partners, Welcoming America works to promote a welcoming atmosphere—community by community—in which immigrants and native-born residents can find common ground and shared prosperity."[17]

In September 2014, the group sponsored "Welcoming Week" to "celebrate immigrants and refugees and the growing movement of leaders and communities that fully embrace immigrants and refugees and their value to the fabric of our country."[18] The group also formed the Welcoming Institute to train up leaders who will engage in "building community support for refugees" across the nation.[19] It runs radio and TV ads and pays for billboards promoting open borders and mass immigration from hostile parts of the world.

David Lubell, executive director of Welcoming America, said his organization brings a new approach to immigration, focusing on resident populations of the receiving communities as much as on the immigrants. His role is to soften up the soil, getting it ready for the planting of the seedlings.

"A lot of groups are trying to water the seed, and not the soil surrounding it," Lubell told the *Huffington Post*, using the exact same language Payne said she heard on the conference call more than a year later. "We're trying to water the soil. Nothing's going to grow just by watering one alone."[20]

Lubell was rewarded for his efforts in December 2014. Obama invited him for a ride on Air Force One and lauded his groundbreaking work on behalf of immigrants, the *Tennessean* reported.[21]

Another player active in funding the propaganda war aimed at getting the American public to embrace its own economic and cultural demise is the New York–based J. M. Kaplan Fund. According to its website, the organization "focus[es] on building robust immigrant integration policies, practices, and programs at the local, state, and federal levels. To that end, we support efforts to improve the pace and quality of integration by working with receiving communities to embrace the immigrants and refugees in their midst. . . . And we advance efforts to ensure that immigrants capitalize on opportunities to live and work in the United States without fear of deportation."[22]

Remember, integration is not the same as assimilation. It encourages immigrants to learn to function within their host community while requiring very little of them in terms of becoming economically self-sufficient or adopting American values such as freedom of speech and equality for women.

A check of Kaplan's list of grants for 2013 shows $145,000 sent to Lubell's Welcoming America for general operations and $15,000 to the Migration Policy Institute for "Refugee Resettlement: Strengthening the System and Containing the Backlash."[23]

As more Americans wake up to the globalist forces trying to change the demographic makeup of their cities and towns without their permission or even notice, the job of containing the backlash will only grow more intense. We'll take a look in later chapters at the growing number of pockets of resistance and how divisive these globalists can be in their efforts to turn Americans against each other at the grassroots level.

Welcoming America avoids the politics of specific immigration policies, targeting instead the social and cultural fears suffered by Americans in changing communities, Lubell told the *Huffington Post*. Of course, the people in these communities are never told that the changes being foisted upon them are being centrally planned by bureaucrats in Washington and the resettlement agencies that contract with the government, enriching themselves with millions in federal grant money in the process.

"Our main goal is to reach those people who are unsure whether immigration growth is a positive thing or not," Lubell said. "And some of them are very reasonable—they're just not getting accurate information about immigration."

The White House report encourages every community in every state to establish an immigration integration plan.

"The reason for the lightning speed on this is the president gave us a timeline, because he is eager for what we can accomplish, eager for outcomes," Muñoz said. "We're making sure the federal government is doing its job and doing its best to lift up cities, mayors and local governments, to make sure others are taking this job on as well, and we have great, great examples to follow of many in this field of building welcoming communities. And the task force's work is reflective of that."

CORPORATE AMERICA ADOPTS OPEN-BORDERS AGENDA

Corporate honchos from some of America's most iconic brands are also involved in the propaganda onslaught, and of course they're on the side of the globalists. Bob Iger, Rupert Murdock, Michael Bloomberg, and Bill Marriott are just a few of the corporate execs working to help cities become sanctuaries for migrants—legal and illegal—while offering money to propagate a rosy view of immigrants' impact on the economy. The corporate executives led by Bloomberg and Disney's Iger have teamed up with the nation's mayors in an organization called the Partnership for a New American Economy.

PNAE announced on March 29, 2016, that it had picked twenty cities from among dozens of competing applications for a grant program based on the strength of their welcoming attitude toward immigrants, refugees, and other "New Americans."[24]

The twenty cities awarded the Gateways for Growth Award were:

- Akron and Summit County, Ohio
- Anchorage, Alaska
- Birmingham, Alabama
- Brownsville, Texas
- Columbus, Ohio
- Detroit
- Fargo, North Dakota
- Houston
- Indianapolis
- Kansas City, Kansas/ Missouri
- Lancaster, Pennsylvania

- Los Angeles
- Macomb County, Michigan
- Nashville, Tennessee
- New Orleans
- Phoenix and the state of Arizona
- Pittsburgh
- San Jose, California
- Salt Lake County, Utah
- Upstate New York region (Syracuse/Buffalo)

At least half are already considered sanctuary cities, and the others will be moving in that direction based on their willingness to compete for a grant that requires greater inclusiveness and cultural diversity. To be eligible for the grants, a nonprofit had to partner with either a local government or the chamber of commerce. The grants are to be used primarily for educating the public on the merits of expanded immigration. These folks have read the polls, which indicate the overwhelming majority of Americans are in favor of holding the level of immigration steady or lowering it. They need to soften up the soil and make it ready to receive more seedlings!

PNAE works with the George Soros–funded National Immigration Forum and Welcoming America to educate Americans about the wonders of mass immigration. They say it creates economic growth and vitality, and the more immigrants and refugees who flow into a city, state, or county, the more prosperity they can expect to enjoy. As we will show later in this chapter, the exact opposite is true.

"These [twenty] communities are leaders in the broader and growing trend to be more inclusive, countering the narrative often heard in the mainstream news," said Lubell, who started Welcoming America in Nashville shortly after Obama was elected to his first term. "Inclusive economic growth strategies that take into account both U.S. and foreign-born communities make cities more vibrant, attractive places for all residents to live, work, and thrive," Lubell added in announcing the grants.[25]

Lubell's job is key. He has worked closely with the White House to soften up the soil in cities targeted to receive an influx of refugees, unaccompanied alien minors (UACs), and other migrants. His organization hosted a national strategy session April 19–21, 2016, in Atlanta in which it shared techniques on how to build welcoming community campaigns.

In the process the ardent Democrat Lubell couldn't resist taking a shot at Republicans who were aligning themselves with the Trump agenda of less illegal immigration and zero immigration of any kind—legal or illegal—from Muslim countries that support terrorism. "The Welcoming movement continues to grow, and hundreds of national and international leaders will gather in Atlanta to exchange ideas and forge relationships," said Lubell's website. "In an election year, heated political rhetoric brings new challenges, but together, we'll explore how to overcome the divisiveness and make the most of this welcoming moment."[26]

Lubell is also a consultant in the Obama administration's "Building Welcoming Communities Campaign." If you live in one of the twenty cities tapped for the grant program, you may want to ask your local chamber of commerce why they are working alongside such a partisan, anti-American hack as David Lubell.

FULL-ON PROPAGANDA ASSAULT

Critics of Lubell, the PNAE, and their funders warn Americans in the twenty chosen cities to expect a massive propaganda campaign that will likely include some of their own elected officials.

Part of the strategy of Lubell and the White House is to co-opt local mayors and city councils and brainwash them with doctored studies and flawed data that suggest refugees and illegal immigrants will bring economic prosperity, when in fact they are a drain on the local taxpayers.

Study after study, both private and public, have shown that refugees, especially those from the Middle East, are heavy welfare users. According to the U.S. Office of Refugee Resettlement, 90 percent of Middle Eastern refugees receive food stamps. More than 76 percent are on Medicaid.[27] And the financial burden on public school systems is extreme, both from the standpoint of having to house more students, which inevitably leads to costly brick-and-mortar projects, and the hiring of more teachers, as well as the special language interpreters and tutors who must be hired.

A government report issued in June 2015 by the ORR shows the unemployment rates of refugees in 2014 well above those found in the general population. The jobless rates for refugees range from 38 percent in Minnesota to 53 percent in Michigan, 54 percent in Texas, 62 percent in Florida, 68 percent in Ohio and 69 percent in California, according to the report.[28]

And many of those who have jobs do not make enough to sustain their families, so they must turn to food stamps and other programs to fill in the financial gaps created by their low-wage jobs. According to the Center for Immigration Studies, the average immigrant has a ninth-grade education and does not have the skills to earn an income that is high enough to offset his use of public services and welfare assistance. So even though these refugees and immigrants may be hardworking people, they're unable to earn wages high enough to support their families. The obvious question for any open-borders proponent would be, how does it benefit the United States to bring in more immigrants who can't afford to feed their children, especially when the United States is $19.4 trillion in debt and has so many of its own veterans and families living in poverty and in need of help?

But with PNAE's money and Welcoming America's public relations expertise, the twenty cities will be working hard to foster an inaccurate view of the recent immigrants who have flooded across the border from Central America, or been shipped here compliments of the Obama administration from a United Nations refugee camp in Kenya or the Middle East. They will pick and choose a few success stories and spin emotionally gripping tales of refugees who have turned into entrepreneurs, knowing full well that these chosen few do not represent the vast majority of refugees.

"They want to manipulate the minds of the community and get Americans to believe mass immigration is going to be good for them, that they're all going to benefit from the influx of more and more migrants," said Ann Corcoran, author of the *Refugee Resettlement Watch* blog. "It's a mind game to soften up the receiving communities."

The mayors and CEOs have different reasons for championing mass immigration, none of which relates to humanitarian zeal to help the migrants.

Mayors know that by attracting new immigrants, legal and illegal, they will boost their political clout in the state legislatures and in Congress. That's because the prevailing method of setting congressional districts—a process called *apportionment*—is based on a head count of a city's total population, rather than counting only American citizens or registered voters. The state of Texas challenged this method, but the U.S. Supreme Court unanimously upheld it in an April 2016 decision.

Mayors are also looking for ways to replace Americans who are not reproducing as fast as they once were. "This is one method by which you can expand the economy and fill economic bubbles by pumping in foreign migrants on top of the rapidly dying and shrinking people of America," says ALIPAC president William Gheen. "It fixes many businesses and industries on paper while contributing to the factors that are behind the implosion of America's current native population. Americans are currently dying more than we are reproducing."

FOLLOWING THE EUROPEAN MODEL

This is the same dilemma European countries have been grappling with for a much longer period, since World War II. To replace their dying native populations and prop up their pay-as-you-go retirement systems, political leaders imported young immigrants from Turkey, Morocco, Pakistan, Somalia, Afghanistan, and Syria.

A recent demographic study shows that American white men and women ages forty-five to fifty-four died at "alarming rates" between 1999 and 2013, the Washington Post reported. "'Drugs and alcohol, and suicide . . . are clearly the proximate cause,' said Angus Deaton, the 2015 Nobel laureate in economics, who co-authored the paper with his wife, Anne Case. Both are economics professors at Princeton University."[29]

Mark Steyn referred to this demographic phenomenon in his book *America Alone*, postulating that it is leading to the death of Europe. The continent has entered a period of "civilizational exhaustion," Steyn said, where the native population loses the will to reproduce and defend its borders.

Now the Obama administration, with the help of Soros and his army of well-funded nongovernmental organizations, is working to "spread the wealth" of immigration from traditional gateway cities such as New York, L.A., Chicago, and Miami to smaller cities and counties such as Nashville, Tennessee; Buffalo and Syracuse, New York; Louisville and Bowling Green, Kentucky; Amarillo, Texas; Athens, Georgia; Boise and Twin Falls Idaho; and Macomb, Oakland, and Wayne counties in Michigan, among others. Many of these smaller-tier cities are at or near the epicenter of large-scale industries that scoop up the cheap refugee labor as fast as the U.S. government contractors from Lutheran Social Services, Catholic Charities, Church World Services, International Rescue Committee, or World Relief can supply it.

Michigan was particularly hard hit in 2016 with a mass influx of Syrian refugees, absorbing more than thirteen hundred in one year. Voter anger over this issue was cited by the Detroit Free Press as one of the primary reasons that Donald Trump was soaring in the polls against Democrat Hillary Clinton in the weeks leading up to the November presidential election.[30]

Global elites have been accused of fomenting the decline of Western civilization by promoting heavy use of birth control, abortion, and sterile same-sex relationships. After several decades, holes in the demographics start to show up, and eventually the dearth of new births leads to a shortage of young people entering the workforce and paying taxes into the system. As the problem of worker shortages grows more acute, the same elites who promoted abortion and tight family planning then come forward with a "fix" for the problem that they encouraged in the first place—replace the missing American workers with people from the Third World in a massive population shift.

"This is a takeover, a socialist overthrow of the United States," Gheen said. "And these [twenty] stronghold cities will give them political dominion over all conservatives and what remains of the countryside, and once this plan reaches a certain level there is no turning back and every socialist dream they ever had will take place, including locking up conservatives that say things they don't like."

But it's much more than just twenty cities.

An organization called Cities for Action includes more than 130 U.S. cities fully on board with the open-borders agenda. On February 15, 2016, in a newspaper editorial commemorating Black History Month, one of the CFA members, Birmingham mayor William Bell, tried to frame immigration as part of the civil rights movement, and to voice support for Obama's executive actions on immigration.[31]

As we shall see, assigning civil rights under the U.S. Constitution to foreign nationals comes straight out of the United Nations 2030 Agenda for Sustainable Development.

The corporate CEOs working with the mayors in PNAE are also

happy to flood cities with immigrants. But they may have different reasons for buying into the same multicultural vision for America. Mayors, as we've seen, are seeking political clout and the increased flow of state and federal tax dollars that comes with greater numbers. But the twin brothers of greedy mayors are greedy corporate execs. Big corporations are in constant search of cheap foreign labor, and they're willing to go to great lengths to ensure access to the most affordable "human capital."

This is where the United Nations comes in, with its plan for global wealth redistribution masked as inclusiveness and sustainability. The UN sees the current massive population shift as a way to redistribute the wealth from the industrialized nations to the developing world.

In UN documents, as well as those coming out of the International Monetary Fund, World Trade Organization, and World Bank, the globalist elites often talk about the need to encourage the free flow of labor or "labor mobility" across open borders. The UN delved into this issue of fighting for the rights of migrants for the first time in its 2030 Agenda for Sustainable Development, signed by some 190 heads of state in September 2015 in New York City.

Many well-meaning libertarian conservatives fall into the trap of believing that open borders will facilitate greater economic activity and creation of wealth. While there is something to be said for well-negotiated trade treaties based on free enterprise, that is not what the globalists have in mind. Their plan goes beyond the free flow of goods across borders. They seek to create a utopian world system in which all countries are equal and none are sovereign. But, as the ever astute George Orwell pointed out in his classic work *Animal Farm*, the equality pitch is a scam. Some animals will always be "more equal" than others.

For equality of nations to take shape, the rich must be brought down at the same time the Third World is brought up. The UN plan to socially engineer the planet into its view of a more equitable and fair global system is cloaked in the language of environmentalism and sustainability.

MASS MIGRATION PART OF THE PLAN FOR "SUSTAINABILITY"

When the UN uses the term "sustainable" or "sustainability," what it really is talking about is a Marxist redistribution of wealth and erosion of sovereignty. The UN's "2030 Agenda for Sustainable Development," which buttresses the now outdated "Agenda 21," sets forth seventeen goals to be reached worldwide by 2030, with the overarching mission of eliminating poverty through a massive program of wealth redistribution. The UN describes this process as nothing short of a global transformation of world systems to bring them into balance, as defined by the UN globalists.[32]

UN migration envoy Peter Sutherland, the former chairman of BP and onetime executive with Goldman Sachs, has stated that sustainable development depends upon a multicultural society, which is a melting pot of migrants and cultures.[33] Sutherland, the European equivalent of George Soros in many ways, is a wealthy banker/investor who believes in open borders and invests heavily in others who will work toward that same goal.

"This is pure smoke, with no substantiation whatsoever," says global governance expert Patrick Wood, an economist who follows the technocracy movement. "Sustainable Development is an economic theory that has never been proven."[34]

Goal 10 in the UN's 2030 Agenda for Sustainable Development is to "reduce inequality within and among countries."[35] What better way to achieve this than to shift people from the impoverished and over-populated Third World into the industrialized and demographically faltering West as refugees while at the same time using secret and corrupt trade deals to ship high-paying American jobs to the poor nations? This is exactly what has been happening for the past forty years with the refugee resettlement program, asylum programs, stunning increases in green-card issuances, and unfair trade deals such as NAFTA, GATT, the TPP, and TTIP.

Goal 10.7 of the 2030 Agenda states: "Facilitate orderly, safe, regular and responsible migration and mobility of people, including through the implementation of planned and well-managed migration policies."[36] (This suggests that the mass migration of Middle Easterners into Europe and the United States is not quite the crisis it is billed as but rather something planned.)

In targeted goal 10.A, the UN 2030 Agenda lays out the preferential treatment to be given to Third World nations: "Implement the principle of special and differential treatment for developing countries, in particular least developed countries, in accordance with World Trade Organization agreements."

The redistribution of wealth is further called for in the following targeted goals:

10.B Encourage official development assistance and financial flows, including foreign direct investment, to States where the need is greatest, in particular least developed countries, African countries, small island developing States and landlocked developing countries, in accordance with their national plans and programs

10.C By 2030, reduce to less than 3 percent the transaction costs of migrant remittances and eliminate remittance corridors with costs higher than 5 percent[37]

While the 2030 Agenda was adopted in September 2015, its major tenets were set forth in a December 2014 document titled "The Road to Dignity by 2030: Ending Poverty, Transforming All Lives and Protecting the Planet." The document describes a "universal call to action" to "transform our world" with "inclusive economic growth" that "leaves no one behind." It also speaks of a transformation that will sweep away the old capitalist order and replace it with a new managed economy, which some see as pure socialism but others say fits in the mold of technocracy.[38]

Whatever one calls it, the UN authors promise us it will be different from anything we've ever seen or experienced.

"Transformation is our watchword. At this moment in time we are called to lead and act with courage. We are called to embrace change.

Change in our societies. Change in the management of our economies. Change in our relationship with our one and only planet," the document states.[39]

Sound familiar? Nobody pushed the *transformation* of America harder than Barack Hussein Obama when he ran for his first term as president of the United States.

It could easily be argued that all of the changes Obama has worked to achieve during his eight years in office were handed to him from the United Nations—that includes his open-borders immigration policy, his Common Core education policy, the sustainable development policies and racial quotas for suburban housing, his antigun policies, and even his push for the destruction of traditional definitions of male and female. Every single one of these policies can be traced to one document or another at the UN. In many cases, these policies were started under previous administrations and taken to a new level by Obama.

USING DATA TO TRANSFORM THE WORLD

The UN's 2030 document also calls for a "data revolution" for sustainable development by which unelected technocrats will use data to manage and engineer the flow of labor and other means of production to ensure growth is occurring in an inclusive manner.

Once all the immigrants and refugees are here, they will need places to live. That explains why Obama implemented the Affirmatively Furthering Fair Housing policy. He literally rewrote the fifty-year-old Fair Housing Act and inserted language demanding that any American city or county that receives federal block grants conform to a federal quota system requiring a certain number of low-income apartments in areas that are considered too wealthy and too white. Those who don't meet the quotas will be hauled into court by the Department of Justice and may even be subject to having their zoning laws rewritten according to federal dictates. All of this will be enforced through new federal data-collection rules imposed on local communities.

"Mechanisms to review the implementation of goals will be needed, and the availability of and access to data would need to be improved, including the disaggregation of information by gender, age, race, ethnicity, migratory status, disability, geographic location, and other characteristics relevant to national contexts," the UN's 2030 document states in Goal 46.[40]

The UN document "demands policy coherence" by all nations in compliance with the "global common good."[41]

To ensure that the level of change takes place, the document makes it clear that special focus will be placed on cultivating young minds. "Young people will be the torch bearers of the next sustainable development agenda through 2030. We must ensure that this transition, while protecting the planet, leaves no one behind. We have a shared responsibility to embark on a path to inclusive and shared prosperity in a peaceful and resilient world where human rights and the rule of law are upheld."[42]

The UN demands for a data revolution to bring about a radical transformation can be seen in several policy initiatives put forth by the Obama administration, from open borders to free Obama phones (a great source of data collection), to Common Core and its obsession with mining data on student attitudes and beliefs, to the Affirmatively Furthering Fair Housing plan. This transformation will take place at the national, regional, and global levels.

The role of expanded migration can be seen in PNAE's lobbying Congress for an increased cap on H-1B visas, which allow foreign guest workers to come and stay up to six years. Companies such as Disney have used the H-1B visa to replace hundreds of American tech workers with cheaper versions from India, China, Pakistan, and elsewhere. Again, this foments a redistribution of wealth from middle-class America to the Third World.

Economist Patrick Wood, author of *Technocracy Rising: The Trojan Horse of Global Transformation*, believes it's highly significant that the UN included the migration issue in its 2030 Agenda. In Wood's article titled "Sustainable development, migration and the multicultural destruction of the nation state," he lays much of the blame for Europe's migrant invasion at the feet of Irish billionaire Peter Sutherland, the EU and the UN. "The 2030 Agenda has for the first time included migration directly. I think that's significant and something that few have picked up on," Wood said.

Sutherland, as you recall, believes a multicultural society is the "pathway to sustainable development."

Lakshmi Puri, deputy director of the UN working group on women, affirmed that in a March 2016 speech in which she said the 2030 Agenda "will be crucial for the economic empowerment of all migrants."[43]

According to Wood, "she was speaking to a convention about migration and she definitely ties the 2030 Agenda into migration and also into the sustainable development movement." Wood said Puri was channeling the dictates of Sutherland, one of the main architects of multiculturalism in Europe. "The other thing I picked up on was her comment about the need to 'leave no one behind.' That's a central theme of the 2030 Agenda but the UN never used it in the context of migration until now," Wood told me.

Puri said, "It's our collective responsibility to deliver on the pledge of the 2030 agenda to leave no one behind." Notably, former president George W. Bush used this same language when he championed the "No Child Left Behind" legislation for U.S. schools. Was it a coincidence? Perhaps so, but he also spoke of Islam as a religion of peace that is not to be feared as he imported thousands of Muslim refugees from Iraq and Somalia.

"These people are determined to get 100 percent of the citizenry on board with everything they're proposing—we see it in education, we see it in immigration, and we see it in the move to go cashless," Wood said. "And yet you cannot point to a single multicultural society in the world that has been successful," he added. "Look at Sweden. Look at France, Belgium. They're all a train wreck."

Soros and Sutherland did not magically receive their utopian visions of a borderless, cashless, data-driven world managed by a largely unelected elite. They inherited it from a long line of power elites dating back through the centuries. I will not delve into that history, as other authors have already plowed that ground, but we will take a brief look at some of the elder statesmen of the global cabal that pushes relentlessly toward the elimination of national borders and the destruction of Judeo-Christian values that underpin Western civilization.

ELDERS OF THE GLOBALIST MOVEMENT

To avoid being called a conspiracy theorist, I will introduce some of our most powerful global elites with minimal fanfare or sensationalist accusations. I prefer to let them speak for themselves and allow readers to make up their own minds whether these men have America's best interest at heart.

Since the formation of the United Nations in 1945, no man has spent more money on the cause of global government than David Rockefeller. The grandson of Standard Oil founder John D. Rockefeller Sr. and son of financial behemoth John D. Rockefeller Jr. donated the land on which the UN was built in New York City. His early career was with Chase Bank, which became Chase-Manhattan Bank in 1955 and moved into a new headquarters in 1960 right across the street from the Federal Reserve Bank of New York in downtown Manhattan. It would later morph into JPMorgan-Chase. His net worth in 2015 was estimated at $3 billion, making him one of the two hundred wealthiest men in the world.[44]

The Rockefeller family is probably worth five to ten times that much if all the money they have hidden in blind trusts and foundations were included. Many of the foundations and NGOs funded by the Rockefeller family are actively engaged in the push for open borders, refugee resettlement, secret trade deals that dilute U.S. sovereignty, abortion, homosexual marriages, and the constant attack on traditional Christian social values.

Following are quotes from Mr. Rockefeller:

Some even believe we [the Rockefeller family] are part of a secret cabal working against the best interests of the United States, characterizing my family and me as "internationalists" and of conspiring with others around the world to build a more integrated global political and economic structure—one world, if you will. If that's the charge, I stand guilty, and I am proud of it.[45]

But this present window of opportunity, during which a truly peaceful and interdependent world order might be built, will not be open for too long. Already there are powerful forces at work that threaten to destroy all of our hopes and efforts to erect an enduring structure of global cooperation.[46]

A close associate of Rockefeller's over the years has been Dr. Henry Kissinger, a confidant and adviser to almost every president since Richard Nixon. Here are some of his words of wisdom.

Today Americans would be outraged if U.N. troops entered Los Angeles to restore order; tomorrow they will be grateful! This is especially true if they were told there was an outside threat from beyond whether real or promulgated, that threatened our very existence. It is then that all peoples of the world will pledge with world leaders to deliver them from this evil. The one thing every man fears is the unknown. When presented with this scenario, individual rights will be willingly relinquished for the guarantee of their well-being granted to them by their world government.[47]

What we in America call terrorists are really groups of people that reject the international system.[48]

[Obama's] task will be to develop an overall strategy for America in this period when, really, a new world order can be created. It's a great opportunity.[49]

Power is the ultimate aphrodisiac.[50]

Another influential globalist who has been around for decades in academic and political circles is Zbigniew Brzezinski. The Polish national authored a key book in 1970 that laid bare the global elite's plans to transform the world by ridding it of traditional Judeo-Christian values of God, country, and family. The book *Between Two Ages: America's Role in the Technetronic Era*, spilled a treasure trove of insights into the mind-set of the global elite.

"The technotronic era involves the gradual appearance of a more controlled society," Brzezinski wrote. "Such a society would be dominated by an elite, unrestrained by traditional values. Soon it will be possible to assert almost continuous surveillance over every citizen and maintain up-to-date complete files containing even the most personal information about the citizen. These files will be subject to instantaneous retrieval by the authorities."

Remember, this was in 1970, long before the advent of the Internet and cellphones.

In more modern times, European Union Commission President, Jean-Claude Juncker, in comments made to the European Forum Alpbach in August 2016, said, "Borders are the worst invention ever made by politicians." He added in reference to the UK's Brexit vote to leave the EU, "In the concentration of globalization and European problems, we must not lose our way."[51]

George Soros, the self-described atheist financier whom we discussed previously, also makes our globalist hall of fame. Soros funds myriad left-wing community organizing groups through his Open Society Institute, including the Center for American Progress think tank headed by former Clinton and Obama aide John Podesta, and has been accused of helping fund the mass movement of Muslim migrants into Europe. He gives billions to left-wing causes, and the open-border agenda is one of his favorites.

In 1998, he wrote, "Insofar as there are collective interests that transcend state boundaries, the sovereignty of states must be subordinated to international law and international institutions."[52] He further believes that "the main obstacle to a stable and just world order is the United States."[53]

Soros has amassed a personal fortune of $13 billion, "which is further leveraged by at least another $25 billion in investor assets controlled by his firm, Soros Fund Management," according to Discover the Networks. "An equally significant source of Soros's power, however, is his passionate messianic zeal. Soros views himself as a missionary with something of a divine mandate to transform the world and its institutions into something better—as he sees it."[54]

"'I realized [as a young man] that it's money that makes the world go round," says Soros, "so I might as well make money. . . . But having made it, I could then indulge my social concerns.' Invariably, those concerns center around a desire to change the world generally—and America particularly—into something new, something consistent with his vision of 'social justice.'"[55]

"Soros's agenda is fundamentally about the destruction of national borders," and this has "been shown very clearly with his funding of the European refugee crisis," reported David Galland and Stephen McBride of Garret/Galland Research:

> The refugee crisis has been blamed on the civil war currently raging in Syria. But did you ever wonder how all these people suddenly knew Europe would open its gates and let them in?"
>
> The refugee crisis is not a naturally occurring phenomenon. It coincided with [Soros's Open Society Institute] donating money to the U.S.-based Migration Policy Institute and the Platform for International Cooperation on Undocumented Migrants . . . Both groups advocate the resettlement of . . . Muslims [from the Middle East and Africa] into Europe [and the West].
>
> In 2015, a Sky News reporter found "Migrant Handbooks" on the Greek island of Lesbos. It was later revealed that the handbooks, which are written in Arabic, had been given to refugees before crossing the Mediterranean by a group called "Welcome to the EU."[56]

Welcome to the EU is funded by none other than the Soros-controlled Open Society Foundations. "Soros has not only backed groups that advocate the resettlement of Third-World migrants into Europe, he in fact is the architect of the 'Merkel Plan,'" according to Galland and McBride.

"The Merkel Plan was created by the European Stability Initiative whose chairman Gerald Knaus is a senior fellow at none other than the Open Society Foundations," they continued.

"The plan proposes that Germany should grant asylum to 500,000 Syrian refugees. It also states that Germany, along with other European nations, should agree to help Turkey, a country that's 98% Muslim, gain visa-free travel within the EU starting in 2016."

One of Soros's loyal friends and partners is Aryeh Neier, who for many years headed up Open Society Institute and the entire Soros Foundation Network. Neier founded the militant Students for a Democratic Society in the 1960s, which led protests against the Vietnam War and openly sought to transform America into a nation built on Marxist ideals. Neier would later become the ACLU's national executive director and then went on to found Human Rights Watch.[57]

Caroline Glick, a former foreign policy adviser to Israeli Prime Minister Benjamin Netanyahu and deputy managing editor for the Jerusalem Post, said in an August 2016 op-ed that no corner of the globe is unaffected by Soros's efforts.

"On the surface, the vast number of groups and people he supports seem unrelated. After all, what does climate change have to do with illegal African immigration to Israel? What does Occupy Wall Street have to do with Greek immigration policies? But the fact is that Soros-backed projects share basic common attributes," Glick writes. "They all work to weaken the ability of national and local authorities in Western democracies to uphold the laws and values of their nations and communities.

"They all work to hinder free markets, whether those markets are financial, ideological, political or scientific. They do so in the name of democracy, human rights, economic, racial and sexual justice and other lofty terms. In other words, their goal is to subvert Western democracies and make it impossible for governments to maintain order or for societies to retain their unique identities and values."[58]

His funding of the Black Lives Matter movement is a prime example, Glick says.

Soros also gave more than $30 million to organizations supporting Hillary Clinton for president, making him by far her largest donor.

FURTHERING THE ACLU-MUSLIM ALLIANCE

Discover the Networks offers this assessment of Soros's influence and ultimate goal. "Both the ACLU and HRW [Human Rights Watch] have long promoted one of the central contentions of Soros's Open Society Institute: the notion that America is institutionally an oppressive nation and a habitual violator of human rights both at home and abroad—indeed, the very antithesis of the type of 'open society' Soros reveres."[59]

Since the 9/11 terrorist attacks, the ACLU has worked hand in hand with the Muslim Brotherhood–sponsored Council on American-Islamic Relations to try to shield American Muslims from being monitored and apprehended for terrorist activity. Any monitoring of radical mosques or known jihadist organizations is portrayed as racial profiling or racial injustice.

So it's no coincidence that Soros provided the seed money to start up Welcoming America, which is the equivalent of Welcome to the EU, his dupe on the other side of the Atlantic Ocean. Different players. Same game plan.

As we saw earlier, Welcoming America is a key player in furthering the false narrative that refugees help boost the U.S. economy. Soros also funds the National Immigration Forum, or NIF, which has established the Evangelical Immigration Table, a group that wraps the open-borders ideology in religious terms such as "social justice" and tries to seduce American pastors into supporting its cause while concealing its Marxist leanings. Jim Wallis, the longtime Marxist president and founder of *Sojourners* magazine, has played a leading role in the Evangelical Immigration Table, yet the organization also draws in a surprising number of good, honest pastors who simply aren't aware of exactly who they have gotten in bed with.

"*World* magazine editor Marvin Olasky laid out in a 2010 article how Wallis and Sojourners had received $325,000 from Soros groups over three grants from 2004, 2006 and 2007. According to [Open Society Institute's] 2007 Form 990 filed with the IRS . . . the 2007 money—a total of $100,000—was for Wallis's Sojourners 'to support the Christians for Comprehensive Immigration Reform Campaign.'"[60]

Immigration reform is always liberal code for amnesty for illegals and open borders for those would-be illegals and refugees who haven't yet arrived.

Wallis at first denied taking any money from the atheist Soros but later recanted that denial. And not only that, he accepted another $150,000 from Soros in 2012.[61]

Harbingers for the future are not good if America is to survive as a country based on Judeo-Christian values. While our government goes on accepting large contingents of Muslim refugees from the United Nations camps, it leaves the Christians coming under persecution from Muslims in the Mideast to fend for themselves.

Those who enter as refugees immediately qualify for a full slate of government goodies that aren't offered to most other immigrants. Everything from subsidized housing to food stamps, aid to families with dependent children, cash stipends, and Medicaid are part of the prize. Within five years they can apply for citizenship and full voting rights.

Regrettably, former presidential candidates Jeb Bush, John Kasich, and Marco Rubio all sang from the same song sheet as House Speaker Paul Ryan, liberal mayors and former mayors such as Michael Bloomberg of New York, Rahm Emanuel of Chicago, and Annise Parker of Houston. The more low-skilled, uneducated migrants, the merrier.

As we've already seen, Muslims come to the United States in various ways—as refugees and asylum seekers, on student and guest-work visas, through the annual diversity visa lottery, on entrepreneur visas and work permits.

But it's not only low-skilled immigrants who are being welcomed with open arms. If you work in a high-skilled job, your livelihood is also up for sale and placed on the bartering block by the globalist politicians in the Democrat and Republican parties. With the full support of the U.S. Chamber of Commerce, these politicians will gleefully send your software development or IT job to India, China, or Pakistan.

Corporate titans such as Disney, Oracle, Harley-Davidson, Microsoft, Southern California Edison, and Northeastern Utilities are exploiting our nation's employer-based visa programs, bringing in skilled guest workers from countries such as Saudi Arabia, India, China, Iran, Kuwait, and Pakistan to replace their American technology workers with cheaper foreign alternatives. Many politicians in Congress, including some with surprisingly conservative reputations, are trying to expand these guest-worker visa programs. These politicians—including, again, Paul Ryan, Jeb Bush, and Marco Rubio—have absolutely no conscience when it comes to stealing the livelihoods of thousands of American workers, nor do they seem concerned about the national security implications of bringing in large numbers of un-vetted professionals from Muslim-dominated nations such as Saudi Arabia, Turkey, United Arab Emirates, Kuwait, Yemen, and Pakistan.

If America wishes to avoid the same path of Europe—and it's already getting late in the game—asking some serious questions of our politicians, and demanding honest answers, is long overdue.

Why is America importing tens of thousands of uneducated, low-skilled refugees from Somalia, Afghanistan, Iraq, Syria, Burma, and other Third World countries and lavishing them with taxpayer-funded welfare? Why are we educating at our universities thousands of young people from Middle Eastern countries known for producing as many jihadists as engineers?

Why are the United Nations and the resettlement agencies pushing for America to accept up to a hundred thousand Muslim refugees from Syria while ignoring the plight of persecuted Christians in that war-torn country who have been driven from their homes and had their property stolen, their men beheaded, and their women sold into sex slavery by these same Sunni Muslim jihadists?

Why are local communities not given a choice as to whether they wish to receive refugees being resettled in their midst at taxpayer expense?

These questions become even harder to answer when taking into account the costs to taxpayers, yet our government leaders make their pitch for these programs with sugarcoated lies and half-truths. By encouraging diversity, inclusiveness, and multiculturalism, America will grow and prosper, they say. Really? Tell that to the veteran who couldn't find a job when he returned from the battlefields of Iraq or Afghanistan. Tell that to the college student who lost out on a job in the technology sector to someone from Pakistan, India, Saudi Arabia, or China. Tell it to an American high school student who received a rejection letter from a university whose enrollment lists were loaded up with foreign students.

This is globalism at work. It destroys American jobs, threatens our security, eats away at our nation's cultural identity, and gnaws at its social cohesion. It seeks to create deep divides within America, pitting the rights of foreigners against the native-born, giving jobs, government subsidies, and special rights to the new arrivals while accusing American citizens who resist of being part of the problem.

Any American who balks at this bitter medicine is instantly branded a bigot, racist, or xenophobe. It doesn't matter that the refugees and immigrants from Muslim lands have little to no understanding or respect for American values; in fact, that's what makes them so useful to their leftist sponsors who share the same hatred for the U.S. Constitution and traditional American values. Would a migrant from Somalia or Saudi Arabia have any understanding, let alone respect, for the First Amendment, the Second Amendment, or the rest of the Bill of Rights? What about support for Israel's right to exist as a nation, which has traditionally been a bipartisan staple of American political thought? It's highly unlikely that immigrants from the Middle East will have anything but contempt for our Constitution or that they would harbor any wishes for Israel other than its annihilation.

Once a resettlement contractor, such as Catholic Charities or Lutheran Social Services, opens an office in your city or town, the flow of refugees will not stop within one or two years. Expect the flood to continue indefinitely, with larger numbers of refugees arriving each year and from more diverse countries.

Schools will be expected to jump into action to accommodate their special needs. That means interpreters and special tutoring services specializing in often obscure foreign languages and dialects, all at tax-payers' expense. A Clinton-era executive order requires public schools to provide lessons to all students in their own language until their English skills are adequate, so there is no way around these hurdles.

The education of native-born American students is bound to suffer as teachers spend more time trying to get the refugees up to speed.

Consider the following Episcopal News Service's (ENS) description of Congolese refugees bound for the United States from a UN camp in Rwanda:

> A Congolese refugee, Zaburiya arrived in Tucson seven months ago with five children, aged 10 to 26, after spending 18 years in a refugee camp in Rwanda.
>
> Illiterate and not speaking a word of English, she became a member of a women's empowerment group operated by Refugee Focus, which *receives support from The Domestic and Foreign Missionary Society's Episcopal Migration Ministries service through funding from the United States government's Office of Refugee Resettlement.*[62]

"Through Episcopal Migration Ministries, the Domestic and Foreign Missionary Society partners with thirty resettlement agencies in twenty-six dioceses nationwide," the ENS further reported. EMM is one of nine VOLAGs that contracts with the State Department to welcome and permanently resettle refugees into more than three hundred U.S. cities and towns.

So we've seen how the network of groups pushing the globalist agenda is wide and powerful, encompassing big business, big government, the United Nations and its affiliated NGOs, along with many of the more liberal-minded Christian churches and Jewish synagogues. What on earth could these myriad and seemingly unrelated groups have in common with the global Islamic movement?

5

UNHOLY ALLIANCE

The precept of the Koran is perpetual war against all who deny that Muhammad is the prophet of God. The vanquished may purchase their lives by the payment of tribute; the victorious may be appeased by a false and delusive promise of peace; and the faithful follower of the prophet may submit to the imperious necessities of defeat: but the command to propagate the Muslim creed by the sword is always obligatory, when it can be made effective. The commands of the prophet may be performed alike by fraud or by force.

—JOHN QUINCY ADAMS

AS WE'VE SEEN, Islam has placed a historic focus on immigration, from the time of Muhammad, who taught Muslims by his own example to migrate and dominate new areas. Al-hijra, as he called it. But the hijra must also be studied in the context of the Islamic teaching of perpetual war against the infidels, or unbelievers. In the Islamic mindset, according to sharia, the world is divided into two sectors, the Dar al-Islam, or the House of Peace, and Dar al-Harb, the House of War. The House of War represents the unconquered nations.

Muslims are to act differently when living in the "lower house," lands not yet conquered by Islam. In this preparation stage, Muslims are encouraged to use peaceful dialogue to buy time and prepare the enemy psychologically for future violent strikes. "They study and know our strategy but we aren't interested in learning theirs," says

Dr. Mark Christian, whom we cited earlier.

Muslim scholars throughout history have stressed that jihad comes in many forms and is not to be limited to violent means. Civilization jihad is just as important and should be waged as a precursor to violent jihad in places still dominated by infidels.

Quran 3:151 states: "Soon shall We cast terror into the hearts of the unbelievers."

"Soon" meaning not yet. Be patient and wait for the right time.

In a military sense, and Muhammad was first and foremost a military commander and strategist, it is necessary to build up your strength demographically and culturally before launching overt attacks. There will be pinpricks of terror, but the full-on assault must wait. Most important is the instruction not to assimilate into the dominant Western culture in which you have settled. Muhammad used this exact same tactic in his migration from Mecca to Medina and across the Arabian Peninsula. At first he was conciliatory and made peace pacts with the elders of Medina. It was perfectly fine, even encouraged, to keep hidden or even lie about his intentions while living among a foreign people in a foreign land that does not live by Islamic law. This is a lesson Muhammad taught by example.

When living among non-Muslims, or *kafirs*, Muhammad taught, Muslims were not to take on the customs or the culture of the native peoples, but they were to reach out to them and try to build alliances with non-Muslim groups that could prove useful in future dealings. This outreach or summoning of non-Muslims to sit and share areas of common ground is called *da'wah*, a strategy still used to great effect today by the Muslim Brotherhood organizations. But, just as in Muhammad's day, these overtures are nothing but a clever ruse meant to weaken the resolve of the unbelievers.

The biggest mistake Christians and Jews make today is to assume that Islam is just another religion seeking a place in society on equal footing with the other great faiths.

Muhammad encouraged Muslims to move into new areas to spread

Islam through da'wah. They refuse to assimilate into the native culture. Enclaves form, and demands for sharia-compliant cultural compromises begin to pop up like popcorn in a popper, slow at first, then picking up steam until the fluffy white puffs overtake the original hard kernels.

The final and natural stage is that once a city, state, or nation becomes significantly Muslim through immigration, it will begin to elect Muslim leaders.

It's already happened in one major Western city, London, England, which elected its first-ever Muslim mayor in May 2016. And it's happened in one small city in Michigan, Hamtramck, which elected the nation's first Muslim-majority city council earlier in 2016.[1]

This begs the question for our friends in the Republican Party: If they still believe in their platform of support for Israel, why do pro-Israel Republicans such as House Speaker Paul Ryan and Indiana Gov. Mike Pence support the importation of tens of thousands of Muslim immigrants every year? Surely they must know that no Muslim supports Israel's right to exist within secure borders.

Pence is a perfect example of what is wrong with so many of our conservative politicians in America today. When GOP presidential candidate Donald Trump first made the statement that he would, if elected, implement a moratorium on all Muslim immigration "until we can figure out what the hell is going on," Pence was one of many conservative Republicans who immediately balked.

Now, when I say conservative Republicans, I'm sincerely talking about the good guys. I'm not talking about the John McCains, Lindsey Grahams, Mitch McConnells, and the rest of the so-called RINOs who regularly sell out their conservative principles for money and political gain. Pence is not that sort of conservative. He seems genuine and most likely is a true Christian. Yet, when Trump made his very astute comment that something was going on within Islam that needed to be figured out before we continue pumping tens of thousands of Muslims into our country, Pence reacted by saying that was "offensive and unconstitutional."[2]

Pence, and the dozens of other GOP politicians just like him, are extremely naive about Islam, but beyond that show an unbelievable lack of knowledge about our own U.S. Constitution.

If I had been the journalist interviewing Pence, I would have asked him to point out for me the section of the Constitution that gave rights to foreign nationals residing outside our country. The undeniable fact is that the United States exercises complete discretion over who is allowed to enter its borders. If it doesn't, we are not a sovereign nation, and I would like to ask Mr. Pence when the United States gave up its sovereignty.

I would also ask him, if he truly supports Israel as he says he does, how he squares that stance with the importation of tens of thousands of Israel-hating Muslims into our country every year. Will the creation of a strong voting bloc of Muslim citizens not eventually affect U.S. policy toward Israel? We already have two Muslim congressmen, one from Minnesota, which has the nation's largest Somali Muslim refugee colony, and the other from Pence's own state of Indiana.

The same could be said with other Republican issues. The GOP is the party that champions religious freedom and freedom of speech without bowing to political correctness. Have Pence and the other naive Republican conservatives ever met a sharia-compliant Muslim who shares these values?

It's well past time for a serious wakeup call within the Republican Party.

But if it chooses to join the political correctness movement, the Republican Party, even its conservative wing, will end up being deceived. Anyone who believes—or even potentially believes—that sharia law is superior to U.S. law is not someone who should be welcomed to America as a refugee or as an immigrant of any type. Unabated refugee influx from sharia-compliant countries is very simply slow-motion suicide.

With Islamic immigration left unchecked at its current rate, the writing is on the wall for America's future. And it's written in blood. Sharia begins with the blasphemy laws. Any Christian or Jew who criticizes Islam will be labeled an extremist and blackballed by the rest of society. The secular leftists will be the first to comply with the new rules and enforce them on others. It gets much worse from there.

Yet, Democrats face a quandary similar to that of Republicans. Have they ever met a sharia-compliant Muslim who shares their values of equal rights for women and homosexuals? I ask my Democrat friends, how does the annual importation of tens of thousands of sharia-compliant immigrants further the cause of women and homosexuals over time?

AMERICA'S FOUNDING FATHERS HAD IT RIGHT

Our founding fathers understood quite well this fundamental incompatibility between sharia and our Constitution.[3]

President Thomas Jefferson sent the Navy to the Barbary Coast in 1801 to stop Islamic pirates' reign of terror on U.S. merchant ships. When Jefferson read the Quran to understand what was motivating the pirates, he learned that the Muslim holy book commanded the faithful to "plunder and enslave" non-Muslims.

In 1814, after Tripoli broke its truce and began attacking U.S. ships again, former president John Adams wrote Jefferson a letter advising that Islam's founder and prophet was "a military fanatic." In another writing, he condemned Islamic law as "contemptible."

His son and future president, John Quincy Adams, went further, arguing that the essence of Islam is "violence and lust: to exalt the brutal over the spiritual part of human nature." He suggested the Quran's commands to fight and conquer other lands "in the cause of Allah" were at odds with democracy, peace, and the Judeo-Christian ethic on which America was founded.

"The precept of the Koran is perpetual war against all who deny that Muhammad is the prophet of God," he added. "The vanquished may purchase their lives by the payment of tribute; the victorious may be appeased by a false and delusive promise of peace; and the faithful follower of the prophet may submit to the imperious necessities of defeat: but the command to propagate the Muslim creed by the sword is always obligatory, when it can be made effective. The commands of the prophet may be performed alike by fraud or by force."

It wasn't until immigration was liberalized in the 1960s that large waves of Muslims began moving to America. At that time, the American Muslim community stood at a paltry 150,000. Muslims did not establish their own political institutions in America until the 1980s, and they didn't elect a representative to Congress until 2007.

While the Republican naivety on this issue remains baffling, it's easier to see why Democrats would support runaway Muslim immigration and are so eager to form political alliances with Islamists.

Hillary Clinton has accepted tens of millions of dollars in donations to the Clinton Foundation from foreign Islamic entities based in Saudi Arabia, Kuwait, the United Arab Emirates, and other wealthy Gulf States. These countries not only ban Christian churches; they forbid women to leave the house without a male relative, and they throw homosexuals in jail or murder them. This is sharia. Hillary Clinton campaigned on a promise to increase the influx of Syrian refugees by 550 percent and would continue the influx from Somalia, Iraq, and Afghanistan, all sharia compliant.[4]

But it's not too difficult to discern what is going on with the Democrats and their love affair with Islam. It's a clear case of "the enemy of my enemy is my friend." The hard-core leftists who rule the Democratic Party and control the major media will be willing to sacrifice what they believe is a temporary inconvenience for the "greater good" of crushing the traditional Judeo-Christian values that they see as oppressive and, believe it or not, every bit as bad as a society based on sharia law.

We saw this pattern play out repeatedly in the final few years of the Obama administration. In Garland, Texas, after Muslim terrorists attacked a "Draw Muhammad" contest, event host Pamela Geller met more media condemnation than the Muslim attackers did. In San Bernardino, California, neighbors and construction workers were afraid to speak out and report suspicious activity at the home of terrorist Syed Farook for fear that they would be called anti-Muslim or Islamophobes.

In Hood River, Oregon, in May 2016, Rev. Michael Harrington, pastor of Belmont Drive Missionary Baptist Church, had had enough. He posted messages on his church marquee that read:

Wake up Christians

Allah is not our God

Muhammad not greater than Jesus.

The other side of the marquee stated, "Only the Bible is God's word . . . Koran is just another book."[5]

It's hard to imagine that such basic Christian tenets would be seen as inflammatory or even slightly controversial as recently as ten years ago. But in today's America, where Muslims carry clout far beyond their numbers, it's considered not only controversial but hateful to quote certain biblical truths.

Within a matter of days, word spread to Muslim groups well beyond the tiny town of Hood River and they had their left-wing "Christian" allies descend on the small church with protest signs saying "Take down this sign."

This church is so small that it often can't muster more than a dozen members for a typical Sunday service. "There may be, on a good day, thirty cars drive by and see our sign," said Pastor Harrington.[6]

But this simple expression of religious opinion was too controversial for some politically correct Christians to tolerate.

The local newspaper covered the story, as did the big-city paper, the *Oregonian* in Portland, and even the mayor intervened with comments that helped stoke what the media had declared a "controversy." Never mind that it was a controversy of their own making and that the sayings were completely within the purview of protected speech under the First Amendment.

Gone are the days when the biggest champions of the smallest person's First Amendment rights are found in the news media. Now, the media are more likely to side with the local politician who seeks to chill public speech or, in this case, what amounts to private speech on private property.

"I am annoyed that in this political season there's a solid case of ugly going on," Mayor Paul Blackburn told the local media in an effort to smear the pastor of the tiny church. "I think it norms up this kind of behavior like 'oh, it's okay to be a bigot now.'"[7]

One can't help but wonder what type of penalty the good mayor would like to impose upon free speech that he considers annoying.

But the story gets worse. Trespassers snuck onto the church property at night and rearranged the letters on the marquee to read, "Holy boobs," among other mocking messages. There were also reports of vandalism that never made it into the local media.[8]

The pastor and his church stood firm and did not buckle to the bullying tactics of the mayor, the media, or their Islamist friends at CAIR, all of whom tried to shut down the pastor's First Amendment rights.[9]

At the same time the Oregon liberals were giving a small-town pastor hell for posting a sign on his own church property, Muslim groups were plastering the roadsides in several states with billboards promoting their faith and targeting Christians and Jews. Some read, "Find Jesus in the Koran," while others talk about Islam being the religion of peace, a blatant lie that any honest inspection of history could easily prove false. Yet no one is saying the Muslims don't have the right to propagate their beliefs, whether accurately reflecting their holy texts or not.

Atheist groups have likewise posted billboards along America's major highways questioning and criticizing Christianity for decades without controversy. Yet when someone put up an anti-Islam billboard in St. Cloud, Minnesota, in early 2016, the owner of the billboard space got a call from the local Catholic Charities representative, who told him to take it down and cancel his contract with the advertiser or risk facing a lawsuit.

"You don't see any protests when it's Christianity being bashed. How come they can put those things up but this pastor can't put a factual, biblically based sign up on his own church property?" asks Pastor Shahram Hadian, a former Muslim who came to the United States from

Iran and operates a ministry based in eastern Washington. "And I'm so glad, thank God, that he's not backing down.

"People are hungry for some courageous pastors. They're like an endangered species. Can we find a courageous pastor anywhere in America? That's, I think, why people are so fired up about this, is we're actually finding one who will take a stand."

There has been much support for the pastor's actions. Fellow Christians from other congregations held a joint worship service at Belmont Drive Missionary Baptist.

"But what's not being reported is the vandalism and the signs being changed," Hadian said. "When if they were defacing a mosque's marquee—that would have been all over the news, and you probably would have had Obama out there with the Department of Justice filing hate-crime charges."

Another case of blatant muffling of First Amendment rights occurred in little Mukilteo, Washington, not far from Seattle, in the summer of 2016.

A local businessman in that community, Peter Zieve, was exercising his freedom of speech by mailing out anonymous postcards informing homeowners that a large mosque was planned in their neighborhood and inviting them to attend local council meetings to oppose it, citing traffic, noise, and other issues. Zieve is the owner of ElectroImpact, a company with about seven hundred employees that supplies cutting-edge machinery to Fortune 500 aerospace companies, such as Boeing and Airbus.

Somehow, the anonymous postcards were traced to Zieve, and an effort was immediately launched to smear him. CAIR used its friends in the media to do negative stories on Zieve, including articles in the *Seattle Times* and coverage by local TV stations that made him out to be a bigot. CAIR also used its always reliable liberal pastors to further pressure Zieve into backing down from his position. A community meeting was held with CAIR officials at Pointe of Grace Lutheran Church in which the Lutheran pastor put forth all the standard lies about Islam being a religion of peace and tolerance. When another pastor, who is a former Muslim, tried to ask what kind of response he should person-ally expect from this peaceful religion after having left its clutches, the imam remained silent and the CAIR representatives started laughing at the pastor.

"He was laughed out of the building," one of the attendees told me.[10]

The honest answer to the question put forth by the former Muslim, of course, is that he could expect to be killed if he had been living in a Muslim country and announced his conversion to Christianity.

After the community meeting at the Lutheran church, Zieve buckled. He sent a written apology to the local Muslim community for having opposed their mosque.

Once again, an American's First Amendment rights had been muzzled. And not only his rights to free speech but his political right to oppose a permit application by a mosque that was up for a vote before his own local government.

Compare and contrast these examples of Muslims playing the oppressed victim and getting away with it to what happened in Lawrenceville, Georgia,[11] on the day after Memorial Day, 2016. A mother and daughter in Lawrenceville, a suburb of Atlanta, were attacked by an unknown Muslim woman simply because they were flying an American flag for Memorial Day. (Read the full story in chapter 10.)

Amina Ali Ahra, a thirty-year-old refugee from Somalia, was arrested on two misdemeanor counts of simple battery after attacking Dami Arno and daughter Brittany at their home.

Arno was sitting in her garage, drinking coffee and talking with her daughter, when Ahra emerged from the woods, grabbed the flag from off the mailbox, and charged at them. The flag was attached to a four-foot-long PVC pipe, which Ahra used to beat Arno outside her own home. The alleged attacker told police she was from Africa, but would give them no other information about her identity.

The Atlanta area has the nation's fifth-largest Somali refugee com-munity, with more than four thousand arriving since 2002. Including those born to their refugee mothers, the total Somali population in the

Atlanta metro area is likely ten thousand strong.[12]

Some neighbors in the area said they were upset that the Muslim woman was only charged with misdemeanor simple battery and not a hate crime. Police said they "did not know the motive for the attack," according to a brief report by the Associated Press, in which the words "Muslim," "Islam," or "burqa" never appeared.[13] But at least the AP filed a report. The national networks ABC, NBC, CBS, and CNN didn't feel the need to report on the incident at all.

The FBI said it looked into the case and didn't see any grounds for a hate crime.[14] The local Atlanta news media totally ignored this aspect of the story and refused to follow up with the FBI's verdict when the family notified them.

What we're seeing is an intentional blackout of all news that puts Islam in a bad light. The media have voluntarily joined forces with the government to protect Muslim refugees and immigrants because to report what is really going on would be too horrific, too difficult for the average American to process. They would start to ask too many questions about why their government, faced with growing Islamic extremism, continues to import more Muslims into American communities at a rate of thousands per week.

"You have a Muslim in a burqa attacking a mom at her home, in her garage, on her property, and all she was charged with was simple battery," Hadian said. "It shows how morally bankrupt we are, how confused we are, and again, it shows you the submission to fear that they would not call this attack in Georgia what it was. It was a hate-motivated attack, and she should be facing felony charges."

And where were the liberal Christians reaching out to the woman and her family after this attack? They were nowhere to be found. Imagine if it had been a Muslim attacked by a Christian. The hard-core leftist "Christians" would have been falling all over themselves to help and console the victim. "We have plenty of delusional Christians who continue to come to the rescue of Islam," Hadian says.

This is the real-life working out of the Muslim Brotherhood plan, laid out in the "Explanatory Memorandum," of "'sabotaging' [Western civilization's] *miserable house* by *their hands* and the hands of the believers."[15]

If you can find someone within your enemy's own camp who is willing to be used and who will do your bidding, that's always more effective than if you pleaded your own cause. "And that is exactly what they are doing," Hadian says. "If they can use us to defeat ourselves, how much better is that than getting their hands dirty? And so how confused are these Christians who think it's an act of love to help Islam, when it's an act of submission, handing our communities over? What I ask these Christians is, have you ever lived in a Muslim country? Have you seen what Islam does to Christian communities? Have you ever talked to a Christian who has lived under that system in a Muslim country and come out of there? If they have, I don't know if they would be doing this."

Hadian believes there is more to the story of businessman Peter Zieve's transformation from someone who opposed the construction of a mosque in Mukilteo into an apologist for the Muslim group sponsoring the mosque. "Something, somehow, got to him, and he flipped his story 180 degrees after this church comes to the aid of the mosque. They have this Kumbaya meeting, and they always use the same line, 'We're not going to be haters.' So if you resist Islam, you're automatically a hater, and exercising voluntary dhimmitude to Islam, voluntary slavery to Islam," he said.

Dhimmitude is the historic condition of Christians and Jews who lived a life of subjugation to Muslims in an Islamic society under sharia law. In return for allowing them to live, the Muslims required the Christians to pay a head tax of 50 percent or more of their income. They could not build new churches or even maintain their churches without the permission of the Muslims, they were not allowed to hold positions of authority in the civil government or military, and they could not evangelize or practice their faith outside the walls of their homes or church. They most assuredly could not criticize Islam in the slightest way without facing prison or death.

Today's Western dhimmi Christian is voluntarily hiding the

gospel message of freedom and forgiveness in Christ out of fear of offending Islam.

"It bothers me that Christians are letting the fear of these labels affect their stand for truth and righteousness, because we don't want to be called a hater or Islamophobe, and so they carry the water for the Muslims," Hadian says. "We'll be your knight in shining armor because you can't protect yourself? Really? CAIR, with all its multimillions of dollars? Why are we apologetic for resisting a mosque?"

Hadian said communities being asked to approve new mosques should put pressure on their city leaders to disclose who's behind the mosque. Where is the money coming from? In at least 75 percent of the cases, it's foreign money coming from Saudi Arabia or it's being financed through the Muslim Brotherhood's North American Islamic Trust. NAIT is based in Plainfield, Indiana, and finances Islamic centers, mosques, and schools across North America.

"It sickens me that Christians are capitulating to this," Hadian said. "And to me it's just a pattern where we're following exactly what happened in 1930s Germany when churches were getting in line to carry the water and follow the mantra of the Nazi Party."

CULTURE CLASH

Americans who are unfamiliar with the fundamental nature of Islam and how it is being given special favor by Western governments dominated by the secular Left, will not understand why we should be concerned about Muslim immigration. Why should we be concerned with such a small demographic that makes up less than 2 percent of America's population? Latino immigration has been going on, legal and illegal, for much longer.

"By that logic America will be a Mexican-Catholic nation long before sharia is the law of the land," one man wrote to me after reading one of my articles.

If we just look at the numbers alone and if we assume that Islam is no different in its fundamental goals than Christianity or Judaism, then that may be true.

But such statements belie a basic ignorance of Islam. Mexican Catholics do not use violence and coercion to implement the tenets of their faith, and they don't wish to make their faith part of the civil government. Under Islam there is no separation between religion and the power strings of government. Islam is one big, universal prescription for all of life that is pushy and coercive by its very nature, as spelled out in sharia. I don't see Mexicans, for example, suing their employers to allow them to have time off work to say the rosary or to allow them to wear religious garb in the workplace. I don't see them pressuring the schools and jails to serve Mexican food, or demanding baptismal fountains in public universities. I certainly don't see them trying to kill people who blaspheme Jesus or the Christian prophets. Muslims make up 1 percent of our population and yet we see them doing all of these things.

Muslim women sue their employers to be able to wear the hijab. Schools, hospitals, and prisons must provide halal meat. Cases of female genital mutilation and honor violence against women are on the rise as Muslims push for separate sharia tribunals to settle their family disputes. Workers demand breaks for Islamic prayer five times a day and Muslim holidays off. Look to Europe to get a glimpse of the future if the tide is not stemmed, say some of the more enlightened Western leaders, such as Geert Wilders of the Netherlands and Prime Minister Viktor Orban of Hungary, who have unapologetically defended their countries' Judeo-Christian heritage.

In England, the number of sex crimes against minors has skyrocketed over the past decade in direct correlation to the rise in the Muslim population, even as the elites operating schools, police agencies, and child welfare agencies have done their best to sweep these cases under the rug with the help of a complicit media. The same has happened with the explosion in the number of sexual assaults against women in Germany and Sweden.

But stalwarts of the faith, such as Franklin Graham and Joel Richardson, have argued that none of these changes could have occurred in Western societies if the Christian church had not abandoned its biblical mandate to not only reach out in love with food, clothing, and shelter, but to aggressively share the undiluted Word of God with all who will listen.

So it's time now to take a look at some of our Christian leaders and how they have offered themselves as useful idiots in the cause of Islam.

CHRISTIAN LEADERS SELLING OUT CHRISTIANITY

Britain's highest-ranking man of the cloth, the archbishop of Canterbury, said Christians should not share their faith with Muslims unless they are asked. Archbishop Justin Welby made the comment at an inter-faith event that included Islamic and Jewish leaders. He insisted Christians should not actively proselytize non-Christians, the UK's *Express* reported.[16]

The comments come as Britain is increasingly being Islamized, with 5.4 percent of its population identifying as Muslim in 2014, dozens of churches being converted to mosques, and the city of London recently electing its first Muslim mayor, Sadiq Khan. Almost every major city in Britain has a Muslim enclave and two boroughs of London are approaching 50 percent. The country has promised to take in at least twenty thousand Syrian refugees over the next five years.[17]

Welby said Christians should be more concerned about "respect for the other," and start by "listening before you speak." They should offer "love that is unconditional and not conditional to one iota, to one single element, on how the person responds to your own declaration of faith; and of not speaking about faith unless you are asked about faith."[18]

Evangelical leaders rebuked the archbishop's comments as unbib-lical, saying they negate Jesus' own words in the Great Commission of Matthew 28:18–20 and many other teachings of Jesus and his disciples, the early church fathers, and the Anglican Church itself. In the Great Commission Jesus said, "Go therefore and make disciples of all the nations, baptizing them in the name of the Father and of the Son and of the Holy Spirit, teaching them to observe all things that I commanded you; and lo, I am with you always, even to the end of the age" (NKJV).

"Christianity has never merely been an intellectual acknowledgement of some particular set of doctrines," said Bible teacher and evangelist Joel Richardson, author of *When a Jew Rules the World*, *The Global Jesus Revolution*, and *The Islamic Antichrist*.[19]

"SHUT THE HELL UP!"

James, the brother of Jesus, made it clear that faith without resulting action is a false faith. "Christians who do not share their faith, may very well not even possess a genuine faith," added Richardson. He continued:

> The message of the world to the Church today is essentially this: 'Shut the hell up and go feed the poor!' The spirit of the age is well pleased when Christians engage in productive social action but remain quiet concerning the reality of sin and the need of all men and women to repent.
>
> They rage when we say, as Jesus so clearly did, that He alone is "the way, the truth, and the life and no one comes to the Father except by [Jesus]." The exclusive message of Christianity drives the world nuts. When Christians withhold the gospel, the message that reveals the only way to life, they are actually placing their stamp of approval on another's spiritual death certificate.

"This is the most hateful act. Those who are genuine disciples of Jesus will not shut up (about the gospel message)," Richardson asserted. "The blind guide archbishop of Canterbury needs to repent himself and begin rightly shepherding his flock or resign."[20]

EVANGELIZING MUSLIM REFUGEES "VERBOTEN"

Archbishop Welby is not the only Christian leader teaching that Christians should keep their faith to themselves or dilute its potency when engaging with Muslims. Pastor Gerhard Scholte of the Reformed Keizersgracht Church, who heads up the refugee task force of combined Amsterdam churches in the Netherlands, told the *Daily Beast* that his church does not promote conversions of non-Christians.

Thousands of Muslim migrants are walking into Europe's churches and seeking to convert to Christianity. Astonishingly, this is not good news to Pastor Scholte and others working to resettle the refugees. They would apparently prefer the converts remain Muslim. "Conversion to Christianity is not promoted in our church, so we see very little of it," Scholte told the *Daily Beast*. "Everyone is a child of God," whether Christian, Jew or Muslim. "Faith should not be conditional," he said, echoing the comments of Welby.[21]

"TAKE DOWN THAT CROSS!"

In Sweden, the world's first lesbian bishop of a mainstream Christian denomination has put forth a call for one of the country's seaport churches to remove its crosses so as to avoid offending Muslims. Bishop Eva Brunne of the Lutheran Church of Sweden has proposed that the Christian symbols of the Seamen's Church in Freeport be removed to make it more inviting for visiting sailors from who practice Islam, according to a report by SVT.se, a Stockholm-based news outlet.

In addition to removing crosses, Brunne's plan calls for setting up a prayer room inside the church that marks the direction of Mecca, thereby accommodating Muslim visitors. It would also make the church less offensive to the tens of thousands of Muslims entering Sweden from the Middle East and North Africa as refugees.

"Making a room available for people of other faiths does not mean that we are not defenders of our own faith. Priests are called to proclaim Christ. We do that every day and in every meeting with people," says Brunne. "But that does not mean that we are stingy toward people of other faiths."

Sweden has "surrendered without so much as firing a shot," said Pamela Geller author of *Stop the Islamization of America*.

"Sweden has lost it," Geller told WND. "It is sacrificing its own heritage to accommodate immigrants who will not be as accommodating to native non-Muslim Swedes. The bishop is paving the way for the Islamization of Sweden."

The Church of Sweden is the largest Christian church in Sweden and the largest Lutheran denomination in the world. The primate of the Church of Sweden is Archbishop Antje Jackelén, the country's first female archbishop.

Robert Spencer, an Islam expert and blogger at Jihad Watch, said, "This is what a society and culture in the midst of suicide looks like. How wonderful and generous and ecumenical and multicultural this is." Spencer suggested that imams in Stockholm and across Europe are likely laughing at the ease with which Christians there are willing to surrender to Islam. "Watch for mosques everywhere to remove their mihrabs and install crosses so that Christians will feel comfortable praying there," Spencer said with biting sarcasm.

Of course, not all Swedes are happy about the bishop's plan. Patrik Pettersson, priest of the Oscars parish in Stockholm, blogged: "The church chapel cannot reasonably be equated with prayer rooms at airports and hospital chapels anyway. The Christian churches and chapels are not public areas at any time."

Seamen's mission director, Kiki Wetterberg, also disagrees with the bishop. "I have no problem with Muslim or Hindu sailors coming here and praying. But I believe that we are a Christian church, so we keep the symbols. If I visit a mosque, I do not ask them to take down their symbols. It's my choice to go in there," she wrote to the newspaper *Dagen*.

"If you think this story sounds too bizarre to be true, then you haven't acquainted yourself with the progressive 'utopia' that is Sweden," wrote UK-based writer Paul Joseph Watson. "This is a country in which some politicians have called for giving free housing, jobs and welfare to returning ISIS jihadists—all at taxpayer expense."

Sweden is also a country that hires ISIS-sympathizers to run its immigration boards, Watson noted. And the country's taxpayer-funded "expert" on Islamophobia, Michael Nikolai Skråmo, also went on to join ISIS.

NETHERLANDS POLITICIAN COUNTERS EU'S MULTICULTURAL "UTOPIA"

Geert Wilders, head of the Dutch Party of Freedom, is one politician who isn't buying into the EU's vision of a multicultural utopia. Wilders has for years been calling for a more aggressive counterjihadist program. His Freedom Party is now the fourth-largest in the Dutch Parliament and continues to gain strength.

"All the politicians are, I have to say, ignoring the problem. They are fooling their constituents (about Islam), even your own president, Mr. Obama," Wilders said in an interview with Jamie Glazov, editor of *FrontPage Magazine*, for Web TV's *The Glazov Gang*. Wilders said he believes Western politicians and diplomats such as Obama, Hillary Clinton, and John Kerry are mischaracterizing the Islamic State, ISIS, as "not Islamic" but rather a group that has simply "hijacked" one of the world's great religions.

"I have to tell you, it's all lies," Wilders said. "The problem we face today in our free Western society is we have imported millions of people from Islamic countries with a background, a culture, an ideology of hate, a totalitarian ideology." Wilders said to stop the Islamization of Western cultures, the nations must stop Islamic immigration, which has led to a steady erosion and degradation of every Christian country where it has been tried.

WEST SHOULD LOOK TO LEBANON FOR EXAMPLE

The West should take its cue from Lebanon. This northern neighbor of Israel was majority Christian until rampant Islamic immigration turned the demographics in the 1950s and '60s. By the 1970s, jihadist attacks on Christian families and Christian-owned businesses were commonplace, and it has been unsafe ever since for Christians to live and practice their faith. Islamic immigration turned Lebanon's capital city of Beirut, once known as the "Paris of the Middle East," into a Third World conflict zone. Europe, short of a 180-degree turn in policy, is now on the same path, Wilders said.

"I believe, if we don't want to see in our own countries happening what we see today in Iraq and Syria, we should fight against the Islamization of our own free society, which means we should stop the Islamization of our society, that we should stop the immigration from Islamic countries. We should expel all the people that have even the slightest sympathy for the Islamic State," Wilders told Glazov, the *FrontPage* editor. "We should encourage the voluntary repatriation of people from Islamic countries. We should de-Islamize our societies in order to stay free. We should not only fight the Islamic State over there, but we should fight the Islamic monster in our own free societies."

THE AMERICAN CHURCH IS FOLLOWING THE EUROPEAN MODEL

The distaste for reaching out to Muslims with the gospel is also alive and well in the American church. Liberal church pastors participating in interfaith associations with imams particularly frown upon proselytizing Muslims. Instead, they talk about building bridges and finding common ground with Islam but in the process present a watered-down version of Christianity.

This falls in line with the Islamists' "Pact of Umar," a treaty signed by Umar II, Islam's third caliph and conqueror of Jerusalem in AD 637. It dictated that Muslims were to rule supreme over the Christians and Jews, who were allowed to practice their faiths only under the oppressive system of dhimmitude, described earlier.

This has been a tenet of sharia law ever since, said Dr. Mark Christian. "Umar did not come up with these rules on his own, it's the sharia law of interrelationships between the three faiths."

One of the tenets of dhimmitude prohibits the erecting of any large symbols or outward displays that are insensitive or offensive to Muslims. Today, in Pakistan, Egypt, and many other Muslim countries where Christians still live and practice their faith under dhimmitude, it is forbidden to erect large crosses outside of churches. These dhimmi churches are also forbidden from ringing church bells or singing with loud choirs. Swedish Lutherans' Eva Brunne, who sought to strip the Seamen's Church of its crosses, would feel right at home.

"We have the cross and the Star of David and who gets upset and is sensitive to any symbols like that? It is the Muslims," Christian said. "Jews and Christians have been living next door on the same streets for years with no problems but history tells us that Muslims are very sensitive to everything, whether it be Christian proselytizing, crosses or even pork in the grocery stores.

"The reality is it is not about sensitivity, it's about making a statement—'we are supreme.'"

A SIGN OF CHRISTIAN APOSTASY?

Carl Gallups, a Florida Baptist pastor, radio host, and author, said this fear of offending Islam is a sign of the apostate church foretold in the biblical book of Revelation. They talk about love, but withholding the truth of Christ is hardly a loving thing for a Christian to do.

"These are the days of apostasy," said Gallups, author of *Final Warning* and *Be Thou Prepared: Equipping Christians for Persecution and Times of Trouble.*

"Can you imagine Jesus ordering His disciples or the church to 'keep your faith quiet'? I guess this archbishop Welby has never read the seven letters to the seven churches in Revelation?" he said. "Wow. It's here, folks."

Joel Richardson agrees and said Welby needs to do some soul searching and repent of his willingness to throw out such a basic Christian dictate as evangelism. "If he does not [repent], faithful Anglicans throughout the world need to remove him," Richardson asserted. "Yes, we Christians will care for the poor, the needy, the outcast, and the afflicted, but we will not shut up. If we remain silent, the very rocks themselves will cry out." (See Luke 19:37–40.)

The Church of England recently launched a campaign to reverse decades of declining membership. How the archbishop's ban on proselytizing Muslims fits into that strategy is mind-boggling, said Gallups. To eliminate or downplay the importance of Christian evangelism, he said, is to give a slap in the face not only to Jesus but to all of His disciples who have gone to their graves as martyrs over the centuries while spreading the gospel in unfriendly places.

"Paul was beheaded, Steven was stoned, Peter was crucified and countless Church fathers were martyred for steadfastly obeying Christ's command to share the good news of the gospel," Gallups said. "This archbishop makes a mockery of their lives."

Iranian-born Shahram Hadian told WND that Pope Francis has put forth the same unbiblical ideas about keeping one's faith hidden. Instead, said Pastor Hadian, "you saw the pope go to the Hagia Sophia [in Turkey] and bow down to pray toward Mecca.

"We have the U.S. Conference of Catholic Bishops saying the same thing," he went on, "that we want to love the refugees and bring them here, feed and clothe them but when you ask them if they have a plan to share the gospel they have no plan to share it because they feel like it's offensive."

Hadian believes this philosophy is proving "disastrous" in Europe, and it plays right into the hands of the Islamists seeking to implement sharia. "Europe has already passed anti-defamation of Islam laws and now, in fact, the archbishop comes out and says 'don't share your faith unless they first ask you.' That's not going to happen for the most part," Hadian said. "Christians are getting orders to keep their faith silent and it's unbiblical, absolutely unbiblical."

SURRENDERING TO ISLAMIC SUBJUGATION

Pastor Hadian has talked to many Christians involved in the refugee resettlement movement who say "the exact same thing" espoused by the archbishop of Canterbury. "They say 'we are going to wait until they ask us, we don't want to push our faith on them.' It really is a surrender," he told me.

"Christians, not Christianity but Christians, are surrendering to Islam. When you're afraid to actually share the gospel, which the Bible says offers the power of eternal life, you are really surrendering ground to this other faith, which is Islam," he continued. "True Christianity will never surrender to Islam. But it's the Christians, or the ones pretending to be Christian, who are surrendering to Islam and it's not biblical. These are not representatives of the gospel. The spirit of God does not retreat, does not surrender ground, the only time it retreats is when Christians give it up."

In fact, when more than a hundred evangelical leaders gathered at the Billy Graham Center for Evangelism (BGCE) at Wheaton College on December 17, 2015, to discuss how American Christians should best respond to the refugee crisis, noticeably absent from their conversation was the importance of evangelism.[22] They issued a statement that talked about providing housing, food, clothing, employment, and education without any mention of spiritual food or guidance.

"That's submission. That's dhimmitude. You are told you can practice your faith, but you're not allowed to share it," said Hadian. "The Pact of Umar is actually where the concept of jizya began. Muhammad said the people of the book must be made subjugated. And oh, by the way, we can break the pact with you at any point, is the Muslims' refrain. Once a formal agreement is made, then they begin to dictate what Christians and Jews are allowed to do. So there you go, Mr. Archbishop of Canterbury. Congratulations for making yourself a dhimmi. Same with the pope. Both have submitted themselves to Mecca."

Paul McGuire, a pastor, author, and former radio host in Southern California who has also appeared as a Fox News contributor, said the UK's Archbishop Welby and Sweden's Bishop Brunne are betraying the gospel, and by doing so are emblematic of the dark spiritual place that much of Western Christendom has entered.

"What is the difference between the Archbishop of Canterbury . . . and the Lord Jesus Christ and the original apostles? The difference is that Jesus Christ and the original apostles were faithful to God, whether men liked it or not," McGuire told me. "Welby's teaching that a Christian should not talk about their faith unless asked, is a teaching that Satan would have invented to prevent men and women from being saved by the Gospel of Jesus Christ. By biblical definition, the Archbishop of

Canterbury is a 'false prophet' and a wolf in sheep's clothing teaching his flock the doctrine of demons."

That doctrine of demons is sweeping the globe, unchecked by a biblical Christian response that fulfills the teachings of Jesus in His Great Commission.

6

EUROPE UNDER ASSAULT

This is but the beginning of what is to come, if Europe does not pull up the drawbridge.

—PATRICK BUCHANAN

IN MAY 2016, POPE FRANCIS, in a meeting billed by Vatican officials as a "summit on the migrant emergency," met with four hundred school-age children in southern Italy to tell them to embrace the migrants who have been flooding into their country.

"Migrants are not a danger; they are in danger," he told them and then called on the children to repeat after him: "They are not a danger, they are in danger."[1]

The pope relayed a tear-jerking story of a six-year-old girl who lost her life trying to cross the ocean to freedom. Hold the child's life jacket, he said, "[A rescue worker] brought me this . . . and, crying, he said, 'Father, I failed. There was a girl, in the waves, but I could not save her. All that was left was her life-jacket.'

"I don't want to upset you," he continued, "but you are brave and you know the truth. They are in danger: many children . . . they are in danger. Think about this girl. What was her name? I don't know: a child without a name. Each of you must give her the name you want to. She is in heaven, she is watching over us."[2]

Francis called on the children to remember their Christian duty when they consider the migrants, and to welcome all as brothers and sisters—much as the biblical story of the Good Samaritan illustrates. Those who don't welcome the migrants into their countries are guilty of hypocrisy, he said, emphasizing that strangers aren't bad people who need to be feared. He encouraged the children to keep their fear of migrants in check because beneath the surface of our various skin colors, we all are children of the same Father.[3]

Under Islam, Allah is not seen as a father, and he most assuredly did not have a son, but that's a small theological inconvenience for a pope sold out to globalism and open borders. *Just love them and they will be nice to us* was the essence of the pope's message that day to the children of Calabria, a region of Italy hit particularly hard by the influx of migrants from sub-Sahara Africa.

That brings us to another scene in Ventimiglia, Italy, that played out in the spring of 2016.

Imagine the surprise of the faithful Catholics at Ventimiglia's Church of St. Anthony when volunteers of a Catholic charity called Caritas told them they couldn't recite the rosary out loud. That's right. Parishioners and visitors were told they must "pray in silence" out of respect for and so as not to disturb African migrants being housed there, reported Virginia Hale of Breitbart London.

According to Breitbart, much of Caritas's resources are spent, not on helping Catholics or other needy Christians, but on "facilitating mass migration to Europe; the organization even boasts of contributing to and seeking to influence European Union "asylum" policies.[4] Caritas Europa reports on its website that it "stresses states' responsibility to ensure that asylum seekers, refugees and other migrants are treated with dignity and are acknowledged as one of the most vulnerable groups in Europe's society."[5]

In the meantime, after one of the female parishioners at St. Anthony requested that the migrants be taken to another church so she could recite the rosary, the parish priest escorted her and the other visitors to another church.[6]

With a population of fifty-five thousand, Ventimiglia has been overwhelmed with hundreds of migrants. More than fifty have been crossing from North Africa into the city every day, hoping that from there they will be able to enter France. The town's mayor, Enrico Ioculano, has said this is "an untenable situation."[7]

Breitbart London reports that in churches across Europe, welcoming migrants has taken precedence over Christian worship. In Germany, an evangelical church stripped out pews, the altar, and the pulpit as well as all symbols of Christianity when offering it as a new home for migrants—so as to make them feel "more welcome in their new home."[8]

The Muslim migrant invasion of Europe is bringing forth a society in which Christians adopt the "cowed posture of dhimmitude," states Ralph Sidway's *Facing Islam* blog, "as Catholics and Protestants convert their churches into migrant housing, then tell their congregants not to pray out loud for fear of disturbing their Muslim guests."[9]

Dhimmitude, as discussed earlier, was Islam's subjugation of Christians during the time of Muhammad and up through the Ottoman Empire of the twentieth century. Christians were allowed to continue practicing their faith, but as second-class citizens with almost no civil rights and at a cost of half—or more—of their incomes. And again, they were not allowed to proselytize, maintain their churches, visibly display symbols of Christianity, or hold positions of authority over Muslims in civil society.

The only difference in Europe today is that Christians are placing themselves under dhimmitude *voluntarily*. And it gets worse.

In Hamburg, Germany, on May 27, 2016, Protestant pastor Sieghard Wilm of St. Pauli Church held a Muslim funeral service in his church for a seventeen-year-old who died fighting as a jihadist for the Islamic State.

The young man had sent an audio message back to Germany shortly before his death, saying he had become disillusioned with the terrorist group. This led to speculation that members of ISIS had executed him.

"We cannot deny this is a difficult situation," Wilm said in response to his critics. "I can tell you as a pastor at St. Pauli, that I have also laid to rest more killers. A man remains a man. Even a person who has offended against someone. Even such a man has relatives who mourn him."

The question is, was it really necessary for a *Christian* pastor to hold a *Muslim* service?

Indeed, there was heated discussion among Germans over the funeral, especially on social media. But Wilm says he wanted to use the opportunity to create a "safe space" for the family of the slain terrorist so they would not have to grieve in private. Furthermore, he claimed, a Muslim service would be a good opportunity for "learning and respect among religions."

According to *Jihad Watch*, the boy had immigrated to Germany from the African nation of Cameroon and was raised as a Christian until he was converted to Islam at age fourteen by Salafist imams, who urge Muslims to live out their faith as it was originally practiced by Muhammad.

He was part of a growing list, numbering in the thousands, of young Muslims who have become quickly radicalized and gone off to fight for ISIS. The largest segment of foreign fighters in the ISIS army comes from Europe, with some estimates exceeding five thousand.[10]

BURSTING ONTO THE WORLD STAGE

The Islamization of Europe has been quietly proceeding for decades, but the story broke onto the world stage with a bang in September 2015, with jaw-dropping photographs and stirring video showing waves of desperate-looking Syrians, Iraqis, Africans, and Afghanis throwing rocks and literally forcing their way into country after country.[11]

But instead of focusing on the aggressive nature of the young, rock-throwing men, the Western media turned their focus elsewhere. One photo in particular had an enormous impact. It captured a small boy's body washed up on a beach in Turkey. The body was that of three-year-old Aylan Kurdi, and the image would resonate around the world. The backers of a borderless world now had a face to put on their cause. This photograph would be shown day after day on CNN and other major networks as the backdrop for the reason Europe and North America needed to open their arms to the fleeing Syrian refugees. A second photograph of a dour-faced policeman carrying the boy's body to shore was equally sensational and effective in steering the public debate toward a solidly humanitarian angle—we were helping desperate widows and orphans, not aggressive young men of fighting age. In the words of the British newspaper the *Independent*, the images of Aylan "sparked international outrage over the refugee crisis."[12]

Why weren't our wealthy Western governments doing more to help these poor, innocent wretches?

The *Independent* ran another story headlined "If these extraordinarily powerful images of a dead Syrian child washed up on a beach don't change Europe's attitude to refugees, what will?" The newspaper also implored its readers to "sign the *Independent*'s petition" to welcome refugees.[13] It was much the same narrative as that put forth by the Associated Press, Reuters, Agence France-Presse, the *Guardian*, the *New York Times*, the *Wall Street Journal*, Fox News, and countless other news outlets.

Then, about a week later, the real story started to come out about Aylan's family. Give Reuters credit for doing what the other news outlets couldn't imagine doing—actually investigating the father's story.

Here is an excerpt from the Reuters article exposing the lies that this father was merely a poor, wretched refugee fleeing war and oppression:

> The father of drowned Syrian toddler Aylan Kurdi was working with smugglers and driving the flimsy boat that capsized trying to reach Greece, other passengers on board said, in an account that disputes the version he gave last week.
>
> Ahmed Hadi Jawwad and his wife, Iraqis who lost their 11-year-old daughter and 9-year-old son in the crossing, told Reuters that Abdullah Kurdi panicked and accelerated when a wave hit the boat, raising questions about his claim that somebody else was driving the boat.
>
> A third passenger confirmed their version of events, which Reuters could not independently verify.

"The story that (Aylan's father) told is untrue. I don't know what made him lie, maybe fear," Jawwad said in Baghdad at his in-laws' house on Friday. "He was the driver from the very beginning until the boat sank."

He said Kurdi swam to them and begged them to cover up his true role in the incident. His wife confirmed the details.

Jawwad said his point of contact with the smugglers was called Abu Hussein. "Abu Hussein told me that he (Kurdi) was the one who organized this trip," he said. . . .

Amir Haider, 22, another Iraqi who said he was on the same boat, confirmed Jawwad's account and identified Kurdi as the driver. He told Reuters by telephone from Istanbul that he initially thought Kurdi was Turkish because he was not speaking, but later heard him talking to his wife in Syrian Arabic.[14]

The truth, which was never reported by the major American and European media, was that Aylan's family was never forced to make the risky voyage to escape any type of physical harm or persecution. In fact, their father was a human smuggler working for profit.

The truth was also reported by the *Daily Telegraph* of London:

The father of the three-year-old boy whose lifeless body washed up on a Turkish beach, rocking the whole world to its core, has been accused of being a people smuggler who captained the fateful voyage.

A woman who lost two of her three children on the vessel made the stunning claims to Network Ten via her cousin, who lives in Sydney, on Friday night. . . .

It was claimed on Friday night that his father Abdullah was a people smuggler who captained the dodgy boat for its entire voyage, capsizing in heavy seas and killing at least 12 people.

Iraq-based Zainab Abbas, via her Sydney-based cousin Lara Tahseen, told Ten News she paid $10,000 for the voyage and Aylan's father was in charge of the boat.

"He was a smuggler, yes, he was the one driving the boat," she said.[15]

The migrants from a growing list of Third World countries also came to Greece and Italy by boat from North Africa. Others walked up from Turkey through Hungary, demanding rail passage to the rich welfare states of Germany and Sweden. More than 3,000 a day were arriving in Greece, and more than 2,000 a day in Italy.

Some 100,000 arrived in the first week of September 2015 in Hungary, forcing a two-day standoff at a train station twenty-two miles from Budapest. The Hungarian government at first refused to let the trains roll toward Austria, as prime minister Viktor Orban said he didn't want to send the message that more migrants would be welcome to use his country as a pass-through. But as the media continued to cover the "crisis," the migrants took off on foot, and Hungary eventually sent buses to carry them to the Austrian border.

For several weeks in the late summer of 2015, CNN, NBC, ABC, and CBS covered the refugee crisis as one of their top stories. Constantly in their news feed were images of perilous boat voyages across the Mediterranean Sea and emotionally charged narratives, clearly intended to tug at the heartstrings of naive and ill-informed Westerners. Rarely was it stated that the overwhelming majority of the refugees were male Sunni Muslims, the same people who were attacking and killing Christians in Syria, Lebanon, Iraq, Egypt, and Libya. No journalists asked the obvious question: Where are the Christians among these refugees, and why aren't Western governments offering to rescue them from the genocidal attacks of ISIS, al-Qaeda, and others in Syria and Iraq, or al-Shabab in Kenya, Hezbollah in Lebanon, and Boko Haram in Nigeria?

Instead they focused on the emotional feature stories of women and children trying to reach Europe, even when they had to look long and hard for a woman or children in the crowd. CNN described one Syrian father gripping his young son as they were reunited on the long journey. "Today he arrived safely in Berlin and is able to build a new future for him and his family."

Facebook and Twitter also lit up with touching stories of refugees as Americans traded the stories with their friends under the hashtags

#EuropeSaysWelcome and #RefugeesWelcome. "Share if you agree that every refugee family fleeing from violence and poverty should be allowed to have a safe and happy life in Europe," read one tweet.[16]

Any European who questioned the wisdom of bringing in more than 1.5 million Muslims, at least two-thirds of whom were young males of fighting age, was immediately cast as a bigot, a racist, and a xenophobe whose voice was not worthy of being heard in the public domain. Germany passed laws allowing its federal government to arrest Germans who posted "hateful" comments about Muslim migrants on social media. Facebook agreed to help the German government crack down on so-called hate speech. In July 2016, the German government conducted predawn raids on sixty homes and arrested forty Germans under the new law. Both sides in the debate have reported being targeted by violent attacks. Thousands of German women have been groped and sexually assaulted by migrants, and some German men have responded by torching asylum centers housing the migrants. German police recorded approximately 200 cases of arson at refugee centers across the country in the first eight months of 2015.[17] Europe's long awaited meltdown was underway.

HOW IT ALL STARTED

Despite the sudden world media focus on Europe and its refugees, the Islamization of Germany began in the 1960s, when the country started welcoming Turkish immigrants. The reason German politicians gave to the German people for this open-doors policy toward the Turks was the same justification that many American politicians, such as Jeb Bush, have given to American voters for a more liberal immigration policy. The Turks were needed to do low-wage jobs Germans no longer wanted to do, but that wasn't the most important reason. More critically, they explain, Turkish workers were needed to support the economy and the future retirement income of German workers.

Why were there not enough Germans to fulfill the country's economic needs? Interestingly, the liberals in Germany, just like the progressives in America, have preached for years that smaller families were morally superior to larger families. That lie, which led to a birthrate below what is needed to replace those who die every year, created the convenient need for a replacement population. German families have a meager fertility rate of 1.4 babies per woman, according to the most recent data provided by the World Bank.[18] That is less than replacement level, so it became clear by the late 1950s and early '60s that Germany would not have enough workers to earn taxable income to support German retirees and continue all the benefits Germans enjoyed as part of the nation's expanding welfare state. In short, not enough worker bees. To replace the millions of Germans lost to contraception and abortion, Germany turned to the Turks, welcoming hundreds of thousands of them into its cities and towns, just as America has turned to the Mexicans, Central Americans, and more recently, to Muslims from Somalia, Iraq, Syria, Afghanistan, and Burma.

The same phenomenon has occurred in France, which has welcomed the North Africans, and in Belgium, Sweden, Norway, the Netherlands, Britain, and Italy.

These Muslim immigrants, unlike their native European counterparts, believe in having babies. Lots of them. Compared to the fertility rates of 1.4 to 1.9 children per woman among Western women, the Muslims have fertility rates of three to seven children per woman.[19]

If current migration trends continue, it is not far-fetched to conclude that Germany, Belgium, and France, which is already 10 percent Muslim, could approach a majority Muslim population within seventy-five years. The United Nations has said the waves of migrants and refugees will not stop anytime soon. The world's refugee population now stands at an all-time record high of 65.3 million and growing, according to the United Nations High Commissioner for Refugees.[20] So the record influx into Europe and increasing influx into the United States has the potential to continue for many years to come.

The German government announced in the summer of 2015 that it would welcome a staggering 1 million refugees and asylum seekers into the country by the end of the year, five times the normal number. Prime minister Angela Merkel said the country could accommodate 500,000 refugees annually "for years." By the middle of 2016, the number had exceeded 1.5 million new migrants in Germany, and a string of violent attacks unleashed by jihadists had Germans on edge.

Just days after the 2016 Würzburg train attack, mentioned in the preface, an eighteen-year-old German-born son of Iranian asylum-seekers shot and killed nine Germans outside a McDonald's at a Munich mall. Then a Syrian refugee killed a pregnant woman in Germany with a machete.

Germany was suddenly enveloped in a climate of fear, feeling betrayed by its own government. Chancellor Angela Merkel and her friends in the German federal government had engineered perhaps the biggest national sellout in history, opting to please their globalist masters over the citizens of Germany. The grand multicultural vision of globalist Europeans was coming apart at the seams, as evidenced by the Brexit vote by the UK citizens who voted overwhelmingly in June 2016 to leave the European Union. The EU's attempt to force its citizens to welcome and pay for the integration of millions of Third World immigrants was causing mass uprisings and could result in anarchy.

THE "HIJRA" INTO EUROPE AND BEYOND

The establishment media portrayed the waves of migrants into Europe as war refugees, and certainly many of them were. But why were so many of them men of military age, between eighteen and forty-five? How come these able-bodied men were not staying home to fight for their beloved countries? Could there be clues in the Quranic text?

Author Robert Spencer knows the answer. "This is no longer just a 'refugee crisis,'" he wrote in *FrontPage Magazine* in September 2015. "This is a hijrah."

As mentioned earlier, the hijrah—or hijra—is the Islamic doctrine of migration, a form of stealth jihad used against non-Muslim nations. Stealth jihad itself is nonviolent, but it sets the stage for violent jihad once Islam has accumulated sufficient strength. "To emigrate in the cause of Allah—that is, to move to a new land in order to bring Islam there, is considered in Islam to be a highly meritorious act," Spencer wrote, citing Sura 4:100 from the Quran.[21]

But all of Europe has not been so quick to roll out the welcome mat for the invading army. In eastern Europe, which has a history of being conquered and then fighting off Islamic rule, the feeling has been much different. The urge to appease has been less compelling. Hungary, the Czech Republic, Slovakia, Serbia, and Poland have all elected leaders who reflect their national will to survive as independent nation-states in opposition to the globalist EU dictates that they import Muslims—and sharia.

Hungary's Prime Minister Orban was lampooned in the European media for writing an op-ed stating that Hungary was blocking Muslim migrants and for constructing a thirteen-foot fence topped with razor wire along Hungary's southern border with Romania and Serbia in order to preserve its Christian heritage.[22] To the globalists running the European Union, the notion that any national leader would dare to guard his national borders against the subjugating onslaught of Islam is seen as dangerous.

But more European leaders should be as astute as Orban, says Clare Lopez, vice president of research and analysis for the Washington, D.C.–based Center for Security Policy.

"Today, it is the nation-state system and any concept of national sovereignty that is under concerted attack by the forces of the global jihad movement," Lopez told me in an interview. "Jihad is not only a violent phenomenon but can be pursued by many other means, including hijra."[23]

The United Nations refugee agency confirmed in the summer of 2015 that 75 percent of the so-called refugees arriving on European soil were men, while only 13 percent were children and 12 percent women.[24]

As word started getting out about the 75 percent ratio, the UN estimates magically began to fall but still remained above 60 percent male in spring 2016.

And while the media mostly blamed the influx on the Syrian civil war, only 20 percent of the 381,412 refugees and migrants who arrived in Europe by sea in the first eight months of 2015 were from Syria. The rest were from all over the Middle East, central Asia, and North Africa.

These demographics do not resemble what one would expect to find among war refugees. Typically, it's the elderly, the women, and the children who flee war-ravaged areas. The few journalists who asked questions and dug a little further beyond the sensational headlines and gripping photographs found out that many of the refugees were actually economic migrants. They were not fleeing war or ISIS persecution but were seeking a better economic life on the European continent.

Patrick Buchanan, the longtime conservative writer and former adviser to President Ronald Reagan, noted in a September 7, 2015, op-ed that Western Europe has been paralyzed by its institutionalized liberalism.[25] He cited James Burnham, who was perhaps the first modern writer to forecast the death of Europe in his 1964 work, *Suicide of the West*, in which he wrote, "Liberalism is the ideology of Western suicide."

"Burnham predicted that the mindless magnanimity of liberals, who subordinate the interests of their own people and nations to utopian and altruistic impulses, would bring about an end to Western civilization," wrote Buchanan.

Serbia, Hungary, Poland, and Slovakia, small nations sensing they will be soon be overrun by Muslim refugees, all took steps to seal their borders in 2015. Interestingly, these are many of the same countries who experienced the scourge of jihad in the earlier Islamic invasions, which they turned back militarily in the thirteenth and fourteenth centuries.

"Their instinct for survival, their awareness of lifeboat ethics, is acute. Yet they are being condemned for trying to save themselves," Buchanan wrote.

At the same time, Pope Francis called on Catholics everywhere to welcome the asylum seekers, and German prime minister Angela Merkel, as noted earlier, also stood up and promised to throw open the doors and welcome them. Some say it was a classic case of Germany trying to appease its own guilt for starting World War II. But Germany's conservative wing was unnerved, holding protest rallies, which have been met by counterrallies of the welcoming Germans. Tensions are growing, cracks in the nation's social cohesion have surfaced, and they are widening.

Some are talking for the first time about the possibility of chaos, loss of order, even civil war.

"This is but the beginning of what is to come, if Europe does not pull up the drawbridge," Buchanan wrote. "For the scores of thousands of Syrians in the Balkans, Hungary, Austria and Germany are only the first wave. Behind them in Lebanon, Turkey and Jordan are 4 million refugees from the Syrian civil war. Seeing the success of the first wave, they are now on the move."

Buchanan was right. A second wave of about 500,000 more refugees started on its way to Germany in 2016.[26] That would mean close to 1.7 million poured into Germany before a string of bloody terror attacks on Germans in the summer forced Merkel to finally consider closing the door. Whether it's too late to save the country remains an open question.

"Also among the thousands pouring into Europe from Turkey are Pakistanis, Bangladeshis and Afghans. When the Americans leave Afghanistan and the Taliban take their revenge, more Afghans will be fleeing west," Buchanan noted.

"Africa has a billion people," he continued, "a number that will double by 2050, and double again to 4 billion by 2100. Are those billions of Africans going to endure lives of poverty under ruthless, incompetent, corrupt and tyrannical regimes, if Europe's door remains wide open?"

"What is coming is not difficult to predict," he said.

Wave after wave is on the horizon as Africans and Arabs flee poverty, factional infighting, and war. "If Europe does not seal its borders, what is to stop the Islamic world and Third World from coming and repopulating the continent with their own kind, as the shrinking native populations of Europe die out?" Buchanan asks.

But he is one of the few writers asking these sobering questions. Most are afraid of being branded Islamophobic or racist.

He went on:

> The Schengen Agreement that guarantees open borders among EU nations is also unlikely to survive this invasion. The old national borders of Europe will be re-established.
>
> And as divisions deepen within and between countries over how many to accept, and when to shut the door, the EU may itself crack up over this most momentous and emotional of issues.[27]

Buchanan's words now seem prophetic. This prediction came true in June 2016 as the UK voted to leave the European Union. The open-borders, mass-immigration policies of the EU were the driving force behind the so-called Brexit vote. And the UK's Brexit success has empowered the secessionist movements already brewing in other countries on the European continent.

Buchanan concluded:

> The scores of thousands of migrants bursting into Europe and the hundreds of thousands and millions coming after them are going to force Europeans to address an existential question.
>
> Who are we? Are we unique and separate peoples of a particular race and tribe, history and faith, language and culture, identifiable to all the world and worth preserving at the price of our lives?
>
> Are we Germans, Russians, Poles, Italians, Spanish and French first?
>
> Or are we simply Europeans, people who live on the world's smallest continent and share a belief in the equality of all peoples and cultures, and in secularism and social democracy?[28]

CULTURES CLASH IN THE NEW EUROPE

At least twelve hundred German women were sexually assaulted in one night on New Year's Eve 2015 in Cologne and other cities, and more than 90 percent of the perpetrators were Muslim migrants, yet this mega-story was almost completely ignored by the U.S. media. It is unconscionable that the media could ignore the assaults on more than a thousand women, but somehow they did.

By September 2016 Germany's migrant rape crisis had spread to cities and towns in all 16 of Germany's federal states, according to Gatestone Institute, which first reported on Germany's rape crisis in September 2015 and again in March 2016.[29]

Germany finds itself in a "vicious circle," the institute reported. "Most of the perpetrators are never found, and the few who are frequently receive lenient sentences." Only one in ten rapes in Germany is reported and only 8 percent of rape trials result in convictions, Gatestone reported, citing Minister of Justice Heiko Maas.

Up to 90 percent of the sex crimes committed in Germany in 2014 do not appear in the official statistics, Gatestone reported, citing André Schulz, the head of the Association of Criminal Police.

"There are strict instructions from the top not to report offenses committed by refugees. It is extraordinary that certain offenders are deliberately NOT being reported about and the information is being classified as confidential," a high-ranking police official in Frankfurt told *Bild*, as reported by Gatestone.

Police and the media showed the same lack of interest in reporting the stories of more than fourteen hundred young school girls in Rotherham, England, who were enticed and groomed as sex slaves by Pakistani Muslims who migrated to the UK.[30] These Muslim men were clever in their plan: a charming, handsome Pakistani boy would make the first contact with the girls, as young as ten or twelve and usually from poor families, as they left school. Or, they might approach the girls at a mall or other youth hangout. Once this boy gained a girl's trust as her "boyfriend," he would have sex with her and hand her off to his "cousin" or "brother." The string of abuse would continue, often for months.

An investigation later turned up evidence that the Muslim sex gangs were operating throughout the UK, not just in Rotherham. In most of the towns, government educators, police, and social workers covered up the crimes and destroyed most of the evidence, reported Britain's

Peter McLoughlin, author of the seminal, meticulously documented book *Easy Meat: Inside Britain's Grooming Gang Scandal.*

I spoke with McLoughlin in an extended interview in late April 2016, about two months after his book release. He said I was the first journalist to contact him.

"So far we're seeing absolutely no interest in the book in England," he told me. "People are buying it, but there have been no book reviews in any newspapers or periodicals, no requests for interviews from media. It's a cover-up."

Between 1988 and 2011 there was virtually no mention in the British media of the problem with grooming gangs.

"One of the things that struck me was that people could deny this was going on when there was no information available," McLoughlin said.

With the publication of *Easy Meat*, the denials are no longer possible.

According to McLoughlin, public officials, from police to child welfare agencies, all did their best to make sure no records were kept that could later be used to show a pattern of Muslim men raping young girls. Rotherham was the exception.

"One of the things the childcare professionals have done is make sure there is no data," he said. "And the reason Rotherham has become emblematic and distinct is that Rotherham by accident had a private organization working for the local government called Risky Business. And what it did was ask these victims for details of who was doing these horrible things to them."

The private agency built case files and took them to police. Thanks to them, "there is data for Rotherham," McLoughlin said.

Strangely, the offices of Risky Business were broken into and many of its files stolen. "So there are indications police officers were involved in the pimping out and exploitation of the girls," McLoughlin said. "One officer who was being investigated died mysteriously in a car crash last year."

With so much information now available, the media and politicians can no longer deny the Rotherham tragedy. So, they attempt to minimize it. That doesn't change the fact that a huge cover-up took place to hide decades of sexual abuse of English schoolgirls by Muslim migrants. Only one female journalist would write about the Muslim gangs with any semblance of honest journalism, and she was accused of being "racist" even though she was a left-leaning feminist, McLoughlin said.

"If Rotherham has this problem with 1,400 victims, and that's a conservative figure, then the local newspaper must have known about it," he said. "And if the same is true in the other towns, and they all don't publish anything about it, then it's like the problem doesn't exist."

But they can't claim ignorance now. McLoughlin's 130,000 words of documentation, photographs, scanned documents, and endnotes stand as an enormous obstacle between the willfully ignorant and the truth. "I got into it from a position of, well, it's a story that's basically being concealed in Britain," he said. "And I have a feeling it's being concealed in other countries as well."

The member of Parliament who represents Rotherham, Sarah Champion, has estimated there could be as many as 1 million victims across the UK. But McLoughlin sticks with his "conservative" estimate of 100,000 to 350,000 victims. "There's an aspect of which I don't wish to believe it's a million victims, because it's too shameful for us as a nation to have allowed something like that to happen," he said. "We effectively have an army of childcare professionals and police officers—it dwarfs the size of the British army—that has ignored and denied this problem for decades."

Even after hundreds of convictions and parliamentary hearings, there is still not "full honesty" about the subject of grooming gangs in Britain, McLoughlin said. The force of political correctness is still too strong to let all of the truth out.

"And what's going on in Rotherham now is the state and the media have turned all their attention on this one town, as if this one town is singularly bad, when there's all kinds of evidence to suggest this is going on in towns across the country," he said. "We just don't have the data in the other towns."

"I think it's the biggest political scandal in 100 years. I don't have any children myself and this is the last thing I ever thought I would do is write a book about this subject," he said. "I work in IT. I spent two years writing this book with the purpose of wanting to preserve for future generations the record of what happened.

"It's such a shocking problem," he added. "The idea that a country would welcome immigrants, offer them every sort of benefit and rights, in some ways superior rights to its own citizens, and then to stand by and let them organize the baiting and prostitution of school girls is just outrageous. If we did not know about this and document it, you would not believe it."

And the problem isn't contained to the Pakistani Muslims. Some of the newly imported Syrian refugees in the UK are already making a name for themselves. Following a freedom of information request by a single newspaper, the *Sun*, it was reported July 31, 2016, that nearly nine hundred Syrian refugees had been arrested over a one-year period across England and Wales for violent crimes that included rapes and child abuse. Among those arrested were four Syrian immigrants charged after two fourteen-year-old girls were allegedly sexually assaulted just yards from Newcastle United's soccer stadium.[31]

IMPORTING A CULTURE OF RAPE

Most Westerners are unaware that rape is deeply ensconced in the Muslim culture dating back to the seventh century and to Muhammad himself.

Daniel Akbari, a former top sharia defense lawyer in Iran before he converted to Christianity and defected to the United States, is a recognized expert in Islamic honor violence and recently coauthored a book on the topic, titled *Honor Killing: A Professional's Guide to Sexual Relations and Ghayra Violence from the Islamic Sources* (Bloomington, IN: AuthorHouse, 2014). According to him, most Islamic migrants "come from Islamic communities in which any association with females other than unmarriageable kin is prohibited and subject to the Islamic punishment of flogging. When these Muslim men immigrate to Western countries where women are free to dress and behave as they wish, they become turbulent."

Their "turbulent" behavior is acted out when they are confronted by Western women. "For their entire lives these men have been taught that the women who do not wear a hijab and show skin are like whores," Akbari told me. "They also assume that only Muslim women who follow sharia rules for women's dress and conduct, wear a hijab, lower their gaze, do not laugh or eat in public, and do not go out of the house without their unmarriageable kin men escorting them deserve respect."

Even when the victim of a sexual assault is a Muslim woman, the sharia court will blame her for the crime if she failed to follow sharia rules for women's dress and conduct, Akbari said. And she must have multiple male witnesses to testify on her behalf.

But what about the non-Muslim woman? The sharia rule is clear, says Akbari. "Merely being a non-Muslim woman provides Muslim men with a legitimate Islamic excuse to justify their sexual harassment."

There are exceptions under sharia for Jewish and Christian women, which the Quran calls "people of the Book," but those exceptions come with a high price.

"Christian or Jewish women who live in lands controlled by Islamic governments are exempted from the rule if they have made a dhimmi contract with the Islamic ruler promising to respect specific boundaries and limitations on their fundamental rights," he said. "And they must pay jizya (tax)."

Not all Muslims know these rules, he said, but the general cultural beliefs about women are deeply ingrained. "Because for centuries all these rules have been practiced in their communities, they know by heart how to distinguish between a woman who deserves respect and the one who does not."

Dr. Timothy Furnish, a historian of Islam who authors the *Mahdi Watch* blog and whose latest book is *Sects, Lies and the Caliphate: 10 Years of Observations about Islam*, said Islam has a very different view of women than either Christianity or Judaism has.

"Islam perpetuates that men should dominate women in sexual matters . . . as per Sura al-Nisa' and the examples of Muhammad, who had as many as 11 wives," Furnish said, citing Quran 4:3, 34.[32] "Also, the afterlife in Islam holds the sexual 'houris' for men, but nothing for women." The houris are djinn-like "sex kittens," available to Islamic men in the afterlife, Furnish explained. Djinn are Islamic spirit beings.

Do these beliefs lead to rape while Muslim men are living here on Earth?

"Not directly," says Furnish, "But it certainly posits females (both humans and houris) as primarily existing to sexually gratify men, and that can lead Muslim men to see all women that way."

IT ALL GOES BACK TO MUHAMMAD

Another scholar of Islam, author and filmmaker G. M. Davis, whose latest work is *House of War: Islam's Jihad Against the World,* devotes a section of his book to Islam's view of women.

"In seventh century Arabic tribal culture, women were seen as commodities to be bought, sold, or otherwise appropriated as one was able, an attitude that Islam has perpetuated," wrote Davis. He cited the example of Muhammad granting permission to a fellow jihadist to take the slave girl Safiya following the massacre of the Jewish tribe Bani Nadir at a place called Khaibar, as documented by hadith narrator Abdul Aziz.

"We conquered Khaibar, took the captives and the booty was collected. Dihya came and said, 'O Allah's Prophet! Give me a slave girl from the captives.' The Prophet said, 'Go and take any slave girl.' He took Safiya bin Huyai."

The real truth is, Muhammad saw Safiya and simply decided he wanted her for himself.

"The hapless slave girl Safiya appears as little more than a prestigious trophy to be haggled over and traded at the will of the victors," Davis wrote. "It is the same mentality that gave rise to the Muslim rape epidemic that has plagued major cities in Sweden and Norway, in which Muslims routinely attack unveiled women."

Muhammad's treatment of the slave girl's husband is even more disturbing—he was tortured with a hot iron on his chest until he told the location of his treasure, then beheaded.

THE NEW SWEDEN: RAPE CAPITAL OF EUROPE

Sweden, a once-peaceful welfare state, has been transformed by one of the continent's most liberal immigration policies following its embrace of multiculturalism. In 2015, Sweden took in more than 162,000 migrants from the Middle East and Africa, mostly from Afghanistan, Iraq, and Syria.[33] That's the largest influx of any European nation on a per capita basis. This open-borders policy is now reaping disastrous results; Sweden's generosity has propelled the country from one of the most low-crime nations into the rape capital of Europe.

The latest rash of sexual assaults took place in June 2016 at Putte i Parken, a free festival in Karlstad. According to the UK's *Express*, police blamed "foreign young men" for the attacks at one of the festivals and arrested at least two unaccompanied migrant youths. All told, police recorded five reports of rapes and twelve of sexual molestation at Bravalla, Sweden's biggest music festival, and another thirty-five reports of molestation at Putte i Parken, where the youngest victim was just twelve. Two of the seven men accused of "aggressive groping" at the second festival were "unaccompanied refugee minors, reportedly living at a nearby accommodation centre."

An anonymous fifteen-year-old girl related that no fewer than five of her six friends had been sexually molested by "foreign youths" during the Karlstad event. One man had come up behind her and started grinding against her, she said. Another young man had groped one of her friends through her clothing.

Alexandra Larsson, seventeen, could not pinpoint exactly who assaulted her at Putte i Parken, but she noted that the group of eighteen-to-nineteen-year-old boys who were standing behind her were "not from a Swedish background. They were probably immigrants," she said.[34]

These reports resemble those made at a Swedish music festival the previous summer in August 2015.

There have also been several Swedish social workers attacked at the nation's asylum centers in 2016, including one in which a twenty-two-year-old Swedish woman was hacked to death by a knife-wielding young Muslim from Ethiopia.[35]

Yet they still keep coming.

POLYGAMY ON THE RISE

Across Europe, another example of Islamic culture on the rise, driven by an influx of Muslim migrants, is polygamy.

The *Telegraph* reported last year that an estimated twenty thousand polygamous Muslim marriages already exist in the UK, despite the fact that such marriages are illegal.

"In 2010, London Mayor Boris Johnson's then 45-year-old ex-wife Allegra Mostyn-Owen married a Muslim man in secret. In an article for the *Evening Standard* she explained her approach to polygamy: 'I realize that I am unlikely to conceive children [at my age] so we agreed that, so long as he chooses a good partner, then I am happy to live together in an extended family.'"[36]

One pro-Islam website, Islam Awareness, provides instructions on how to facilitate or obtain polygamy where it remains illegal. Imam Ahmad Hulail of Frankfurt, Germany, advises:

> With regard to the Muslim man who has a second wife, I believe . . . that he has to follow the channels of law in order to legalize his second marriage in the country he lives in. There are some Muslim brothers who did so through the legitimate channels. They submitted documents to the European countries they reside in to the effect that they have second wives according to the Islamic Law and that the first wives agree to that . . . I know a Jordanian Muslim who managed to get residence for his two wives in a European country.
>
> If the attempts to legalize the second marriage fail, the person could document his (second) marriage in one of the Islamic centers, yet, his marriage then would not be regarded legitimate under the

law of the country concerned. The problem he might face in the future is regarding getting birth certificates for the children from his second wife. But I think there are some flexible European laws concerning registering names of the children born even from illegitimate relationships.

I advise the Muslims who live in the Western countries to demand their rights in that regard. Foreign non-Muslim minorities who live in the West managed to get approval to exercise their rights pursuant to their religious rituals . . . Muslims can follow in the same footsteps to get legitimate approvals from the Western countries to exercise the rituals of their religion freely.[37]

TROUBLES IN THE UK

As in the United States, the leftists in the UK have strategically planted Islam and Islamic principles into the public school system where they can take root with young minds. The idea is not necessarily to get students to convert to Islam, but to brainwash them into being more welcoming of diverse religious cultures. And just as in America, Islam is always presented in British schools as a religion of peace, its dark side completely ignored.

In April 2015, officials at the Lostwithiel School in Cornwall, England, publicly humiliated nearly a dozen students ages eight to eleven whose parents had refused to allow them to participate in a school trip to a mosque in Exeter, citing fear of Islamic terrorism. According to Breitbart, school officials forced each of the noncompliant pupils to give an explanation for his or her absence during the student assembly.[38]

The infiltration of the prison system is also a problem in the UK. An April 15, 2015, article in *Newsweek* magazine reported that the "extreme views of a 'racist, homophobe and anti-Semite' who supports killing non-Muslims and 'stoning adulterers' are being made available to prison imams and prisoners throughout England and Wales, with the blessing of [prison] authorities."[39]

This is a problem that has been festering in American prisons for decades. Violent black youths are targeted for conversion by radical imams with the full support of the U.S. government.

ISIS PROMISES TO INFILTRATE WITH AN "ARMY"

An ISIS smuggler in his thirties revealed to the website BuzzFeed in February 2015 that the terror group has successfully smuggled thousands of jihadists into Europe, hidden among the thousands of incoming refugees.

The Islamic State operative, sporting a neatly trimmed black beard, "spoke exclusively to BuzzFeed on the condition of anonymity and is believed to be the first to confirm plans to infiltrate Western countries" the *Express* reported (although similar statements have been made through unconfirmed ISIS Twitter accounts).

According to the smuggler, ISIS had been actively smuggling covert gunmen across the 565-mile Turkish border and on to wealthier European nations, taking advantage of Western nations' generosity toward refugees to infiltrate Europe. The clandestine operation has been a "complete success."

ISIS fighters use local smugglers to blend in and travel within the ranks of a tidal wave of migrants flooding into Europe, both by boat from North Africa and on land through Hungary and Austria into Germany, Belgium, and Sweden.[40]

But the story of ISIS penetration of the refugee ranks went lightly reported in 2015. Instead, the mainstream media were so interested in finding heart-wrenching tales of desperate refugees on the run or of refugees reunited with their families that they missed the *story of the century*, an Islamic invasion of Europe that will have violent repercussions decades into the future.

But after the aforementioned photos of the drowned refugee boy hit the mainstream media, the chorus grew predictably louder in America for President Obama to "do something" to help Europe, which could only mean one thing: accept more Syrian refugees into the United States.

The chorus was answered on September 20, when Secretary of

State John Kerry announced that the United States would increase its total refugee intake from 70,000 in fiscal 2015 to 85,000 in 2016 and 100,000 in 2017. The ceiling on refugee arrivals for fiscal 2017 was later raised further by the lame-duck president to 110,000. Most of the increase would be in the form of Syrian refugees, 12,587 of them in fiscal 2016 and up to three times that many in 2017.

The "welcoming" movement financed by billionaire globalists like George Soros tried to deny or discredit any cautionary warnings that terrorists were sneaking into Europe amid the ranks of war refugees, even though ISIS itself had promised to use the historic movement of refugees to infiltrate the West. As I've just shown, an ISIS operative had already disclosed that the terror group had assembled an army of some four thousand trained fighters inside Western Europe.

Whether it was in Europe, Canada, or the United States, the leftists and globalists seemed to be reading from the same script. They would say that it was far easier for an ISIS fighter to get into a Western nation by other means than as a refugee, so all the noise being made by conservatives was merely a cynical attempt at fearmongering. We were turning the American public against these desperate refugees and trying to scare them out of doing their humanitarian duty simply because we were Islamophobic and hateful.

As the number of bloody jihadist attacks in our nation and across Europe started to mount in the summer of 2016, it became clear the warnings of conservatives would be borne out as anything but fearmongering. Our worst fears were about to come true.

Meanwhile, German officials admitted that by late September 2015, 7,900 radical Islamists had infiltrated their country. Other young Muslims who came to the country merely to find economic opportunity would be targeted for recruitment into violent Islamic movements after they arrived.

"There is a big worry that Islamists in Germany, on the pretext of offering humanitarian help, could try to take advantage of the migrants' situation to convert and recruit those seeking asylum," Hans-Georg Maassen, the president of the BfV domestic intelligence agency, told the UK's *Independent*.

"Our attention is particularly focused on unaccompanied young refugees who could be easy prey for Islamists," he said.

According to the *Independent*, "the remarks came just hours after police raided eight properties in Berlin, including a mosque association, that they suspect were being used by Islamists supporting fighters in Syria.

"The comments will also feed into a divisive debate in Germany about how the country should deal with an influx of" nearly 1.7 million Muslim migrants.[41]

Astonishingly, Maassen said in late 2015 that there was "no proof yet" that violent Islamists had infiltrated the ranks of refugees filing into Germany.[42]

By the summer of 2016, that would change. It started on July 18 with the Würzburg train attack, discussed earlier. ISIS claimed responsibility. Four days later came the Munich shooting, carried out with a Glock pistol. This was followed by the Reutlingen knife attack on July 24. On the same day, a twenty-seven-year-old Syrian who had been denied asylum detonated a backpack of explosives at the entrance to a music festival in Ansbach, killing himself and wounding fifteen others. Again, ISIS claimed responsibility.

France was also enduring a bloody summer. Less than two weeks after the vicious July 14 truck attack that killed eighty-five people in Nice, two ISIS attackers entered a Catholic church in the northern French town of Saint-Étienne-du-Rouvray and slit the throat of eighty-year-old Jacques Hamel, a priest who was celebrating an early-morning mass. They also critically injured a nun and took four people hostage before police arrived and killed them.

So on top of the already out-of-control rape epidemic and anti-Semitic attacks, Europe was now cast into a dark era of bloody jihadist attacks against civilians of all faiths. All of this chaos was given scant coverage by the American media, which focused on Hillary Clinton's choice of Tim Kaine for her vice presidential pick and on the Democratic National Convention.

In Sweden the rape epidemic had been going on for years when it opened its borders to more Muslim immigrants than any other European country on a per capita basis. So, Swedish authorities tried to school their male Muslim immigrants on the proper way to treat a Swedish woman. They posted signs in public pools and bath houses explaining that men are not free to touch women's breasts in Sweden just because they are wearing bikinis and swimming in the same pool with men.

In Germany many school officials put the burden on the girls themselves, sending out special instructions for them to cover up and dress modestly, as their new Muslim neighbors come from a different culture that doesn't acknowledge the same social mores.

The situation became so absurd that even the liberal *Washington Post* found it worthy of a story. Under the headline "Germany is trying to teach refugees the right way to have sex," the *Post* reported that the German government is "rushing to integrate hundreds of thousands of asylum seekers, offering them language classes and the prospect of work. But in a country known for its matter-of-fact acceptance of public nudity and creative forms of lovemaking, it is also trying to teach the mostly-Muslim migrants about the joy of sex."

The *Post* went on to tell its readers:

> Germany's Federal Center for Health Education has gone live with a sexual education website for adult migrants. Using highly graphic diagrams and images, the $136,000 site outlines everything from first-time sex to how to perform far more advanced sexual acts.
>
> After a rash of sexual assaults allegedly committed by suspects including asylum seekers on New Year's Eve, the Germans have been on a mission to re-educate migrants, especially males, about sexual norms in the West. In Munich, public pools, for instance, published cartoons warning migrants not to grope women in bikinis. Also in Bavaria, public money is partially funding sexual education classes including lessons for male migrants on how to correctly approach German women. . . .
>
> . . . There are also explanations—which advocates say are needed

for some refugees—on the need to respect gays and lesbians. . . .

Sexual intercourse is fully illustrated here, along with a suggestion to "vary movements in speed, rhythm and intensity" and a special tip that it can be enjoyed while "lying, sitting, standing or squatting."[43]

As if that weren't already the height of ridiculous, the pope of Rome added to the year's absurdities when he offered his version of the sublime.

Pope Francis seemed to put himself at the epicenter of Europe's migrant welcoming party from the very beginning. He initiated a PR stunt in April 2016 in which he agreed to house about a dozen Syrian refugees in the Vatican. One month later, Francis weighed in with his most shocking comments to date.[44]

In an interview published with the French newspaper *La Croix*, Francis argued that Jesus' call to spread the gospel differs little from the jihad waged by radical Islamic terrorists.

Attempting to explain how ISIS' "war of conquest" has bred an unjustified fear of Islam in general among Westerners, the pope said, "It is true that the idea of conquest is inherent in the soul of Islam. However, it is also possible to interpret the objective in Matthew's Gospel, where Jesus sends his disciples to all nations, in terms of the same idea of conquest."

Now, that's a favorite liberal trick right there: drawing moral equivalency between Islam and Christianity!

Pope Francis, in classic Jesuit form, blamed economic issues for the gap between Christianity and Islam, saying Western capitalism "has descended into the idolatry of money" and is therefore partly to blame for Islamic terrorism.

"The initial problems are the wars in the Middle East and in Africa as well as the underdevelopment of the African continent, which causes hunger," the pope explained. "If there is so much unemployment, it is because of a lack of investment capable of providing employment, of which Africa has such a great need.

". . . The great majority of humanity's wealth has fallen into the hands of a minority of the population.

"A completely free market does not work."

In the same interview the pope hailed the election of a Muslim mayor, Sadiq Khan, in London and said the mass Muslim migration into Europe was "necessary" due to the "grave problem" of Europe's faltering birthrate. His comments were roundly condemned by conservative media sites such as WND, *Gateway Pundit*, and Breitbart News but were largely ignored by the mainstream media.

"Where in the Bible does it describe the apostles beheading infidels and selling sex slaves? Must have missed that part in my Catholic upbringing," mused Jim Hoft in a May 20, 2016, post for *Gateway Pundit*.[45]

But not all Catholic leaders were shilling for Islam as Europe's migrant crisis worsened in the autumn of 2016. Others were sounding an alarm.

The UK's *Telegraph* reported on September 14, 2016, that an Austrian cardinal who is considered one of the frontrunners to be the next pope, warned of an "Islamic Conquest of Europe."[46]

Cardinal Christoph Schönborn made the dire warning in a speech at the Holy Name of Mary church festival marking the 333rd anniversary of the Battle of Vienna in 1683 in which Christian forces defeated the Muslim Ottoman Turkish army. He said: "Will there be an Islamic conquest of Europe? Many Muslims want that and say: Europe is at its end."

"God have mercy on Europe and on thy people, who are in danger of forfeiting our Christian heritage," the cardinal reportedly prayed.

The cardinal said the impending conquest was already being felt "not only economically, but above all, in human and religious matters."

Meanwhile, the pressure on the United States to step up and relieve some of the pressure on Europe by accepting more Syrian refugees continued to increase.

David Miliband, the CEO of International Rescue Committee, issued a statement September 2, 2015, on the organization's website demanding that the United States up its game and accept more Syrian refugees. He suggested 65,000 should be taken in by the end of 2016, and he chastised the Obama administration for agreeing to take "only" 8,000, a figure that was later upped to more than 12,000 in 2016 and will surely continue to rise each year beyond that.

"The US has historically been the world leader in recognizing the moral obligation to resettle refugees," said Miliband,[47] who moralized about the need to take in poverty-stricken refugees while hauling in $600,000 in annual compensation as head of a "nonprofit" IRC. His two top deputies at IRC also earn more than $250,000 each and the IRC staff includes eleven executives earning at least $200,000 a year. In short, more refugees mean more money for IRC.[48] "But in the four years of the Syria crisis there has been inertia rather than leadership," Miliband continued, speaking of the U.S. government. "As the German government calmly says that it expects 800,000 refugees and asylum seekers in 2015, it is vital for the US to step up its response."[49]

Not to be outdone, the Lutheran Immigration and Refugee Service issued an e-mail alert to its supporters in September 2015 asking them to pressure the Obama administration to increase the number of foreign refugees accepted into the United States from 70,000 in 2015 to 200,000 in 2016. LIRS said it wanted Obama to bring in 100,000 from Syria alone.[50]

Like the IRC, the U.S. Conference of Catholic Bishops, and the Hebrew Immigrant Aid Society, the Lutheran group gets paid by the federal government for every refugee it resettles in U.S. cities. Of course, they didn't tell their supporters that, nor did any of the media that dutifully reported their demands.

It is interesting to note that in all the pleas by the nine resettlement agencies for Western nations to take more refugees from Syria, no mention was ever made by any of them for Islamic nations to step up to the plate and help their own desperately needy brothers and sisters.

As Amnesty International pointed out, the "six Gulf countries— Qatar, United Arab Emirates, Saudi Arabia, Kuwait, Oman and Bahrain—have offered zero resettlement places to Syrian refugees."[51]

Instead, it is Europe's problem and, increasingly, America's.

PLANS TO CONQUER EUROPE FROM WITHIN

The jihadist smuggler interviewed by BuzzFeed said ISIS has laid ambitious plans for the future of Europe. "It's our dream that there should be a caliphate not only in Syria but in all the world," he said, "and we will have it soon, God willing." "There are some things I'm allowed to tell you and some things I'm not," he said, but he did reveal that the ongoing undercover infiltration of Europe was just "the beginning of a larger plot to carry out revenge attacks in the West in retaliation for the US-led coalition airstrikes."

The revelation came just days after a spokesperson for the Islamic State called on Muslims in the West to carry out terror attacks.

The jihadist told Western followers that if they had the opportunity to "shed a drop of blood" in Western countries—then they should do so.[52]

Yet, as Europe was drowning itself in the refugee flood in 2015, Melissa Fleming, spokeswoman for the United Nations refugee agency, assured Europeans that all was well and they should continue to lay out the welcome mat for more refugees.

Germany and Sweden were taking 43 percent of the asylum seekers in the EU, Fleming said. "If you look proportionately to population, smaller countries such as Austria are taking huge numbers of asylum seekers where other countries are taking very few," she told Reuters. In her opinion, the twenty-eight EU members must offer more resettlement places for refugees, especially those seeking to join family members. "We honestly believe if correct measures are taken this is something that Europe can handle," Fleming said. "It's a bigger number than last year, yes. But it's not going to turn Europe upside down."[53]

All this was happening amid reports that Europe has recorded massive increases in attacks on Jewish synagogues, its empty churches were being turned into mosques, and Muslims were settling into enclaves where police are hesitant to go.

Is it any wonder that the next phase of Islamization would involve outright attacks on the public and that Fleming's 2015 assurances that

Europe would not be turned upside down were about to be exposed as pure idiocy?

Perhaps the most bizarre turn of events came when the German police and media tried to spin each one of the attacks as "not related to terrorism." Remember: the reason most often cited for Muslim immigration was that Europe needed to import a young worker class that would offset declining birthrates and support elderly retirees. Apparently when Europeans agreed to that deal, they also agreed to accept hundreds of churches being converted to mosques, out-of-control rapes, and a reluctance by police to admit when a rape or jihadist attack takes place out of fear of inciting Islamophobia.

We've seen the same tendency by the U.S. government and media to whitewash jihadist attacks, labeling them workplace violence or merely a disturbed young Muslim with anger issues.

Occasionally the attacks are so brutal that they can't be hidden by the PC media, like the beheading of a young mother and stabbing of her son at an IKEA store near Stockholm, Sweden, in 2015.[54] This was widely reported throughout Europe, but most of the establishment media failed to point out that the killer was Muslim.

LESSONS FOR AMERICA?

America is a nation of immigrants, so any criticism of immigration, especially legal immigration, has historically been viewed with skepticism. But, with the rise of Muslim immigration from the Middle East and other regions, the sacred place that legal immigration has held in the American psyche is starting to change. This was proven by the rise of Donald Trump's candidacy for president, which changed the game and shook up the deck that the globalists are accustomed to dealing with. The issue of legal immigration and the difficulty in vetting particularly Muslim immigrants has now been thrust before the American public for the first time.

Despite record immigration over the past twenty years, escalating to the breathtaking rate of 1.1 million legal immigrants annually, America remains roughly evenly split on the issue of immigration and whether it should proceed at the current level. Within the Republican Party, however, the tide of public opinion has clearly turned, resulting in the wave of support for Trump in the 2016 GOP presidential primaries.

We'll take a look next at the blowback associated with the awakening American spirit that has risen up in more than a dozen communities across the land. This movement is still relatively small but growing fast.

These communities are being called *pockets of resistance*.

7

"BUILDING COALITIONS"

We are the community that staged a revolution across the world. If we can do that, why can't we have that revolution in America?
—KHALILA SABRA, MUSLIM-AMERICAN SOCIETY

AS 2015 WAS COMING TO A CLOSE, few Americans were aware of the violence and mayhem that were about to be unleashed on the country, most of it connected in one way or another to Islam.

First came the San Bernardino attack, discussed in chapter 2. Next came the June 2016 Orlando nightclub shooting, again perpetrated by a Muslim. Then, on July 7 Micah Xavier Johnson, aka "Micah X," stood on the rooftop of a parking garage and opened fire on a group of police officers who were patrolling a Black Lives Matter protest in Dallas. A dozen officers were wounded, five of them fatally, following an extended, military-like shootout on the streets of a major U.S. city. It happened again ten days later in Baton Rouge, Louisiana, when Gavin Eugene Long shot and killed three more officers and wounded three others. Both shooters had left evidence of connections to the Nation of Islam and radical black nationalism.

More cop shootings, all of them appearing to be premeditated, occurred in that same month in Georgia, Missouri, Tennessee, and California.

While reading about Johnson's connections to the Nation of Islam,

I could not help recalling the words of that radical group's leader one year earlier, in July 2015. Nation of Islam leader Louis Farrakhan told supporters during a visiting sermon at Mt. Zion Baptist Church in Miami that violence was indeed the answer to solving the problem of police shootings of young black suspects.

"I'm looking for 10,000 in the midst of a million," Farrakhan railed. "Ten thousand fearless men . . . to rise up and kill those who kill us . . . stalk them and kill them and let them feel the pain that we are feeling."[1]

In full context, Farrakhan's speech was an obvious call to murder white cops. Yet, in a story I broke for WND, the U.S. Attorney's Office for South Florida said it had listened to Farrakhan's sermon and, astonishingly, found the hate-filled rant to be well within the bounds of protected speech under the First Amendment. (Compare that reaction to the response of Attorney General Loretta Lynch in the wake of the San Bernardino attacks, in which she threatened to crack down on free speech by Americans who speak critically of Muslims.)[2] After an outcry from First Amendment advocates and some members of Congress, Lynch "recalibrated" her statement.[3]

Meanwhile Obama had invited the radical Black Lives Matter leaders to the White House, giving them national credibility they could only have dreamed of obtaining given their violent protests dating back to the uprisings in Ferguson and Baltimore in 2015.

Obama also bent over backwards to defend Islam after every major attack in Europe and the United States, and there were many in the final two years of his presidency.

"It's very important for us to align ourselves with the 99.9 percent of Muslims who are looking for the same things we're looking for," Obama said in an interview with CNN's Fareed Zakaria.[4] Exactly where our mathematician president got that figure is a mystery, since scientific surveys by Pew Research Center have shown that 53 percent of the world's 1.6 billion Muslims want some form of sharia law to reign as the supreme law of the land.[5] According to "Worldwide Trends in Honor Killings" in *Middle East Quarterly* (Spring 2010), 91 percent of honor killings worldwide are committed by Muslims.[6] Honor killings are most often committed against women and girls over issues of premarital or extramarital sex. Twenty-seven percent said they believe apostates, or Muslims who leave the faith, should be executed.

Hooray for our president for pulling an arbitrary, make-believe number out of thin air, and tossing it to the gullible American public as if it were fact.

Then you had Secretary of State John Kerry stating in July 2016 that air conditioners and refrigerators posed a bigger threat to the United States than Islamic terrorism.[7]

Hillary Clinton said, with a straight face, that "Muslims are peaceful and tolerant people and have nothing whatsoever to do with terrorism."[8]

Any woman who believes Hillary is telling them the truth should put on a sun dress, perfectly acceptable in almost any church, and try walking into her neighborhood mosque and watch the "tolerant" Muslims' response. Or maybe she should try to get into a cab driven by a sharia-compliant Muslim cabbie while carrying a bottle of wine, or perhaps her pet Chihuahua. See how tolerant he is.

So while our leaders lie to us, the cult of Islam continues to be emboldened. And worse yet, it is now reaching out to form alliances with angry blacks in the Black Lives Matter and black nationalist movements.

Obama and Lynch, while fueling the violent reaction of blacks to police shootings, were working on the other side to militarize and globalize U.S. police agencies through the United Nations Strong Cities Network. This network is focused on stamping out "violent extremism,"[9] taking the emphasis off of Islam as the inspiration for 90 percent of global terrorism.

So the seeds of violence have been planted. America seemed, on the eve of 2016, to be plunging into a new hell, similar to the old hell of the 1960s race riots, only this time with the added evil of political Islam inserting itself in the middle as instigator, urging the Black Lives Matter crowd to attack not their own communities, as blacks did in the

'60s, but white cops and communities. It is whites, after all, who are oppressing them and keeping them down, just as they have oppressed the world's Muslim community. Too bad America's black community doesn't research the history of Islam in Africa. If they did, they would find the racist tendencies of Arab Islamic invaders who swept in and enslaved thousands of native blacks, building a thriving slave trade that continued right up until the mid to late twentieth century in several African countries.

Meanwhile Farrakhan's vitriolic rant has started to resonate.

Fatal cop shootings spiked 78 percent in the first half of 2016 compared to the previous year, according to the National Law Enforcement Officers Memorial Fund. But more alarming yet was the increase in ambush-style attacks like the ones that killed nine officers in Dallas, Baton Rouge, and San Diego over a period of two weeks in July.

Thirty-two officers died in shootings in the first half of the year, including fourteen who were killed in ambush-style attacks, according to the report. That compares to eighteen officers fatally shot in the line of duty in the same period of 2015, and only three ambush-style deaths.

"That's a very alarming, shocking increase in the number of officers who are being literally assassinated because of the uniform they wear and the job that they do," Craig W. Floyd, who heads the officers fund, told Fox News.[10]

As the cop shootings piled up in July, my mind flashed back to another story I had covered a few months earlier. This time, it was a speech by Muslim Brotherhood operative Khalilah Sabra during the annual convention of the Muslim-American Society on December 28, 2015, in Chicago. Sabra openly called for an Islamic-inspired revolution in America. The MAS and its sister organization, the Islamic Circle of North America, are both Brotherhood front organizations.

Sabra, the executive director and project developer for the Muslim Society of America's Immigrant Justice Center, left little to the imagination regarding her organization's strategy to spawn violence on American streets, flexing her influence with the growing Muslim population.

"Basically you are the new black people of America . . . We are the community that staged a revolution across the world," she told her Muslim audience, referring to the so-called Arab Spring revolutions that brought death to thousands in Tunisia, Libya, Egypt, and Syria. "If we can do that, why can't we have that revolution in America?"[11]

Nihad Awad, executive director of the Muslim Brotherhood off-shoot CAIR, was even blunter in suggesting, at the same conference, that the U.S. Muslim community embrace Black Lives Matter. He said "Black Lives Matter is our matter. Black Lives Matter is our campaign."

While I agree that police conduct in some of the shootings of young black men has been deplorable, each case must be evaluated independently. In other instances, the police clearly acted professionally while confronting a legitimately dangerous situation that could have cost them their lives. We must also remember that blacks are not the only ones who have suffered at the hands of trigger-happy police. I have personally reported on cases during my many years as a newspaper reporter in which whites were unnecessarily brutalized or gunned down by the law. We have good and bad apples working in law enforcement—and they come in all colors—just as in any other profession.

Nevertheless, Black Lives Matter and the Muslim Brotherhood are working together to exploit legitimate concerns with police shootings, but not all police shootings, only those involving blacks.

Remember our earlier discussion, in chapter 2, of the Brotherhood's strategy? Its "Explanatory Memorandum" encouraged Muslims to, among other things, develop "a mastery of the art of 'coalitions.'"[12] These coalitions, of course, would be with friendly, non-Muslim groups on the left. In short, by working closely with these leftist allies, they could gain far more influence and accomplish more of their agenda than if they worked alone.

The Muslim Brotherhood is clever enough to know that the easiest people to manipulate for its own purposes are young, angry black men who have been taught to feel oppressed. Look for Brotherhood operatives to continue to tap into the American racial divide, using it to their own end and recruiting more young black men into their fold, either as Muslim converts or as rock-throwing thugs who can be used to stir the pot of racial dissension in our cities.

"We have direct evidence of Muslim Brotherhood–Hamas working with anarchists and Black Lives Matter," former FBI counterterrorism specialist John Guandolo told me in a report for WND. "You have Nihad Awad saying, 'Black Lives Matter is our matter,' and '2016 is our year to make our mark.'"[13]

The move to bring black Americans into the Islamic fold actually predates CAIR and ISIS by quite a few generations, noted William Kilpatrick in an article for *Crisis Magazine*.

"Black Muslim organizations such as Louis Farrakhan's The Nation of Islam have been recruiting blacks to their unorthodox brand of Islam for decades," he wrote. "The vast majority of blacks have resisted the temptation to join, perhaps because of NOI's overt racism, its anti-Semitism, and its criticism of Christianity. In any event, it seems that the Black Muslim movement is being gradually displaced by traditional Sunni Islam. That's because Sunni Islam has a much better claim to legitimacy—it being a worldwide religion that traces its roots back not to a 1930s Detroit preacher named Wallace Fard Muhammad, but to a seventh century prophet named Muhammad."[14]

Guandolo sees a further coming together of the Muslim Brotherhood entities and the forces of radical revolutionaries associated with Black Lives Matter. And the BLM thugs don't necessarily need to convert to Islam to be effective revolutionaries in the hands of the Brotherhood.

"Sabra is a senior executive in the Muslim Brotherhood, but she also represents the Department of Justice in their executive office of immigration review, and she's saying we had a revolution in the Middle East, why can't we have one in the U.S.?" Guandolo said. "That is astonishing. These two movements are taking parallel paths."

Guandolo still works in law enforcement and once commanded a SWAT unit in Washington, D.C. He told me, "Most SWAT teams are in no way prepared for what is coming. And I'm not talking about their equipment. They are just not mentally prepared for real, raging battle, a battle that can last eight to 10 hours on the streets. They're not prepared for that, but that's where we are heading."[15]

Indeed, CAIR's Nihad Awad has told American Muslims that it's time to flex their political muscles. "Turn your Islamic centers, mosques, into [voter] registration centers," he told his Muslim audience at the aforementioned convention, heading into the pivotal 2016 election year.[16] The vast majority of Muslims vote Democratic, despite their ultraconservative, sharia-influenced views on marriage, homosexuality, the melding of church and state, and alcohol and drug use. The reason is clear: they share an agenda with the American secular Left—born of a hatred of conservative Christianity and a desire to see it weakened and ultimately cleansed from every Western city, replaced by a single dominant, Islamic faith. The Left sees Islam as a battering ram against Christianity, and the Muslim Brotherhood is more than happy to help erode what's left of Christian influence over American life. Christianity's demise means Islam's rise, which has been the pattern in Europe.

While the global Islamic movement has been largely focused on the Muslim world—trying to get Muslims to be sharia compliant and to support jihad in places such as Egypt, Syria, North Africa, and Asia—a transition is taking place. Formerly moderate Muslim countries, including Malaysia, Indonesia, Turkey, and Jordan, are being pressured to become more hard-line. Turkey has already gone over the edge under Islamist president Erdogan.

"Their focus, per their stated strategy by leaders of the Muslim Brotherhood since 2010, really was focusing on the Muslim world. But this is the year that their strategy is supposed to turn," Guandolo said. "They're entering that time where they turn their focus to the West.

"So just imagine that instead of 400 fighters in Europe ready to launch attacks, just imagine if it were 10,000 of them going into Italy and storming Rome. We think that's incomprehensible but I would say we need to prepare for that. That day is coming. Our leaders have no clue about the history of the West's battle with Islam. The West has fought nine wars with Islam. It's getting ready to happen again."[17]

Against this backdrop of rising racial tensions in the United States and terrorism in Europe, with President Obama coddling violent black thugs and the Muslim Brotherhood stirring the pot, let's look at a few case studies of how the forced Islamization of U.S. cities is changing the very fabric of communities. We'll see Muslims lashing out in hostility toward their American neighbors, and often being protected from any real consequences by local and federal authorities. These are the stories your local newspaper doesn't like to cover. Nor will you see them reported on the evening national news. Where does this hostility come from, ask yourself, and would this type of activity be occurring if Muslim immigrants were assimilating into American culture?

8

TRANSFORMING SMALL-TOWN AMERICA

We're all afraid to say anything against the Muslim faith, the Islamists; nobody dares to say anything. We're all afraid to be labeled.

—OWATONNA, MINNESOTA, RESIDENT

OWATONNA, MINNESOTA, WAS ONCE AN all-American town. Located straight down Interstate 5 about an hour south of Minneapolis, it had a little over twenty thousand residents counted in the 1990 census and was in a state of population decline. It was a microcosm of small-town, working-class America. There are towns like Owatonna in every state taking the brunt of globalist policies that ship jobs overseas through unfair trade deals negotiated in secret by politicians named Bush and Clinton. The problem of an aging, declining population was remedied when the federal government started allowing mass numbers of illegal immigrants through the southern border while also importing large numbers of refugees. This artificially boosted the population with a low-skilled, welfare-dependent class that speaks little to no English and insulates itself from the broader community.

Things started to change in the mid-1990s. That's when Catholic Charities, operating out of an office in nearby Rochester, began funneling Somali refugees into Owatonna and a local window manufacturing plant, AmesburyTruth, started hiring the refugees through a placement agency.

A local citizens' group immediately formed, educating themselves on the resettlement business and informing others about the demographic changes that were about to take place without so much as a public hearing being held by their local elected leaders.

"We had meetings every month," one longtime female resident and former activist told me. "We used the term 'foreign nationals' coming in to do us harm, rather than saying Muslim radicals, but 99 percent of those that want to do us harm are Muslim."

At first the meetings drew big crowds, with upwards of 150 people filling the local high school auditorium.

"People were so disgusted with the numbers of refugees as well as the illegal aliens," the woman said. "We started with our local city council and mayor. Our mayor at the time, as long as you didn't mention his name, he was all on your side, but he didn't want to be publicly connected to our movement."

As local residents realized that none of their elected officials were serious about addressing their concerns, and that to continue standing up against the influx of refugees could cost them their reputations, they began to drop out of the resistance movement.

"We were labeled radical; we were labeled radical, not the Muslims! We were called xenophobes," the woman told me, asking not to be identified for fear of retribution. "We lobbied our congressmen, but you only get to talk to their interns and their aides, and they're pretty much all young people right out of college and very liberal. While we were in Washington, one of the congressmen ran into the office and said he had X number of minutes to get to the floor for a vote and asked his intern, 'What am I voting on, and how am I voting?' I realized then that the interns were in charge and we were not getting anywhere with our congressmen."

Back home in Owatonna, the pressure also got turned up on the resistance movement. Pro-immigration groups sent representatives to the town to put down the uprising and they had plenty of help from local churches.

"The pastors' wives at two of the local Lutheran churches wrote letters to the editor in the local newspaper saying how evil we were and used scripture quotes to make their case," she told me.

Many residents who worked at local companies affiliated with the chamber of commerce were told by their bosses that they should stop attending the anti-immigration meetings. One of the former leaders of the resistance told me she continued only because she was self-employed.

"I remember years ago when the Hmong refugees came to our state, churches sponsored them, and you would sign up to work with this refugee family and those people were integrated into society much quicker than these Somalis, much quicker," the former activist said.

The resettlement agencies grouped the Somalis together in neighborhoods where they could walk almost everywhere they needed to go. The older Somalis did not need to master English or learn to drive, and many worked in nearby factories, including the AmesburyTruth window plant.

Residents say the Somalis are allowed time off work to pray no matter what shift they are working. "What that did was it created tension between the American worker and the Somali worker," the former activist said.

The Somalis often did not put out the same amount of work as their American counterparts, either.

This is how it played out at many factories: If you're Somali and you have a thousand widgets you're required to put through in your eight-hour shift, but you're only putting through six hundred, your American coworker is going to notice that and start asking questions.

If you mention to your boss that Mohamed didn't pull his weight and that's why your shift came up short of its goal, all of a sudden you are told you're a racist or a xenophobe.

"So that American worker is now getting frustrated," the former activist told me.

Then comes the issue of water spilling all over the floor in the employee bathrooms when Somalis use the sinks to perform their ceremonial washings, which are required by sharia before a Muslim can pray. The water spillage creates an unsafe environment, and before long the Somalis demand footbaths, where they can safely wash before praying in fulfillment of Islamic rituals. The Somalis also demand a special room in which to pray. Many of the American workers get fed up and quit. To fill the vacancies, the factory hires more Somalis.

Nearly two dozen Muslim Somali Americans filed discrimination charges with the U.S. Equal Employment Opportunity against AmesburyTruth and Doherty Staffing Solutions in Owatonna in April 2016. They alleged they were denied a place to pray at the manufacturing plant and lost their jobs for trying to practice their religion.[1]

The Minnesota chapter of CAIR is leading the effort on behalf of the twenty-one former workers, who were terminated in May and June 2015.

The employees were told that if they could not comply with the plant's break schedule or could not wait until their shifts were over to pray, they could not continue working, the *StarTribune* reported. A number of workers were told to go home and wait for the company to create special accommodations but were never called back to work, according to CAIR Minnesota. Some employees were fired for "violating the bathroom policy" by spilling water on the floor.

Observant Muslims pray five times daily—at dawn, midday, afternoon, sunset and at night. Before prayer, they are required to wash their faces, hands, and feet with clean water, which can be performed in a restroom sink but increasingly in special Islamic footbaths.

AmesburyTruth's Owatonna plant employs eight hundred workers and specializes in making windows, hinges, locks, and other hardware used in casement windows.

"The window company has demands for prayer times and a room to wash their feet. A non-Muslim would say, 'I don't get that time off, with pay; why should Mohamed?'" my activist friend explained. "You can't say that. Now you're being a xenophobe or racist. So a lot of good, solid people have quit work; they don't last there. There are Help Wanted signs everywhere in this town."

In the schools, there are also divisions that didn't before exist.

Little Mohamed Jr. gets released from class to go and pray while little Johnnie must work on math problems or study for his upcoming test. Mohamed gets passed along to the next grade. The American students recognize the favoritism toward the Somali students. Somali students form cliques and harass the American kids. They also harass the Hispanic kids. The Somalis aren't assimilating. Nobody is getting along.

Students complain. Parents complain. Rarely is anything done to discipline a refugee student.

"I've given up," the former activist told me. "Our governor, Mark Dayton, he is so liberal. Nothing is going to change."

Dayton is an heir to the extravagantly wealthy family that founded the Dayton Hudson Corporation. He lives in a secure mansion with armed security guards to protect him. Yet, he told citizens at a town hall meeting in St. Cloud in October 2015 that if they aren't comfortable living with Somalis in their towns, they should "find another state."[2]

This sounds eerily similar to the statement by a German regional governor who in October 2015 told residents of the small town of Lohfelden, which was being forced to absorb four hundred Muslim migrants, "If you don't like it . . . you can leave! We have, as Germans freedom, and you are free to leave if you do not agree."[3]

This is how native Germans are being treated in their own country—by their own government. That same disrespect is now being shown to American citizens as the mass importation of Muslim "super citizens" overtakes their communities.

A couple of weeks after Governor Dayton publicly disrespected the taxpaying citizens of his state, the state's attorney general weighed in with legal threats against Minnesotans who question the wisdom of importing thousands of welfare-using refugees into their communities.

Attorney General Andrew Luger, in an open letter in the Minneapolis *StarTribune* on November 2, said, "The current wave of Islamophobia needs to be stopped in its tracks. Minnesota has a thriving, patriotic and entrepreneurial Muslim population. By collectively rejecting attacks on Muslim Minnesotans, we can set an example for the rest of the nation."

For anyone who reads Luger's full letter, it becomes obvious that the "attacks" he is speaking about amount to nothing more than verbal criticisms of Islam. He didn't mention a single physical "attack." While he lectured Americans about speaking ill of Islam, members of the Muslim faith were carrying out attacks on non-Muslims across the world, but Luger did not have a single word of correction for his Muslim listeners, only for law-abiding Americans who would dare speak the truth about a violent and intolerant religion. Luger had the audacity to threaten legal action against any Minnesotan who makes such verbal "attacks" on Islam.

"Given my role in the enforcement of civil-rights laws, I have two means of addressing Islamophobia," he wrote. "First, my office can bring civil-rights lawsuits when any group—including Muslims—is the victim of discrimination."[4]

Anyone who criticizes Islam is now guilty of Islamophobia, according to Minnesota's highest law enforcement official. This can only be interpreted as a veiled threat against activists in St. Cloud and other areas of the state who have been asking questions and pushing back against the infusion of Somali Muslim refugees into their communities without their input, to the point where they are being asked to build new schools and hire more teachers, which of course means higher taxes.

What Luger did was put Minnesota residents on notice that followers of Allah have become a protected class in their state. Unlike Christianity, which is open for criticism by any and all who feel inclined to disparage its beliefs, Islam has been placed above all other religions, protected from criticism whether deserved or not. What we end up with is the de facto establishment of Islamic blasphemy laws, which prohibit criticism of Islam or its prophet. In Muslim states, such as Pakistan, Christians are imprisoned, tortured, and killed for violating these blasphemy laws, in accordance with sharia. In many parts of America today, we should consider ourselves lucky. Violating the Islamic blasphemy laws will only get us sued by our own government.

So we see refugee resettlement divides communities. People start locking their doors, they lose trust in their elected officials, and eventually they become the target of those same elected officials, who blame them for the division and threaten them with punitive legal action.

The U.S. attorney for Minnesota has joined forces with the Muslim Brotherhood to "silence the truth and suppress the God-given rights of American citizens," observed Guandolo, the former FBI counterterrorism specialist.[5]

Fear is the ultimate weapon. If the leftist politicians can instill fear in their communities, in their states, they have won the prize. They have silenced the majority of hardworking Christian and Jewish families and empowered the minority—Islam. And they have sowed the seeds of discord in the process. A once peaceful town is now divided. Nobody trusts anybody.

"Even the dog catcher, nobody is trusting him," an Owatonna resident told me. "We're all afraid to say anything against the Muslim faith, the Islamists; nobody dares to say anything. We're all afraid to be labeled."

Residents of the Linden Hills neighborhood of Minneapolis told me similar stories. They have suffered attacks on their dogs, which Muslims consider "unclean," and the women have been the targets of verbal threats from Somalis up to and including rape, but when they complain to police, they either aren't taken seriously or the authorities don't follow through.

"We got nowhere in Owatonna," the activist said. "Wouldn't you think somebody would have listened to 150 people? No, the next day we were labeled as these horrible people. Some people were found out and were told not to come back to these meetings. If you go to another meeting you will lose your job.

"We have to be ever so politically correct. And I'm assuming in every town around here, Austin, Bloomington, St. Cloud, it's run the exact same way."

Many of the parents have also seen how the teenage Muslim boys show disrespect for the American girls, "and they are not appreciative of that as a mom," the former activist told me.

She said more moms come to school to pick their daughters up at the end of the day because the girls told their moms they "didn't like the vibes" they were getting from the Muslim boys on the bus. "They don't speak the language when they talk to each other, or they use that as a crutch when you know darn well they speak English," she said.

Some Somali students want to assimilate and become Americans, but they run into obstacles from their families. Somali teens, for instance, are forbidden to work in many of the traditional, entry-level jobs in the community, including at restaurants and grocery stores, because they would come in contact with pork, a food deemed unclean by sharia-adherent Muslims.

"You won't find a Muslim bagging groceries in our town, because they sell pork, and they might touch the package of pork," the former activist told me.

The activist's husband works in a job that brings him in contact with many apartment complexes in the area. When school is out for the summer, he sees many of the Somali kids at home with nothing to do. "It's like the parents are condemning them for wanting to become Americanized," the activist said. "They don't usually get up before noon. They're up half the night. That's when they go to the grocery store. The women work. Most of their men don't."

Owatonna has had three coffee shops open in recent years, only to later go out of business. The activist says the pattern has become clear.

"Muslim men gather there," she said. "While Americans are waiting for their coffee, these Islamist men, you know they're saying slandering things about you but they're speaking Somali. You can tell by the intonation of their voice they are hostile. We have one coffee shop open now and it will be closing shortly; I guarantee it. It's the way they overtake something. They don't assimilate."

The Somali students must get up to pray at daybreak, and again pray at noon. Some don't get to school until after the noontime prayer. If you are an American student you have to be in class by a certain time or you fail. The students see the double standard and know it is not fair that Mohamed doesn't have to show up for school on time. They're essentially told, "Oh well, he's had a tough life; get over it."

As the Muslim community grew in Owatonna through refugee resettlement, they wanted a bigger mosque. The Christian Family Church was outgrowing its facility, and a service-oriented institution showed interest in buying the building. The Muslim group offered to pay a higher price and the church sold them its building. It was converted from a church into a mosque. Drive by the mosque during prayer times and you will often find black plastic bags over the windows.

Two elderly ladies from Owatonna decided to visit the mosque to find out what was being taught. They showed up for regular prayer time and asked to be seated. "We just want to sit in," they said.

"No, no, no. That's just for members only," the imam told them.

"So after a while it's like, these people, they're not being open and honest with us, and they're not trying to help us get to know them, so why should we care about them?" the activist said.

The lawsuits over prayer times at the window factory in Owatonna mimicked those that had earlier haunted the Tyson poultry processing plant in Shelbyville, Tennessee. That drama was chronicled by fearless newspaper reporter Brian Mosely of the Shelbyville *Times-Gazette* and later made the subject of a pro-refugee documentary, *Welcome to Shelbyville*. Similar lawsuits have been filed against employers in Dearborn and Troy, Michigan, and almost every community targeted for mass numbers of Muslim refugees.

Kevin Anez, marketing director for the window maker AmesburyTruth, declined to comment on the Minnesota case because it was a pending legal matter, but issued a statement saying the company did nothing wrong.

CAIR-Minnesota's civil rights director, Amarita Singh, told the *StarTribune* that Muslim employees have the "constitutional right" to have employers accommodate their religious practices.

"These employees were working on an assembly line in a manufacturing plant," Singh said. "They wanted to pray, and the company said they were not able to accommodate them because if they step away they can't keep the production line going."[6]

Jaylani Hussein, CAIR-Minnesota's executive director, told the *StarTribune* that more than 50 percent of the organization's casework now comes from these types of workers' rights cases filed by Muslims.

In typical CAIR fashion, Hussein cast the Muslims as poor, persecuted minorities being picked on by evil American companies, and they are being singled out and targeted in greater numbers, Hussein told the *StarTribune*, often in reaction to suicide attacks by extremists.

Okay, so let's get this straight. Islam is the only religion that includes an organized war against civilized Western society, called jihad, while also seeking to undermine Western civilization through nonviolent cultural jihad, but CAIR expects Western society not only to afford Islam the same rights as other religions but to extend those rights to a special status, making Muslims a protected class of "super citizens" to whom we "regular Americans" must bow down. This not only flies in the face of the U.S. Constitution, which requires all citizens to be treated equally under the law, but it makes for an excellent formula for national suicide.

When's the last time, for instance, you saw a Catholic sue his employer for time off on Good Friday, let alone every day of the week, for time to attend mass morning, noon, and night?

Devout Catholics, in case CAIR isn't aware, also don't walk into restaurants and nightclubs and blow people away while shouting "Jesus Christ is greatest!" They don't massacre them at gay bars or ax them on trains either.

Over time, the constant slander and name-calling took its toll on the activists of Owatonna. The crowds of 150 people at their events got smaller and smaller.

"It came down to ten or twelve of us toward the end, and we finally said, 'Oh my God this is ridiculous,'" the frustrated activist said. "Because when your own government doesn't care enough to help you, the tax-paying citizenry, after a while it's like, why should we care? We've given up. We realized no government official was helping us. They just don't care. We tend to think somebody's palms are being greased, somewhere."

That's exactly the wrong approach to take, say activists in other areas who are still holding their elected officials' feet to the fire, demanding accountability and transparency in the costly refugee resettlement program. Activists have won some battles, at least temporarily, in communities such as Spartanburg, South Carolina, and Twin Falls, Idaho, which were in line to receive Syrian refugees but have thus far not received any, or very few, because local activists quickly organized and educated enough of the masses on the corrupt, secretive, and deceptive nature of the resettlement industry.

In South Carolina a secret plan to resettle hundreds of refugees, including Syrians, was hatched in late 2015 by the federal government, left-wing nonprofits, and a Baptist preacher who had the backing of Republican governor Nikki Haley. Despite all of that power, activists caught wind of the plan in March 2016 and started an intense pushback. Their efforts included social media campaigns, a lawsuit by the family of Brian Bilbro against the state and resettlement contractor World Relief, and educating local residents by speaking at Tea Party meetings, Republican women's groups, and conservative churches. The plan to secretly import Islam into South Carolina against the will of its people is still on the books, and the liberals will not give up, but their main weapon—their secrecy—has been stripped away. Residents are demanding full information and transparency. These two things—information and transparency—will always slow down the process of Islamization.

Typically, the way the resettlement program works, the ball starts to roll when one local official, either the mayor or a member of the city council, secretly meets with a representative of a resettlement agency. Also included in the meetings will be a member of the governor's office or the U.S. State Department.

That's how things played out in tiny Rutland, Vermont, in the spring of 2016. Rutland, population seventeen thousand, had never received refugees before and does not have a single mosque. There was no public hearing, let alone a public vote on the matter. The mayor, Chris Louras, held secret meetings with a federal contractor, the United States Committee for Refugees and Immigrants, a subcontractor, Gov. Peter Shumlin, and federal officials over a period of weeks to discuss the resettlement of hundreds of refugees, including many from jihadist-infested Syria. A backroom deal was cut and later "announced" to the public.

Louras hid his refugee resettlement plans from voters, police, school officials, and even the board of aldermen. The mayor did share his secret dealings with one board member—aldermen president William Notte. In a matter of weeks Notte received a call from the mayor.

"The next time I heard about it was when I was contacted by the mayor to tell me everything was a go, and that there was going to be a press conference a few days later to announce the refugee resettlement," Notte told Watchdog.org.[7]

Notte said he was "stunned" at how quickly the plan came together. After it was announced, hundreds of residents turned out at council meetings to protest. They felt as though their elected leaders had sold them out, and didn't even have the guts to do it at an open meeting. They had simply announced the plan that had been hatched in secret with the feds to transform their town.

Mayor Louras insisted that the majority of his town supported his plan and were eager to welcome the refugees. Apparently the majority of his board of aldermen didn't agree. They voted 7-3 in July 2016 to send a letter to the U.S. State Department saying they did not support the plan because it had been hidden from the public.[8]

In some cities, such as Spartanburg, South Carolina, the conspirators never even make an announcement directly to the people at a press conference or meeting of the local government. The news that their town has suddenly become a federal resettlement community simply appears one day in a bland feature story in the local newspaper that explains little about the true scope of the program. The article will typically focus on one or two families and won't say that this is the beginning of a steady influx from the Third World that will continue indefinitely.

Either way, once the deal is done, your town will be permanently transformed in a matter of a few years.

A parallel community within a community was set to be planted in Rutland by outside globalist influences all because one naive mayor thought it would be neat to help a few refugees. He had zero knowledge of Islam or sharia, and what little knowledge he was given was tainted with lies spoon-fed to him by those who would profit from the resettlements.

The mayor committed his town to a difficult future, torn by immigrants who won't come to Rutland excited about assimilating into the community. And even before the refugees arrive, the mayor has created a fracture in his community between those who wish to welcome them and those who would rather they stay in the Middle East.

The fracture will only widen over time if the federal government makes good on its promise to bring Syrian refugees to Rutland. A mosque will soon be opening, funded by either Saudi Arabian cash or the Muslim Brotherhood's North America Islamic Trust—bet on it. The mosque will start out small and keep a low profile until it is ready to expand into a much bigger facility and leave a bigger public footprint. It will likely seek to build within a residential area, causing friction with loud calls to prayer and overflow parking on Friday evenings and during Ramadan at all hours of the night. Mosque members will take over public parks, scowl at local residents, attack their dogs, and speak slanderous words against them in a language the locals don't understand. They will treat their women like property and demand special privileges for their children at school and on the job. The school district will ask for a bond issue funded by higher taxes because it requires more space to educate the artificially inflated population of school-age kids coming from the Middle East. Arabic will become the dominant foreign language spoken in the schools, eventually outpacing Spanish, and there will be other obscure dialects as well spoken by refugees out of Africa and possibly Afghanistan or Burma. Expensive linguistic translators will be hired in the schools and at the local E-911 center. But this will all happen so gradually that few in Rutland will realize what's going on until it's too late.

All of this will happen because of one mayor, who will likely be no longer in office by the time the people of Rutland start noticing all the new problems in their town. The transformation will be too far advanced at that point. The parallel society will have grown and spread its wings to the point where it wields considerable political clout and is deemed untouchable by the purveyors of political correctness. To even mention some of the obvious problems will cause any resident to be branded a racist and an Islamophobe. That resident could lose a job or get kicked out of his church.

Missoula, Montana, is another all-American town targeted for Syrian refugees by the federal government, invited in by its liberal city council. Residents there are engaged in a pitched battle with their state and local elected leaders, trying to get them to stop rolling over for the feds and inviting resettlement contractors to form a beachhead in their communities. Experience tells us that once a resettlement office opens in your community, the influx of refugees will never stop, and rarely will it even slow down.

What are the stakes, you ask? Let's move on to a couple of other cities, one in Minnesota and one in Michigan, which leave little to the imagination about what can happen when citizens give up the fight. The first, Bloomington, Minnesota, has been completely subjugated by its local Muslim population. The other, Hamtramck, Michigan, shows the ultimate fate of every American city that bows to Islamic demands.

9

ROLLING OVER FOR ISLAM

We are walking around like zombies sending text messages on what we had for lunch, when the world is at war. The Chaldeans are aware of it . . . The question is, when will people here wake up and realize it?

—DICK MANASERRI, ROCHESTER, MICHIGAN ACTIVIST

IN BLOOMINGTON, MINNESOTA, we find another city kowtowing to Islam. While its citizens are continuing the fight to reclaim their city from corrupt politicians, it's getting late in the game.

A radical mosque known for breeding terrorists has been granted special privileges by the city of Bloomington, which allows its members to take over a public park and treat it as their own, to the exclusion of other residents, according to complaints filed by a citizens group.

The Friends of Smith Park started a petition drive and took its case to the Bloomington city council with a formal complaint on July 25, 2016.

At issue is the Dar al-Farooq mosque, which has a record of turning Somali refugees into jihadists for ISIS and other terror groups.

At least half a dozen known Somali terrorists have attended Dar al-Farooq in recent years, including Adnan Farah, twenty, and his brother Mohamed, twenty-two, who pleaded guilty in April to providing material support to ISIS. The mosque is headed by Waleed Idris al-Meneesey, who preaches hatred of Jews straight from the Quran and the hadiths.

Now it has come to light that Bloomington city officials have given al-Meneesey and his sharia-compliant followers special privileges that violate the town's conditional-use permit, or CUP, and that are not offered to any other religious group, said attorney and retired lieutenant colonel Larry Frost. By doing so, Frost said the city has exposed itself to potential lawsuits from churches and synagogues in the area that have not been afforded the same rights.

"According to your police officers, you've privileged Dal al-Farooq worshipers above all other religions. You've made Smith Park a Dar al-Farooq-only zone after the park is already closed, excluding citizens of all other faiths and those of no faith," said Frost, who represents Friends of Smith Park.[1]

The council members sat mum during Frost's comments.

The list of abuses and alleged violations by Dar al-Farooq, which was allowed to build in a residential area, is long. They range from dumping asbestos in the trash to having three to five times the occupancy allowed by its conditional-use permit, making excess noise, shining car lights, and producing overflow parking at all hours of the night during the month of Ramadan—and to a lesser extent every weekend. The mosque members take over the adjacent public park and force out residents of nearby neighborhoods, often staying in the park well after the posted closing time of 11 p.m.

Neighbors have been told by mosque workers to get out of Smith Park "because the park belongs to [the Muslims]," said one local woman.

Another local resident, Matilda Zumba, who lives in a neighborhood near the mosque, approached the city council with an interpreter. She said she has two small children who are always playing outside. "I'm very afraid because there is a lot of traffic and a lot of speeding and the people of Dar al-Farooq don't respect our speed limits and the safety of our children," Zumba told the council. "I'm also now afraid to take our children to the park because there are many people there who do not respect the rights of our own children to play there.

"A lot of times the other children don't want to work together to share with our children. Sometimes their parents are there and they may shout at them but they don't do anything, they just continue to let their children interfere. The park is very important to the Spanish community especially and we met there a lot, but now we don't because we don't feel safe."[2]

Mosque attendees have flooded the neighborhood with offsite parking, blocked driveways, and walked through neighbors' yards without permission. The city has told neighbors if they park in joint-use parking, the neighbors have to "hurry to the sidewalk" and get out of the parking lot so it would be available for the mosque.

One supporter of the neighborhood group witnessed mosque abusers using joint-parking areas to practice driving at 1:30 a.m.—by using city garbage cans as obstacles. When the witness came to film the event, three young mosque members confronted him, one demanding to know what he was doing and telling him he could not film the offending car or its license. Later, a police officer told the witness that "only mosque members can use the parking lots after normal park hours"—in other words, the public space is reserved for use by one particular religion after it's closed to the public.

The city took more than three years and sixty-seven drafts to complete the conditional-use permit with the mosque. Built into that contract is a requirement that the city use a laborious five-phase, six-month enforcement process to correct any Dar al-Farooq violations.

"Clearly that's a non-enforcement clause," Frost said. "The city has to give this amazing provision to every new church applicant, and I would argue, every current CUP holder can demand the same. Why? Because you are privileging Dar al-Farooq above other religions.

"One of your own council members said 'I feel like we're punishing applicants that came after Dar al Farook,' because you required them to do things that Dar al-Farooq is not required to do."[3]

The city council granted a conditional-use permit to Dar al-Farooq, enabling the mosque to operate in a residential neighborhood, then failed to enforce either the CUP or the joint-use agreement allowing the mosque to use Smith Park. As a result, the neighbors of Smith Park have been reduced to second-class status, unable to use and enjoy a public park adjacent to their neighborhood.

Mosque actions violating the CUP and JUA were not stopped because the city attorney insisted that the federal Religious Land-use and Incarcerated Persons Act, commonly called RLUIPA, did not allow the city to enforce the CUP/JUA, effectively making the neighborhood around Dar al-Farooq a zoning-free area. The city attorney also told council members that enforcement of the CUP could result in lawsuits against council members in their private capacities. Both legal ideas are flatly false, said Frost.

"Your own city attorney, former attorney, told you that you had to do that, but you made a grave legal and moral error when you signed a CUP and then didn't enforce it, because that's not what RLUIPA says," Frost told the council.

RLUIPA is a federal statute that requires local governments to issue permits for houses of worship equally when it comes to construction projects.

"But once you have the CUP you're no longer in the permitting phase—it is not a legal permitting issue," Frost said. "Despite what your previous city attorney said, you can enforce the CUP and you must."

Friends of Smith Park are asking only that all city council resolutions concerning Dar al-Farooq be enforced, including retroactive enforcement where legal and appropriate—exactly as would be the case for all other religious institutions with a conditional-use permit.

A MOSQUE IS NOT JUST A HOUSE OF WORSHIP

Most Americans believe a mosque or Islamic Center is simply a "Muslim church," when in fact it operates much differently, said Debra Anderson, coordinator of the Minneapolis chapter of ACT for America, which is working with the citizens of Bloomington.

"In Islam, the prophet Mohammad is viewed as the perfect example of a man," she said. "Anything he did is considered the example for all Muslims to follow for all time." Mohammad used the first mosques as political and military bases as well as houses of worship. "It has been from the mosque that devout (Muslims) have waged their war of global conquest, slaughtering non-Muslims who refuse to surrender to Islam and producing a trail of blood and tears across world history," Anderson said.

Turkey's Islamist president, Recep Tayyip Erdogan, once said, "The mosques are our barracks, the domes our helmets, the minarets our bayonets, and the Muslim faithful our soldiers."

Bloomington's Dar al-Farooq is just one out of 83 mosques in Hennepin County. There are 163 mosques, Islamic centers, masjids, and prayer spaces in Minnesota at last count, Anderson said.

"How many are in your county? Who is the Imam? What are they teaching? Are they teaching that 'Allah is our objective; the Prophet is our leader; the Quran is our law; Jihad is our way; dying in the way of Allah is our highest hope'?" Anderson asks, referring to the motto of the Muslim Brotherhood and the Muslim Student Association.

In an e-mail alert, Anderson said three civilian Minnesota women, two of whom are grandmothers in Bloomington, have been "doing the work that our FBI and law enforcement agencies used to do before all their training manuals were purged of anything deemed offensive by the Muslim Brotherhood . . . before our military, intelligence, and law enforcement institutions became 'sensitive' to blasphemy laws as dictated by Islamic Sharia law. Yes, the country is in great trouble. You are needed. Please, stand with these American patriots in Bloomington in their effort to protect and preserve the safety and livability of their neighborhood from this radical mosque that is clearly demonstrating their utter disregard for American law, their neighbors . . . and more importantly our national security."

If enough Americans don't wake up and stand their ground against refugee resettlement, more cities will find themselves subdued, even sub-jugated by Islam's heavy-handed tactics of nonviolent civilization jihad as waged by the Muslim Brotherhood. That's what happened in another city in Michigan that has been active in the Muslim immigration game for a lot longer than most. Hamtramck has been importing Muslims since the 1970s from Bangladesh, Yemen, Iraq, and Bosnia. It represents the future of every city now facing a refugee resettlement influx.

SHARIAHVILLE, USA

A city on the outskirts of Detroit known since 1920 as a thriving Polish community has been fully transformed by globalism and the federal government's Islamic immigration program. The bulk of the change has occurred over the past twenty years, but it started in the 1970s with the globalization of the auto industry and mass immigration.

Hamtramck, known affectionately as "Poletown" by Michiganians for its bustling district of Polish restaurants, markets, and beautiful Catholic churches, became the nation's first city to elect a Muslim-majority city council in November 2015—sending three Muslims to join one incumbent who was not up for reelection. In butcher shops that once offered juicy Polish sausages in refrigerated display cases, female customers wearing hijabs now purchase halal meats blessed by an imam. The sound of church bells has given way to the chant of a Muslim holy man giving the call to prayer in Arabic.

Many of the storefronts have been converted to mosques, and the call to prayer is blasted over loudspeakers five times a day. Poletown has been transformed. Some residents of neighboring communities now call it "Shariahville."

Within hours of the historic election, Muslim political organizer Ibrahim Algahim was caught on video giving a chilling warning: "Now we show the Polish and everybody else, that . . ." he said, as cheers drowned out the rest of his words.

And now it's spreading. The city of Sterling Heights, about fourteen miles to the north, is on the front lines of a contentious battle between the Muslim community with its progressive backers, and those who would rather not see their city transformed in the image of Hamtramck.

The Sterling Heights planning board voted 9–0 to reject plans for a mega-mosque on September 11, 2015, before a packed chamber of distraught residents. Hundreds of residents who could not fit into the meeting chambers stood outside and cheered wildly as the vote was announced that the mosque had been defeated. The mosque was proposed to be built in the middle of a neighborhood heavily populated by Iraqi Chaldean Christians.

Chaldean Christians are all too familiar with persecution at the hands of sharia-compliant Muslim communities back home in Iraq.

Sterling Heights is home to one of the country's largest Chaldean Iraqi Christian communities. Since the 2003 U.S. invasion of Iraq, which overthrew Saddam Hussein, these ancient Christian communities have seen their priests and family members kidnapped and murdered, their churches firebombed, their husbands beheaded, and their wives raped and sold into slavery by Muslims. The Chaldeans once made up nearly a third of the city of Mosul in northern Iraq but today live as refugees in Lebanon, Turkey, and the Kurdish-controlled areas of Iraq.

Dick Manasseri, an activist who lives in Rochester, Michigan, said the Chaldean community is nervous, having come to America to escape Muslim violence, only to find out their adopted country is now inviting their killers into the very same state, even the same communities where they live.

The Obama administration has secretly planted nearly twenty-eight thousand refugees in more than a hundred Michigan towns since fiscal year 2008. Most of them have been placed in seven counties in southeastern Michigan, with Oakland and Macomb counties getting the highest number—9,173 and 5,852, respectively.

"They were picked by the United Nations and secretly resettled by [the] U.S. State Department, the Catholic Bishops and Lutheran Social Services, moving bodies like FedEx and getting paid per head," Manasseri said of the religious groups that help the government resettle refugees. "You have people from 31 different countries that must be dealt with in Lansing, for instance, and that means the local community picks up the cost, we have a massive growth of Medicaid in Michigan."

Nahren Anweya, a Chaldean Christian who escaped Iraq, has joined Manasseri's grassroots campaign, called Secure Michigan, and is addressing some of the audiences.

"She is not Pamela Geller, just a well-spoken person talking from her personal family experience, and that made a big impression on us, that we are walking around like zombies sending text messages on what we had for lunch, when the world is at war. The Chaldeans are aware of it," he said. "The question is, when will people here wake up and realize it?"

But the battle is not over in Sterling Heights. The city council still has the option of approving the mosque, and a local Muslim group has sued the city. The Obama Justice Department weighed in, telling the *Detroit Free Press* that it has an open investigation into whether the city has violated the Muslims' civil rights by denying the mosque.[4]

On November 6, 2015, just a few days after Hamtramck's historic election, Republican governor Rick Snyder was on hand to celebrate the city's Bangladeshi corridor. Bangladeshis, along with immigrants from Yemen, make up the majority of Hamtramck's Muslim community. The corridor is being branded Banglatown, and Snyder sees it as a potential tourist destination.

"The branding of Banglatown as a cultural tourism destination is a priority for Global Detroit, (the Bangladeshi American Public Affairs Committee) and the Economic Development Committee of the Detroit City Council Immigration Task Force," says a statement issued by Global Detroit.[5]

Global Detroit is an organization whose goal is to improve economies by "welcoming, retaining and empowering" immigrant communities. It is an affiliate of George Soros–funded Welcoming America, introduced in chapter 4.

"Hamtramck contains one of the nation's densest Bangladeshi populations and offers the only U.S. voting ballot in Bengali, the so-called 'Bangla ballot,'" boasts the Global Detroit statement.

"The governor was part of a celebration of that event, so it was duly recognized by the governor who is really twisted on this subject," Manasseri said. "He somehow doesn't make a distinction between economic development and the influx of people who practice Sharia. It seems he's very much in favor of Shariahville, as I call it, and wants to see it spread all over Michigan. And so we're working against that at the grassroots level for the whole state."

Governor Snyder also addressed the Islamic Society of North America's annual convention in August 2014, despite the fact that ISNA is a known front group for the Muslim Brotherhood. Snyder, ironically, did take the opportunity to mention Israel's right to exist, a comment that infuriated ISNA leaders, causing them to put out an "action alert" for all Muslims to call the governor's office and complain.[6]

Manasseri's group has created a website and is collecting signatures for passage of a resolution that would halt refugee resettlement in Michigan.[7] He said requests for presentations before clubs and groups are growing in light of the migrant crisis in Europe, where the number of rapes and assaults has exploded around the refugee camps and teachers in Germany are warning girls to dress modestly and not to engage young Muslim men in conversation.[8] Those Americans who are paying attention to what's happening on the ground in Germany, Sweden, Belgium, France, and the UK are beginning to "wake up," he said.

"At the grassroots level, it's still a small minority but our presentation is resonating. I think we have a long way to go," he said.

Manasseri went on to say that Western women hold the key to that wake-up call. "I think, this is largely a women's issue," he said. Unfortunately, "the women are either occupied or they're not paying attention. When women are challenged for their own safety, then maybe they'll get it. There are certain communities up here where you can really get a feeling for what Sharia looks like. We have communities that look like the Middle East, and I can't believe that women won't wake up at some point and fear for the safety of their children."

Manasseri believes the battle will be difficult as long as those on the other side include governors, mayors, and the chamber of commerce. "We have a really tough nut to crack. We basically have a game of chicken going on with the governor of Michigan and the grassroots that are waking up," he said.

Hamtramck's election of a Muslim-majority city council has prompted articles in *USA Today*, the *New York Times*, the *Washington*

Post, and the *Wall Street Journal*.

And the 2015 election wasn't the first time Hamtramck, a city of twenty-two thousand, has drawn the attention of the national media. In 2004, when the city council allowed a mosque to broadcast its call to prayer from loudspeakers, they opened up a divide that some say never fully healed. Opponents claimed it was an intrusion of Islam into their lives. They lost that battle, and many of the Polish residents who felt uncomfortable with the new Hamtramck headed for the exits.

In 1990, the city was 45 percent Polish, down from 90 percent in the 1970s. Today that figure has dwindled to 15 percent as the Polish Catholics started having fewer children, and many of the younger Poles moved to the suburbs at the same time the Muslims were moving in from Bangladesh, Yemen, Bosnia, and Iraq. They have large families and bring their extended families from abroad.

When the Muslim prayers were allowed to go public on loudspeaker in 2004, only one city council member was Muslim along with about 25 percent of the population. That capitulation was the beginning of the end of Poletown. Today it is estimated that half of Hamtramck is Muslim. According to University of Michigan–Dearborn professor Sally Howell, Hamtramck might have become the first American city to have a Muslim majority in 2013.

"The growth is taking place in these Muslim communities, and they are transforming the city scape," Howell told the *Washington Post*. "It's become much more visible in the last 15 years."

The Islamization of Poletown has been decades in the making, spilling over from Dearborn, a Muslim enclave to the south, and aided by Wayne State University, which like most universities has imported hundreds of Islamic students over the years, many of whom graduate and go on to get green cards and eventual citizenship in the United States.

The top three vote-getters in the 2015 election were Muslim, two were incumbents—Anam Miah and Abu Musa—and the third, Saad Almasmari, is a twenty-eight-year-old college student who emigrated to the United States in 2009 and became a citizen two years later.

OBAMA JUSTICE DEPARTMENT'S HEAVY HAND

While Hamtramck lost its battle over the loudspeakers in 2004 and had its die cast with the new Muslim-majority local government, the fight rages on in neighboring Sterling Heights.

"The proposal in Sterling Heights was sloppy. It was very close to the residential area and the response was slow, almost like someone wanted it to be rejected and so the DOJ could come in and chill the whole community as far as any push back," Manasseri said.

The DOJ is already sending signals to the city council that it had better conform to the wishes of the local Muslim community and grant the mosque permission to build.

"It's a well-known fact that CAIR has the DOJ on speed dial," said Karen Lugo, an attorney with expertise in mosque projects.[9] She said the DOJ will often begin to intimidate by requesting that local government officials turn over all e-mails involving correspondence with Muslim groups seeking to build a mosque or school. Often, this is enough to scare them into submission, as they seek to avoid a lawsuit with the federal government.

In Pittsfield Township, Michigan, a few miles outside of Ann Arbor, another controversy has been festering over the township's rejection of a large Islamic school, recreation center, and prayer room proposed right next to a residential neighborhood. In that case, the township denied a rezoning of the parcel following a contentious council meeting that lasted until one thirty in the morning.

According to court documents, the township said the project did not involve a "small-scale school" as required by the township's master plan, traffic would be disruptive, and noise and light from outdoor activities would also be disruptive to the adjacent residential neighborhood.

The mosque proposing the large school in Pittsfield Township is the Muslim Community Association of Ann Arbor and Vicinity, headed by a well-known radical imam who was investigated by the FBI in 1999 for ties to Osama bin Laden. A native of Damascus, Syria, Imam Moataz Al-Hallak was a founding member of the Islamic Society of Arlington, Texas, and moved to Michigan in 2005.

Al-Hallak's name was first mentioned publicly in conjunction with the investigation of bin Laden's involvement in the 1998 bombings of the United States embassies in Kenya and Tanzania, the *New York Times* reported.[10]

Al-Hallak was never charged in the case but, according to the *Times*, a federal prosecutor in Manhattan told Judge Leonard B. Sand that the government had specific concerns about him.

"'Moataz Al-Hallak has served as a contact between members of the bin Laden organization," the prosecutor, Patrick J. Fitzgerald, said at the time, according to the *Times*.

One of the defendants in the terrorism case, Wadih el-Hage, wanted to call al-Hallak from jail, seeking his support for bail application, something the imam's lawyer said was purely for religious reasons. El-Hage had attended Al-Hallak's mosque in Arlington.[11]

On October 26, 2015, the Obama Justice Department intervened in the local affairs of Pittsfield Township and sided with the Muslims, as it has in so many of the mosque battles in communities across America. The DOJ filed suit in federal court in Detroit alleging civil rights violations.[12] The township capitulated and settled out of court for $1.7 million.[13]

Next, we'll look at another small town that is being Islamized, slowly but steadily, by refugee resettlement, and how one family was brutally made aware of just how hostile some refugees can be when it comes to the central symbol of American pride.

10

PIERCING THE SILENCE IN RURAL GEORGIA

If someone would have told me you would have to defend your neighbor from a Muslim attacking her with her own flag, I would have laughed at them, but my sense of security has been shattered.

—KATIE BOROWSKI, LAWRENCEVILLE, GEORGIA

DAMI ARNO, FORTY-TWO, lives a quiet life with her husband and two children in a small Georgia town thirty-two miles northeast of Atlanta. She helps her husband, Jimmy, in his auto repair business and is in the final throes of raising two teenagers, Chuck and Brittany.

They live at the end of a sleepy little street in Lawrenceville, Georgia, in a community of twenty-one very modest three-bedroom brick ranches and split-level homes built in the 1970s. In communities like this, people still love to fly the American flag, especially in the period between Memorial Day and Independence Day.

"We have only two streets, both dead-end, and we're all very close-knit, we all talk to each other, we all know each other, we all barbecue together and all watch each other's animals when someone goes out of town," Dami Arno told me. "This is your all-American, 1950s-style neighborhood. We've got a great group of neighbors. We work hard; we keep our yards clean; we like each together. I guess it's just a normal neighborhood for us. I always knew if my neighbors heard something bad happening or someone went and got them that they would be there for me in a heartbeat."[1]

That faith in her neighbors would be tested on May 31, 2016, the day after Memorial Day. It was on that morning, just after 9 a.m., that the Arnos' peaceful community would be violated in a most unexpected way. While sitting in her garage, drinking coffee with her daughter, Brittany, they got the surprise of their lives.

"We were sitting there in the garage, just talking about what had happened the night before, when the neighbors told us what had gone on, how they had seen a woman in a colorful hijab walking through our neighborhood," said seventeen-year-old Brittany.

Then she pointed to the family's large flag flying from a flagpole mounted on their mailbox. (You may remember parts of this story from chapter 5.)

"Look how pretty that flag looks blowing in the wind," she told her mom.

That's when it happened.

"We turned around, and there she was," Brittany said.

A tall, muscular black woman bolted out of the woods behind the Arnos' house. Only her eyes were visible, peering from behind her black burqa.

"She just stared at us and then casually walked over and yanked the flag out, like it didn't even faze her. Then she comes running at us, charging at us. My mom came out of the garage to meet her at the sidewalk and stopped her at the sidewalk before the flagpole hit her in the face."

The attacker, later identified as thirty-year-old Amina Ali Ahra, took hold of the four-foot PVC pipe that had served as the flagpole. In her hands it became a weapon similar to a police night stick.

Ahra stands six foot three. She is a refugee from Somalia who Dami would later learn had been resettled in the Lawrenceville community by her own government, one of more than 132,000 Somali refugees distributed into more than two hundred U.S. cities and towns since the 1980s. Dami had never seen this woman before and had never encountered any affront so personal and so violent.

As her mom struggled to fight off the woman, Brittany ran inside and called 9-1-1. "I told my brother to grab the gun. I said, 'Quick, grab the gun. Mom's in trouble.'"

Chuck, who is only fourteen, grabbed the family pistol from the drawer. Brittany ran back outside, and her mother was still fighting with the intruder.

"I'm answering questions from 911, and then I see she is going for my mother's throat, trying to grab my mother's throat," she said. "That's when I jumped in and pushed her away from my mom. Her hands were huge; they fit around my mom's throat."

The Muslim woman, now stripped of her flagpole weapon, took off her shoe and used it to strike Dami and Brittany.

"She just kept saying 'shoe, shoe,' like she wanted her shoe back. I had snatched her shoe from her and threw it because she had hit me with it," Brittany said. "I said, 'You're not getting this shoe back that you hit me with!'"

Chuck emerged from the house with the .38-caliber revolver and pointed it at the Somali woman, wondering if he would have to pull the trigger.

"I haven't really been in an actual fight before," Brittany said. "Me being a teenager, I've been in conflicts and confrontations, but I'd always tried to talk it out. My daddy taught me how to fight, but I'd never had to apply it to a situation until then."

Dami was equally shocked but reacted on impulse to defend her daughter.

"She didn't utter a word, just came at me swinging that flagpole towards my head," Dami told me. "I've never been in a fight in my life, but my momma bear instincts kicked in, and I grabbed the pole and yanked it, eventually wrestled her down to the ground. The neighbors said I had her in a headlock, but I honestly don't remember."

They were still fighting off their attacker when the woman who lives next door heard yelling and screaming coming from outside. Katie Borowski looked out her window and saw her friend was in trouble.

"I heard yelling and a commotion going on outside and I looked out and saw Dami defending herself from this very large woman who was attacking her," Borowski said. "I could not stand there and let it go down like that. This is my neighbor and my friend . . .

". . . So I came over and helped defend Dami. I held one arm and Dami held the other. At one point she did reach for my throat. She grabbed the front collar of my shirt as I pulled back."[2]

(Borowski later told me that she had been outside the night before and had seen the woman, with her Muslim "head wrap," walking around the neighborhood. "I didn't pay too much attention to it because I just figured she's visiting someone in the neighborhood and I didn't want to report it and be seen as singling anyone out [because of their race or religion].[3]")

Chuck aimed the pistol at the attacker but saw that she was being subdued by his mother and Borowski. He never pulled the trigger. A male neighbor also arrived on the scene to help detain the Somali woman.

"The four of us sat on her until the police arrived," Dami said.

According to Dami, once the Lawrenceville responding officer arrived he told them he could not remove the assailant's burqa "because that would violate her civil rights."

The Atlanta area is among the top five U.S. destinations for Somali refugees, having received more than 4,000 since the September 11, 2001, terrorist attacks, according to the U.S. State Department's Refugee Processing Center. Lawrenceville has received 24 Somalis, but nearby Atlanta has received 1,203, and neighboring Clarkston has received 437; Decatur, 1,039; and Stone Mountain, 1,096.

Just within the last few years, a mosque opened not far from the Arnos' neighborhood.

LIVING IN FEAR

Like her neighbors, the Arnos, Borowski told me she is on edge now and "living in fear."

"It's very disconcerting. I don't sleep well at night," Borowski said. "My husband works nights and I've purchased a firearm and I will defend myself and my children. This used to be a sleepy little neighborhood but it's sad, the times we live in. If someone would have told me you would have to defend your neighbor from a Muslim attacking her with her own flag, I would have laughed at them, but my sense of security has been shattered."

Even more disconcerting and shattering to this neighborhood's sense of security is the way law enforcement, on both the local and federal levels, treated the Arno family as victims of a violent crime. The Arnos called their local police chief, Randy Johnson, twice, and left a voicemail message seeking information on their attacker. He ignored them.

When I called Johnson to ask about this, he seemed surprised and denied he'd ever heard the voicemail.

Jimmy Arno told me he was very unhappy with the misdemeanor charges filed against his wife's attacker.

Johnson's department filed only two counts of simple battery against Amina Ali Ahra, along with one charge of giving false information to police about her name and address. Johnson did have the good sense to turn the case over to the FBI for potential federal hate-crime charges, since Georgia has no hate-crime laws of its own.

But after "investigating" the case for more than a week, the FBI dismissed it.

I use the term "investigating" loosely. The FBI agent assigned to the case never interviewed the victims, either in person or over the phone. He never interviewed the multiple witnesses. He never visited the scene of the crime, and he never, to my knowledge, interrogated the perpetrator.

Obama's FBI and Homeland Security apparatus once again showed its bias in acting as defender of Islam rather than protector of Americans.

I talked to a federal law enforcement agent who asked me to withhold his name from publication for fear of losing his job. He said he was not surprised by the outcome of the investigation. He told me the Obama administration has a deep-seated, built-in bias against Americans who are attacked by Muslims.

The federal agent told me Ahra may have mental health issues, which made it unlikely for federal prosecutors to charge her with a hate crime.

"But if you want an example of someone who is radicalized you can't get a better one than someone walking up and grabbing someone's American flag and beating them with it," said the agent. "I assure you if it were the other way around there would have been federal hate crime charges filed," he told me.

"The FBI agent [assigned to the case] never contacted our family. We finally reached him and he told us there was no hate crime and I am not entitled to any information on this woman who attacked me in my own home," Dami Arno said. "He wouldn't even tell us whether or not she was legally here in this country."

Ahra's country of origin, Somalia, only became known because one of Dami Arno's friends was employed at the local sheriff's office in Gwinnett County. She told Dami that Ahra is a native of Somalia living in the United States on either a green card or visa. I tried to confirm her immigration status and was given the runaround.

The Gwinnett County Police told me to check with the sheriff's office. I called the sheriff's office and was told that information would have to come from the federal Immigration and Customs Enforcement, or ICE. An ICE official told me they did not have any detainers against Ahra for previous crimes, but they could not verify her status or how she entered the country. That was confidential.

The media's reaction was also telling in this case. Two local TV stations, Fox 5 Atlanta and 11 Alive (the NBC affiliate), aired initial reports on the attack but never followed up when it became apparent the FBI was doing nothing to ensure equal justice under the law. The local newspaper, the *Atlanta Journal-Constitution*, a bastion of liberalism and staunch supporter of President Obama, initially ran a brief story on the attack, but never followed up.

No national television networks picked up the story except one brief mention on Fox News.

While an obviously dangerous immigrant's status was being guarded like a state secret by the feds and complicit media, the victims in this case were virtually ignored by their local police and media, then completely insulted by the FBI's so-called investigation.

It appears, once again, that the America-hating immigrant was part of a protected class, treated with more dignity and respect than the victim who was American through and through.

The Southern Poverty Law Center, which brags about its self-appointed status as monitor of hate crimes and hate groups, was nowhere to be found in Lawrenceville, Georgia, in the wake of the attack on the Arnos for no other reason than that the attacker did not like their American flag. No, this family did not fit their agenda.

Dami Arno said she and her husband will not lie down and be passive. "All he [FBI agent] kept saying was 'I can give you no information, I can give you no information.' We're not ones to roll over. We're going to stand up and fight."

She said the family has been in contact with a state legislator who is working on legislation that would provide some sort of punishment for refugees or immigrants guilty of violent crimes against Americans— something besides a mere simple-battery misdemeanor.

"I was like everyone else. I didn't realize what was happening until I was slapped in the face with it, and she was standing there waving the flag and trying to attack me and my children, and I said, 'Wait a minute; I have to look into this and find out what is going on,'" Dami told me after she'd had several weeks to reflect on the attack on her home. "And what I found out was very scary."

Dami said she wanted to believe the government. She wanted to believe the Somalis were just like every other immigrant, and still resists the temptation to paint them all with a broad brush. Surely there are many honorable Somalis, but her sense of trust in the government's vetting system has been shattered.

"It's not like they have it plastered all over the place in Lawrenceville; unless you start looking and are aware, it's not going to slap you in the face," she said. "Now that my family has been attacked I'm aware but most aren't.

"I was totally under the belief that our government was protecting us and they were only letting in the people that were vetted and should be let in, like the local media are telling everybody; I bought into all of that. When I was faced with the woman standing in front of me, I knew we were not being protected, and then when the report came back from the FBI and said there was no hate crime committed, I knew something was up, and that was when I woke up and said, 'I've got to do something, because this can't continue to happen.'

"Now is the time for American citizens to stand up and open their eyes. As long as our government continues to let these refugees in, un-vetted, and let these mosques spread messages of hate, they are going to do it, and the only ones who are going to stop it are the American citizens who stand up and say enough is enough."

Jimmy Arno said he was proud of the way his son handled himself, not firing the gun but ready to fire if neighbors had not assisted his mother. "He did everything right. He showed restraint by not shooting her. He did everything he was supposed to do," Arno told me. "Now I just want my government to do what it is supposed to do."

But he isn't expecting President Obama to commend his son for his bravery or to call his wife to offer a consoling word.

Jimmy told me the attack has changed the family's outlook on life. The peaceful subdivision on the outskirts of town has changed too.

"We don't move to a different room in the house without asking, 'Do you have the gun?' I call home 10 or 12 times before lunch to make sure my wife and kids are okay. I shouldn't have to do that. I shouldn't have to mow the grass with a gun strapped to my side."

More than a month after the attack, Dami Arno told me she and her daughter still have nightmares about the attack and how it could have turned out differently.

"I mean, how many times do you stand there and watch someone attack you from your own driveway, and how many times does your fourteen-year-old boy have to pull a gun?" she asked.

Jimmy said he did get one small bit of satisfaction. When he rushed home early from work, the police still had Ahra on-site in their patrol car.

"I grabbed a brand-new flag and put it on the flagpole and put it back up, right there with her watching. It had to happen," he said. "It was important for her to know, okay, you're not going to come in here and stop us in this neighborhood from flying the American flag . . .

". . . My wife is 42 years old and never been in a fight before in her life, but the flag, here at this house, it means something."

His wife agrees. The flag is to be defended.

"We've got to figure out what we can do to stop them [from attacking] because, as an American, I'm not going down like that and not giving up," Dami said. "The people who fought and died to make us free are just too important to just give up and let them win."

Whether Dami and Jimmy Arno knew it or not, they, by standing up to the federal cartel that is bent on destroying their community, were well on their way to forming what is called in the resettlement industry a "pocket of resistance."

Dami has taken on an activist role in her community, trying to educate others and watching more closely what her local government is doing.

She is not alone. There are many more communities across America that are waking up and fighting back. Let's look at a few other "pockets."

11

TRAGEDY AND COVER-UP IN IDAHO

Islamophobia ended in Orlando. My first handgun class is on Saturday.

—A TWIN FALLS, IDAHO, RESIDENT

WHILE IN LAWRENCEVILLE the Arno family found themselves thrust suddenly into the position of having to defend themselves against a rabidly anti-American Somali refugee, some residents of other American cities have warned their public officials ahead of time that bad things happen when a community tries to absorb large numbers of refugees from countries hostile to America and who do not wish to assimilate into American culture.

One city that has a number of activists on high alert for the safety of their communities is Twin Falls, Idaho.

Some two hundred to three hundred residents organized a protest rally in October 2015 against the expected arrival of refugees from the Middle East, when word leaked out of a secret meeting that up to three hundred Syrians fleeing the Syrian civil war were destined for the southern Idaho city. A smaller number of residents held a counter-protest, easily tossing out words like "racist" and "Islamophobe."

The activists approached their elected city leaders and asked them to join their fight against the importation of Syrian refugees, whom they believe will not be properly vetted by the U.S. government. Obama's own FBI director, James Comey, and his director of national intelligence, James Clapper, admitted as much to Congress.

Idaho governor Butch Otter was one of more than twenty-four governors, most of them Republicans, who called on Obama in November 2015 not to bring any Syrians into their states, again citing the problems with vetting people from a failed state where the United States has no access to reliable law enforcement data on refugees.

But whether Syrians were sent to Twin Falls or not, the city was already up to its ears in refugees from other jihadist hotbeds, including Iraq and Sudan. The small city of 24,000 people had received 161 Sudanese refugees and 76 Afghans since 2009, along with 377 Iraqis since 2008 and 68 Bosnians in 2002–03. Almost all of these refugees were Muslim, fueling the growth of the local Islamic community, as evidenced by the brand-new mega-mosque that opened in Twin Falls in 2015.

On the afternoon of June 2, 2016, the worst possible nightmare visited a local family living in a low-income apartment complex in Twin Falls.[1] It was about 3:30 p.m. when eighty-nine-year-old Jolene Payne was sitting on her front porch at the Fawnbrook Apartments and noticed something strange. She saw a boy standing at the entrance to the communal laundry room. The door to the room was cracked just wide enough for the boy to point his camera phone in and film something going on inside.

The retired nurse got up from her comfortable rocking chair and walked over to see what was going on. When she flung open the door, she was shocked at what she found.

A small girl, five-year-old Jamie (not her real name), who knew Payne as "Grandma Jo," was standing inside, naked. She had a deep scratch on her neck and was soaked in urine. Two boys, ages seven and ten, were in the room with her, also naked. The older boy with the camera, age fourteen, was filming a sexual assault in progress. Little Jamie has developmental special needs.

"I knew there was something going on because the boy [with the phone camera] was acting funny, he was taking pictures but he was telling the two younger boys what to do," she told me. "It was like he was coaching them."

This alert grandmother gave me the exact same account she gave police on the day after the incident. Strangely, I was the first member of the media to interview her, even though I was in Atlanta and she was in Idaho! Where were the local media and why weren't they doing their jobs, investigating this horrific crime against a helpless little special-needs girl?

"I opened that door and I almost fainted when I saw what was going on and I'm a nurse," Payne told me. "What a pitiful thing for a poor little girl to go through."

She ordered the boys to put their clothes on and took the girl to her parents' apartment, then called police. Payne said the "little white girl" was humiliated. The littlest boy told her, "We didn't do it; he told us to," pointing to the older boy, who ran off before police arrived.

"They're just kids that have a mother and they moved here from overseas. The women don't even talk any English, some of them do, but others don't. They wear long dresses and long black things on their heads," the grandmother told me.

"I saw two boys and one little girl scared to death," she continued. "I told them boys you better get your clothes on. She was scared to death, crying 'Grandma Jo, Grandma Jo, help me.' I'm not her grandmother but that's what all the kids around here call me."

Later, the little girl's mother, Laney Shelly (not her real name), told me, "It all happened in 10 minutes. I was outside playing with her and had to use the restroom real fast and by the time I got out she was gone. I was freaking out."

The two older refugee boys were taken into custody at a juvenile detention center in Twin Falls but released less than a week later.

Activists and concerned citizens packed the local city council chambers in Twin Falls on June 20 and again on June 27, demanding answers. Some bloggers were first to report the story nationally on June 18, followed by a report by the conservative website Infowars on June 19.

Local newspapers, which had remained silent, reacted in anger and disgust.

The *Spokesman-Review* of Spokane, the *Times-News* of Twin Falls, and the *Idaho Statesman* of Boise all ran follow-up articles, the first of these accusing "anti-Muslim and conspiracy-oriented websites" of reporting a "false story" about the rape of little Jamie at the Fawnbrook Apartments. There were, in fact, some details Infowars got wrong about the incident, having reported that "Syrian refugees" had gang-raped the girl at "knife-point." The suspects were actually Sudanese and Iraqi refugees, and no knife was found at the crime scene, although Jamie told police the boys had one. Yet, despite the fact that the bulk of what was reported was true, and that I had filed a completely accurate story for WND one day after the Infowars report, the refugee advocates went into full spin mode. The local media piled on.

Zeze Rwasama, director of the College of Southern Idaho Refugee Center in Twin Falls, told the *Spokesman-Review* he was "stunned by the false story."

"We have not resettled Syrians in this area," Rwasama said. "Now, it's not because we don't want to resettle them, I want to make that clear, just because they have not come our way yet. But it is very surprising that people are pushing the Syrians in this area. That shows me that probably there's a different agenda that I don't know of. If there is a story to tell, then the story should be all accurate."

Adding insult to injury, Jamie's parents were denied basic public records about their daughter's rape for more than a month, including the 911 transcripts, the police report, even her medical records. The owner of their apartment complex immediately sent eviction notices to the two families of the refugee boys charged with Jamie's sexual assault. But the family of one of the boys was still living right next door to Jamie's family more than two months after the rape.

"The child [perpetrator] does still live here next to us. I don't let her play outside [for long at a time], and my child feels like a prisoner in her own home," the girl's mother, Laney Shelly, told me in a phone interview.

Shelly watches her daughter play outside each day, but she has a rare liver disease, and the prescription she takes for the condition makes her sensitive to the sun. "I can't be out there but five minutes at a time with my medication," she said. "She doesn't understand why she can't go outside and play."

"We've started her in counseling, but she's still traumatized really bad. She'll tell me 'those are bad boys, those are all bad boys.'"

Shelly, twenty-eight, is a stay-at-home mom whose other child, a son, is autistic. Her fiancé works as a chef at a nearby hotel and does not have health insurance.

The crime against their daughter was more horrific than the local prosecutor, Grant Loebs, made it sound in his statements to local media, she said. And Shelly is also disappointed in the way local news agencies have covered the story.

"The local media, I feel like they're against us, because they get the wrong story and they switch it around," she told me. "I won't even talk to the local media. I just think everything they say is B.S."

The Twin Falls community has been mostly supportive, she said. A group of citizens held a rally on a local bridge one Saturday and made a stop at the apartment complex to show their support. A GoFundMe account has been started, and many have made donations to help them raise enough money to hire a lawyer and to move to a better apartment away from the perpetrators.

As it turns out, the oldest of the three refugee boys, the fourteen-year-old from Sudan, captured the entire incident on a video about four minutes long. And what Jolene Payne had said was true. "Two of them were naked and the one videotaping was coaching the others on what to do," Shelly said, adding she could not bring herself to watch the video, but her fiancé did.

"He is missing a lot of work because it is hard for him to work, and when he goes to counseling we have to pay for it out of pocket," she told me. "He needs the counseling. It was hard for him to stay back because when this happened he wanted to hurt somebody. That is his baby."

According to Shelly, it took over two hours for the police to arrive from the time of the first 911 call following the child's assault. The local police chief denied this at a city council meeting, claiming officers had arrived in a "timely" fashion.

"As victims it just makes us feel like they're treating us like we're the criminals. I called the victim's advocate a few times to get the records and she said 'I told you several times now you can't have nothing.' And she's like 'why do you want this stuff?' And I tell her because it's my daughter and I want to know and I have a right to it under our Constitution."

'NOBODY SHOULD BE STUNNED'

Despite Zeze Rwasama's comment about being "stunned" by the assault story, nobody should be "stunned" when a criminal report involving refugees gets covered up by police and buried by the media, says Ann Corcoran, who has been following the refugee program for the past nine years with the blog *Refugee Resettlement Watch*. It happens all the time. It was only because of the local activists' persistence in prying information from their public officials and sharing it with bloggers that the Twin Falls rape ever saw the light of day.

"They got the nationality wrong and a couple of other minor points, but it was otherwise spot on," Corcoran said of the initial reports by bloggers.

"And," she continued, "there is no doubt that if local residents, criticized by their elected officials, hadn't pushed this story out to the public, with a few small errors like the nationalities of the perps, the whole case would have been swept under the rug."[2]

WND published my first story about the Idaho rape on June 20, the day after the Infowars article had hit the Drudge Report. Five more of my stories would be published in the days ahead, shedding more light on exactly what happened at the Fawnbrook Apartments and how honest bloggers and activists were being smeared in the media.

While the local media reacted shamefully, the national media ignored the story altogether. They were acting remarkably similar to the way European media reacted to the earlier mass sexual assaults by migrants on women in Germany, Sweden, and the UK.

Cover-ups of refugee crimes, especially sex crimes, are endemic across Europe. The Idaho case shows the same tendency of the establishment system—including politicians, police, prosecutors, child welfare advocates, and media—to do everything in its power to hide these crimes.

Twin Falls Mayor Shawn Barigar scolded his local residents at the June 27 city council meeting, saying they should not spread the "false narrative," the "fiction" put out by irresponsible bloggers and Internet journalists.[3]

The mayor and his allies tried to discredit the entire story even though a set of facts, reported from the beginning by WND, lay indisputable—a small, special-needs girl was raped by one refugee boy from Iraq while another stood by waiting his turn and a third was busy filming the entire assault.

OBAMA APPOINTEE COMES TO DEFENSE OF MUSLIM COMMUNITY

The real stunner in this story came late on Friday, June 25, 2016. That's when the Obama Justice Department's U.S. attorney for Idaho, Wendy J. Olson, issued a threat to the Idaho public.

Keep in mind this was a local criminal case being handled by local police in Twin Falls. As a federal prosecutor, appointed in 2010 by President Obama, Olson had no role in this case.

But that didn't stop her from inserting herself into the local drama. She issued a statement on a Friday evening, calling for calm in the Twin Falls community and urging people to let the police chief and local prosecutor do their jobs. Fair enough. But that was just the window dressing. The real point of her Friday-night bombshell was found a little lower in the press release. Olson said: "The spread of false information or inflammatory or threatening statements about the perpetrators or the crime itself reduces public safety and may violate federal law."[4]

I was relaxing and sipping coffee on Saturday morning when news of her press release came into my e-mail box. While Saturday mornings are normally leisurely off time for me, I almost choked on my coffee as I read Olson's statement. It was eerily similar to that of the Obama-appointed attorney general Loretta Lynch, who, on the day after the San Bernardino terrorist attack, issued a warning to Americans that she would "aggressively prosecute" any anti-Muslim speech that was "edging toward violence."[5] Lynch was forced to walk back the comments a few days later after First Amendment advocates universally expressed outrage.

I immediately started writing up a new story for WND about Olson's comments. My story was finished by 2:30 p.m. Saturday and immediately picked up by the Drudge Report. It went viral, with 1 million views and more than 6,150 reader comments.

I reported a second story on Monday, also picked up by Drudge, which quoted three constitutional scholars, all saying Olson's comments were outside the boundaries of the First Amendment and taking her to task for threatening to chill the local community's free speech rights.

By Tuesday Ms. Olson, taking a cue from her boss Loretta Lynch a few months earlier, was walking back her statement, saying people had "misinterpreted" her remarks, which were never intended to be a threat of arrest. Sorry, but very few were buying that argument.[6]

ADOPTING OBAMA'S "VIOLENT EXTREMISM" RHETORIC

I researched Olson's background and found this wasn't the first time she had come to the defense of criminally deviant Muslims in Idaho while threatening local residents that they had better keep quiet about Islam. On July 10, 2015, she had issued a statement about "building resilient communities" after meeting with law enforcement, the ACLU, and other groups to discuss "anti-refugee" and "anti-Muslim" sentiments in Idaho and across the country that she deemed were seeking to "divide communities."[7]

Olson used the language of the United Nations–sanctioned "Strong Cities Network," or SCN, which was announced by Attorney General Lynch at the UN in September 2015. That's when Lynch called for building "resilient communities" in the fight against "violent extremism."

The SCN attempts to globalize law enforcement agencies, connecting U.S. cops with those overseas to combat violent extremism in all its forms. By changing the narrative from Islamic terrorism to the more generic "violent extremism," many conservative leaders viewed the SCN initiative as an attempt to single out and silence traditional Christian conservatives under the guise of branding them "right-wing extremists."

On July 8, 2015, just over two months before Lynch's UN announcement, Olson said her staff met with representatives from the refugee community, refugee support agencies, the Idaho Muslim community, the Boise Police Department, the FBI, the Intermountain Fair Housing Council, the ACLU, and Stand Up America to discuss community responses to recent terrorism cases in Idaho and across the country.

"We are at a critical time in our nation and in our own community—from the shooting at the Emanuel AME Church in Charleston, to anti-refugee and anti-Muslim sentiments expressed by groups and individuals in Idaho, to defiance in parts of some states to the Supreme Court's decision to legalize same-sex marriage in *Obergefell v. Hodges,*" said Olson's statement. "There are many currents that seek to divide communities. Instead, we have to come together. We need to stand up and form strategies against those who espouse extremist ideologies and recruit others to engage in violent acts in our communities on their behalf. We want to mentor our young people, educate parents, identify solutions, and form closer relationships between refugees and Idahoans who have been here for generations."[8]

The only real answers to the divisive problems noted by Olson are for refugees already here to assimilate into American society, and for the U.S. government to stop importing more unvettable refugees from sharia-compliant countries that hate America.

PROTECTING MUSLIMS AGAINST "BIAS"

Olson said the objective of the July 8 meeting was to reassure members of the refugee and Muslim communities that with the federal terrorism trial in *United States v. Kurbanov* scheduled to begin July 13, "law enforcement officers will be vigilant in protecting them against bias crimes."[9]

Olson had called this meeting and issued her statement ahead of the trial that ended up convicting Fazliddin Kurbanov, a Muslim refugee from Uzbekistan, of conspiring to blow up U.S. military installations with homemade bombs being made in his Boise apartment. An Idaho jury convicted Kurbanov on terror charges in August 2015 following a twenty-day trial and two days of deliberation. "Prosecutors also said he tried to provide computer support and money to the Islamic Movement of Uzbekistan, which the U.S. government has identified as a terrorist organization," reported the *New York Daily News*.[10]

Kurbanov, a Russian-speaking truck driver, is just one of dozens of refugees who have been tried and convicted on terrorism charges. More than forty Somali refugees have also left the United States to join foreign terrorist organizations, including al-Shabab and ISIS.[11] Two Iraqi refugees living in Kentucky were charged and convicted in 2011 of providing material support to al-Qaeda.[12]

This is just the tip of the iceberg. Congressional data show hundreds of terror plots have been stopped in the United States since 9/11— mostly involving foreign-born suspects, including dozens of refugees. The files, if publicized by major media, would have further stoked the debate over the Obama administration's push to admit thousands more refugees from Syria and elsewhere, a proposal Donald Trump vehemently opposed on the 2016 campaign trail.

"[T]hese data make clear that the United States not only lacks the ability to properly screen individuals prior to their arrival, but also that our nation has an unprecedented assimilation problem," senators Jeff Sessions and Ted Cruz told President Obama in a June 14 letter obtained by FoxNews.com.[13]

Yet, in the run-up to that Kurbanov trial, Olson was wanting to make sure there was no backlash against Muslims, even as more United Nations–selected refugees from sharia-compliant Muslim countries were being secretly planted in hundreds of U.S. cities and towns.

Corcoran noted that many major media outlets, including the *New York Times*, rushed out to Idaho to cover the "Islamophobes" who were protesting the arrival of refugees in October and November 2015. But those same media outlets were nowhere to be found when a little girl was sexually assaulted by refugee boys in her own apartment complex.[14]

And it isn't the first such case brought to light, either. I reported on July 9, 2016, another case involving a Syrian refugee who was charged with molesting a thirteen-year-old girl at a public pool in Lowell, Massachusetts, near Boston. The suspect, twenty-two-year-old Emad Hasso, was allegedly running his hand up the young girl's thigh when a lifeguard saw the assault and intervened. Hasso had only been in the country two months, one of eighteen Syrian refugees delivered to Lowell compliments of the Obama administration.

Prosecutor Sam Miller reported that the teen said a man had approached her, touched her upper thigh, and asked her age. The girl told him she was too young for him and walked away. Hasso then allegedly followed the girl around the pool. While swimming, he again approached her, touched her upper thigh, and asked her age. The girl responded that she was a "little kid, leave me alone." At that point other people at the pool, including the lifeguard, saw some of the interaction between Hasso and the girl and called authorities.[15]

In 2009 an eight-year-old girl was gang-raped by four Liberian refugee boys ages nine to fourteen.[16]

And in May 2015 a forty-nine-year-old Iraqi refugee was arrested for the rape of a grade school–aged girl in Kennewick, Washington. He allegedly raped her repeatedly over a six-month period and was to stand trial in July 2016, but he jumped bail and hopped a plane to the United Arab Emirates two days before his trial was to begin.[17]

There are likely untold numbers of other sexual assaults by refugees that were swept under the carpet from public view.

At the June 20 Twin Falls City Council meeting, the *Spokesman-Review* reported that several local residents spoke out against the resettlement of refugees in their city. They cited the rape in their own community and the emerging news about out-of-control sexual assaults by migrants against women in Germany and Sweden. "ISIS is here," one woman warned. The citizens of Twin Falls also objected to the city's approval of a new mega-mosque, and charged that a Muslim woman had spit on someone at a local grocery store.[18]

The mayor admitted that things could have been handled better and with more transparency while still guarding the identities of the juveniles involved.[19]

The criminal case against the three refugee boys in Twin Falls was sealed by a judge, but that didn't justify the denial of basic information to the victim's family.

If all this hedging, covering up, and conflating of the issues sound familiar, it should. Remember the stories of slack police investigations and silent media in Rotherham, England, in the face of repeated rapes by Pakistani Muslim "sex grooming gangs," which victimized more than fourteen hundred young English school girls from poor families over a period of fourteen years. This travesty played out in Rotherham spread to other cities as well, and the full extent of the tragedy may never be known.

WATCH THE PROPERTY TRANSACTIONS

Tiffany, a Twin Falls resident who asked me not to reveal her real name, shared with me how refugee resettlement has changed her neighborhood. Her story squares with what I've been told by residents in other towns being Islamized—there's a disturbing pattern in the property transactions being recorded at the local courthouse.

"I live in a beautiful subdivision called Rock Creek in the quiet town of Twin Falls," she told me.[20]

Immediately upon moving into her rental home on Knoll Ridge Road in July 2014, she noticed that her neighbors did not appear to be Americans, and she witnessed a pattern of incidents that she found "unnerving." She began to document these incidents.

On July 28, 2014, at 11 a.m., twenty to twenty-five cars were parked along her residential street. Most were midsized white sedans, and some had blurred-out plates. No women and children were visible. Cars pulled up, and men, all Muslim between the ages of eighteen and sixty-five, walked into the neighbor's house in pairs. They scoped out the neighborhood for about ten minutes. A "lookout" directed all the men, single file, across the street to a different house on Knoll Ridge Road. Several men were on cell phones. A large, gray-haired man speaking in perhaps Turkish or Russian stopped and looked directly at Tiffany and mentioned her house number in English. Their cars blocked her driveway and were parked directly in front of her house. She had no exit.

"I'm home with my son and a daughter. I call my husband, who's at work. I call a friend. I get a non-emergency police number. I call the police and report the suspicious gathering of easily 30 to 35 Middle Eastern men," Tiffany wrote in her journal. "They are all dressed in pants, collared shirts, no jeans. By 11:25 the group has dispersed. A few kids return to the street. My dog was injured this morning from some unexplained puncture wound to his snout. These are men I have never seen."

She said she reported the activity and the attack on her dog to the FBI. The agency did not follow through with a thorough investigation. "As I documented these activities, I began to wonder, who are the people in my neighborhood? If they give you their name, it is an Americanized version, and they are vague about their places of origin," she said.

She went to the public parcel website for her neighborhood and discovered that of the 136 homes in her subdivision, 31 were owned by people with Muslim-sounding names, bringing Muslim occupancy to approximately 22 percent. A small adjacent neighborhood, Bosero Way, is home to about 35 percent Muslim families.

Tiffany sent me copies of the recorded land deeds.

Strangely, many of these families own multiple properties. The imam, Bakhritdin Yusupov, who is Russian born and Turkish speaking, has owned a house on Caswell since 2008, but now there are five under the Yusupov name in the neighborhood. Salim Shaoo owns two, the Mametovs two, Fakhratov/Fakhratova owns three, Sharafov owns five, the Sobi (Sobbi) family from Iran owns six plus a valuable large plot of land near the canyon. And one of the homes is still owned by the College of Southern Idaho, home to the CSI Refugee Program in Twin Falls.

A white windowless cargo van sits parked in the wrong direction, never moving for months. The home is listed under a Murat Yusupov. No pictures can be found of Murat, and no one seems to be able to find any information on Imam Bakhritdin Yusupov before 2008.

Tiffany noted that when large gatherings happen next door, the police no longer come when called. They explained that they don't want to appear to be "profiling."

"Why do I care?" she asked. "I could move, and we most likely will next summer, sadly, never to purchase here due to this rampant influx of refugees. The housing market is tight right now. Lots of developments are currently breaking ground in once-empty fields on the west side of town. Muslims are seeking contractors, but asking for greatly reduced [50 percent] rates. One neighbor on Knoll Ridge has their home for sale. They bought at the height of the market. Then the Muslims moved in all around them and they fear they will have to rent it out and may never recoup their investment. These 'refugees' aren't hungry, poor people running for their lives. They are well funded, well established, and generally quiet. Haven't we heard that before? The Boston bombers were 'all-American boys.' San Bernardino shooter Syed Farook was quiet, hardworking, educated. So was the Chattanooga shooter, Muhammad Youssef Abdulazeez. Almost without exception, the neighbors of every terrorist has claimed they 'were so nice and would never do that.' I'm not going to be *that* neighbor. Islamophobia ended in Orlando. My first handgun class is on Saturday."

OFFSHORING INDUSTRY WITH HELP OF GOVERNMENT AND CHURCHES

There is another lesson to be drawn from Twin Falls, and that stems from the Chobani yogurt factory, which employs more than six hundred people and gives 30 percent of those jobs to foreign refugees.

If one looks at many of the smaller- to medium-sized cities being flooded with refugees, there is often a meatpacking plant, a window factory, a yogurt plant, or some other industry at the heart of the operation that is more than happy to make use of the steady flow of cheap refugee labor. And the U.S. government and its mostly religious resettlement contractors, such as Catholic Charities and Lutheran Social Services, are all too happy to serve as virtual headhunters for those industries, bringing the cheap labor from the Third World directly to their doorstep in places such as Twin Falls, Idaho; Bowling Green and Louisville, Kentucky; and Willmar, Owatonna, and St. Cloud, Minnesota.

It is the same principle that led to the offshoring of the American textile industry after President Clinton signed the North American Free Trade Agreement (NAFTA was negotiated by Clinton's predecessor George H. W. Bush). Only under this arrangement, businesses no longer need to go through the trouble of navigating a foreign government's rules and regulations for constructing a plant and employing foreign nationals. They can have the Third World labor advantage brought directly to them, without the expenses and headaches associated with operating an overseas factory.

Amarillo, Texas, is one of many towns with factories acting as magnets for refugee labor. Tyson Fresh Meats Inc., Cargill, and other companies operate large meatpacking plants in Amarillo.

12

AMARILLO, TEXAS:
A BRAVE MAYOR PUSHES BACK

Refugee resettlement is not about "humanitarianism"! It is about globalists and greedy industries wanting to improve their bottom lines—the social and economic condition of your towns and cities be damned.

—ANN CORCORAN, *REFUGEE RESETTLEMENT WATCH*

WHILE MOST AMERICAN CITIES SEEM content to bow to every Muslim demand and subdue themselves to Islam, there are some exceptions. Mayor Paul Harpole of Amarillo is pushing back, forming his own pocket of resistance.

Amarillo made it into the national spotlight in June 2016 when a male refugee who had emigrated from Iran in 2003 took two coworkers hostage at a local Walmart. The fact that he was a refugee came as no surprise to those who track the federal government's robust refugee resettlement program.[1]

Amarillo is bursting at the seams with refugees from Africa, Asia, and the Middle East, and its mayor has pleaded repeatedly with the government to stop sending refugees to his city. But they keep coming. The schools are stretched, and the local police department is having a hard time getting a handle on the rising crime.

Mohammad Moghaddan, an Iranian refugee who became an American citizen in 2010, was shot and killed by sheriff's deputies after he had taken the two Walmart employees hostage. Moghaddan, fifty-four, was a current employee of the store, and his actions were quickly declared a case of "workplace violence" by the sheriff's office.[2] The hostage taker, armed with a handgun, was shot dead by a SWAT team as terrified shoppers were ushered out of the store.

The city's mayor has been on a crusade since 2011 to get the U.S. State Department, working with the United Nations, to put a damper on the number of refugees flooding into his city.[3] So far, Mayor Paul Harpole has had little success.

Whether the event in the summer of 2016 was terrorism or "workplace violence," Amarillo, a city of 240,000, has had its share of crime. Adding to the problem is the fact that it has the highest per capita ratio of refugees of any city in the world, says Harpole. "The City of Amarillo gets more refugees per 100,000 population than any city in the world," Harpole testified on April 21, 2016, before the state Senate's Committee on Health and Human Services, which held a hearing on refugee resettlement. He cited figures from per capita comparisons of other U.S. cities that suggest Amarillo should take in between 65 and 90 refugees a year. Instead, he said, "We get about 500 a year."

The refugees are stretching the city's ability to keep up with their needs. Worse, said Harpole, Amarillo is creating "small ghettos. A group of Somalis came in to say they had elected a mayor of their community. Then another faction claimed they had their own leader. We come to find out that rival tribes—slaves and masters—were being settled together."

Catholic Charities of the Texas Panhandle has been the main resettlement contractor in Amarillo for years. It agreed in 2011 to bring in 35 to 40 percent fewer refugees after the city leaders complained, but the U.S. State Department was not to be deterred. It simply picked up a second contractor to fill in the gap, said Ann Corcoran, who was introduced in chapter 4.

That second contractor is Amarillo's Refugee Services of Texas office, which works through Church World Services and Lutheran Immigration and Refugee Services. Corcoran says many of the refugees the State Department and its contractors send to Amarillo are placed in jobs in area meatpacking plants. Food giant Cargill is one of the biggest employers in the area.

"Like so many meatpacking towns in America, federal refugee resettlement contractors [established] a foothold there years ago, mostly working as 'headhunters' for the meatpacking industry, and have continued to pour Third-Worlders into Amarillo despite pleas by elected officials to stop," Corcoran said. The bottom line is to keep wages down, and this is why Republicans in Congress typically go along with the Democrats in supporting the refugee program. Even as they talked tough against Syrian refugees in late 2015, they voted to fully fund President Obama's expanded refugee program, which was buried in the $1.1 trillion omnibus spending bill.

"Refugee resettlement is not about 'humanitarianism'! It is about globalists and greedy industries wanting to improve their bottom lines—the social and economic condition of your towns and cities be damned," Corcoran says.

FLOODING IN FROM THE MIDDLE EAST

Not only does Amarillo have the highest ratio of refugees in the world, but it has the highest ratio of Middle Eastern refugees of any city in America. Amarillo has become home to more than one thousand Mideast migrants. When you take into consideration Muslim migrants from outside the Middle East, it's much more.

According to the State Department's Refugee Processing Center database, a total of 4,892 refugees have arrived since 2002 from the following countries, all of which have strong Muslim refugee populations.

Refugees sent to Amarillo from Muslim strongholds since 2002:

Afghanistan: 39	Iran: 674
Bosnia: 11	Iraq: 393
Burma: 2,923	Somalia: 584
Burundi: 97	Sudan: 99
Eritrea: 72	

Taxpayer activist William Sumerford recently told Watchdog.org that refugees in Amarillo are stretching local services. "Police say crime is a chronic problem in the resettlement enclaves," Watchdog's Texas Bureau reported, adding that the city currently fields 911 calls in forty-two different languages.

"Hospitals, welfare, police, you name it, are strained. That all comes back on our city budget," Sumerford said.

Amarillo's school system is particularly vulnerable. "Our education system is overloaded with kids who can't speak English," noted Sumerford.

More than fifteen languages are spoken in the Amarillo school system, and when you include the different dialects, the number balloons to seventy-five, according to Harpole's testimony before the state legislature.

"We have 660 (refugee) kids who don't speak English, and the U.S. Department of Education says they have to be at grade level within one year. It's a ludicrous requirement—they don't even know how to use the bathroom," Mayor Harpole reported. According to Watchdog. org, Washington pays schools only $100 per refugee student per year.

The Amarillo City Commission has been considering a plan to halt further refugee settlements, but so far no city or state has been successful in ending a federal resettlement program once it gets started. The state of Texas sued the federal government, seeking a stronger role in the resettlement process, as did the state of Alabama. Both states lost their cases, but Tennessee has the strongest legal case against the feds, preparing a suit on Tenth Amendment grounds alleging the program is a violation of state sovereignty.

Harpole says he isn't optimistic about the city's authority to push back.

"We've been a giving community, and it's a huge disservice to bring in refugees in numbers that we're not able to handle."

"Federal law requires the Obama administration to work with Texas in the refugee resettling process," Katherine Wise, spokeswoman for

Texas Attorney General Ken Paxton, told Watchdog.org. "The response by the Obama administration makes it clear that it has no intention of cooperating with us."

The most active congressman to stand against the refugee resettlement program is Rep. Brian Babin, R-TX, who represents the Houston suburbs. He introduced a bill in July 2014 that would halt the arrival of all refugees until a full audit of the program's costs and risks to national security can be completed. The GOP-controlled House under Speaker Paul Ryan ignored Babin's bill, even though it garnered eighty cosponsors. Instead Ryan, while speaking out against Syrian refugees, quietly negotiated a deal with the Democrats that fully funded President Obama's expanded refugee program.

Ryan also argued against Donald Trump's plan to put a temporary pause on all Muslim immigration.

The United States is scheduled to bring in 85,000 foreign refugees in 2016 and 110,000 in fiscal 2017—with about half of them coming from Muslim-dominated countries.

But the full picture of Muslim immigration is much more troublesome. According to the Center for Immigration Studies, Sen. Jeff Sessions, and other sources, the United States issues more than 120,000 green cards every year to people from Muslim countries. If temporary visas are included, such as those issued to college students and guest workers, the number balloons to more than 240,000 per year.

Refugees, however, are the most entitled of all immigrants. They qualify for all federal welfare benefits on day one of their arrival and are granted green-card status within a year. They can qualify for full citizenship, including voting rights, within five years.

If this makes you angry, it should. Ann Corcoran has spoken around the country on the federal government's placement of refugees into unsuspecting local communities. She told me the two issues that most infuriate residents are the secrecy of the program and the priority given to foreigners over our own Americans in need.

"I'm sorry. I shouldn't be so cynical, but honestly why are

foreign-born poor people needier and more deserving than American-born disabled, impoverished and struggling in the eyes of these 'good Christians?' Is it somehow more charitable to care for immigrants than their own neighbors? Are 'refugees' somehow cooler than our own poor people (of all colors)?" [4]

Remember, these religious organizations working for the federal government are not using their own charitable dollars, but rather *your* tax dollars!

13

WHAT'S GOING ON IN MINNEAPOLIS?

They slowed the car down, waved at my husband with the windows open and played a recording of what sounded like a woman being raped, blasted it from their car speakers.

—SARAH PENSKEY

Note: The name of the victim in this story has been changed to protect her safety.

SARAH PENSKEY WAS IN HER GARAGE, unpacking boxes on a sunny morning in late June 2016, when she was approached by several bearded Somali men in their early to mid twenties. It was the last week of Ramadan, and the men were wearing traditional Islamic robes. The uninvited visitors to this posh Minneapolis neighborhood known as Linden Hills—situated among tall trees just off of Thomas Beach on Lake Calhoun—ground to a halt beside Penskey's house that morning. They came in a white RAV 4 Toyota and a dark-colored van, catching her unawares as she walked out of her garage to put something in her trash can.

Just the day before, another group of Somalis had driven through the neighborhood and approached her as she was turning on her sprinkler, but they were younger, in their late teens and dressed in basketball shorts.

"Hey, you have a beautiful house," they had said. "You're beautiful too. Can we move in with you?"

Penskey thanked them dismissively and walked back into her house.

The older group that showed up the next day was not so subtle. Nor would they be so easily dismissed. "Hey . . . Hey . . . Hey!" they yelled as she was taking out her trash.

"Yes?"

"We want to live in your house. We want to marry you."

"No, I already have a husband, but have a good day," Penskey replied.

The men starting jostling each other and yelling things that were hard to understand. At least five other cars were driving recklessly through the narrow streets, setting off bottle rockets, their passengers hanging off of the door frames, some even riding on the hood, yelling, "Jihad!"

They ran over some neighbors' lawns and reportedly beat up one resident's dog.

"Do you know sharia law?" one of the robed men yelled at Penskey.

Having lived overseas, Penskey knew about sharia and its rules for man-woman relationships and Muslim–non-Muslim relationships.

"Yes," she said, walking back toward her garage.

"We can kidnap you and rape you!" the man shouted back at her.

She shut the garage door and ran inside to call police.

"I didn't yell at them. I didn't do anything, just tried to shut the door and get back inside, so it's like there were some bad apples one day, and then there were some really bad apples the next," Penskey told me in a phone interview. Her husband was not home during either of her first two encounters with the Somali men.

Many neighbors called police on the second morning of what some are calling the Somali "wilding," a day of brazen intimidation that started in Linden Hills using fireworks and fake guns and spread to the adjacent beach on Lake Calhoun.

"On the second day, multiple neighbors were running out, trying to get license plate numbers, and were on the phone with the police. They were running outside, barefoot. One woman came and swept up her child and took her back in the house," Penskey said. "Imagine six cars driving fifty miles per hour through a residential street, then slamming on the brakes, driving on lawns, exploding fireworks. They almost hit one child and actually did hit one of their own."

Several of the Somalis carried black flags that Penskey said resembled the ISIS flag.

One Somali reportedly threatened a man in his sixties who had photographed the immigrant's license plate, and demanded that he erase the picture.

Police took up to three hours to arrive. The dispatchers told Penskey they didn't have enough officers on duty to confront twenty or more men. The police did periodic drive-bys to monitor the situation. When they did show up, the worst offenders were gone. The police report says officers arrived to find a female victim, Penskey, who was "very distraught and alone. Crying."

She had called 911 three times that day. An officer arrived once earlier but only wrote a minor traffic ticket to one of the rioters. The main instigators had fled before police got there.

POLICE: "THIS IS A VERY UNUSUAL CASE"

John Elder, public information officer with the Minneapolis Police Department, told me there had been no arrests in the incident as of this writing.

"There remains an active investigation, and I am very limited in what I can say due to the fact that it is an active investigation," Elder said. "We continue to work with the community, and continue to interview folks, but no arrests have been made at this point."

I asked if any arrests were anticipated.

"I can't comment on that," Elder replied.

"Is this type of activity common in Minneapolis?"

"This is an unusual case, yep," the officer said.

The case is being investigated as a situation involving potential terroristic threats. Penskey said the FBI have also visited her and are taking the case very seriously.

DAY 3: MEN IN ROBES RETURN

The terrorizing of Linden Hills didn't stop after the second day. The men returned for a third straight morning, June 28, and this time Penskey's husband was home, standing out in the yard as they approached.

This time, it was the younger group of Somalis who came, but within minutes, the older provocateurs were back too, with their robes and their duffel bags, their flags and their bottle rockets, shouting their threats in this strange form of jihad.

But this time they had a surprise for the targets of their terror.

"They slowed the car down, waved at my husband with the windows open, and played a recording of what sounded like a woman being raped, blasted it from their car speakers," Penskey said. "Then they parked their car, and my husband came upstairs and said, 'Call 911 now, and stay away from the windows.'"

The robed Somalis scared vacationers off the beach that morning, reportedly using their duffel bags as fake guns, pointing them at families and pretending to shoot them, one by one. The sound of exploding bottle rockets crashed through the heavy morning air.

"The beach emptied out real quick. It was about 10 a.m., and there weren't a lot of people out there. But those who were got up and immediately walked toward the parking lot yelling, 'Call the cops!'" witnesses told me.

"The problem is this escalated so fast, but it was more at the beachside on the third day," Penskey said. "They said something inappropriate to my husband, turning on the recording of a woman being raped, or having loud sex, and just waved at him and smiled, a threat, to my husband. What was he to think? He was just furious and came upstairs and said, 'You can't leave the house today.'"

Police arrived much faster this time, within three minutes. But, again, the older ones, who were the main instigators had already driven away.

Even in liberal-minded Minnesota, where the sight of bearded Somalis in Islamic attire is considered part of the multicultural norm, the beach-goers' reactions reflected the level of aggressiveness that was on display.

"They're not accepted on the beach that way. You have beards and you're dressed in long robes and using a duffel bag like you're shooting a machine gun," Penskey said. "People left. People left the beach. I don't think people realize how bad it is in Minnesota and what type of backdrop we have here."

FEDS IMPORT 132,000 SOMALI REFUGEES OVER THIRTY YEARS

As you may recall from chapter 10, the federal government, working with the United Nations, Catholic Charities, and Lutheran Social Services, among other agencies, has imported more than 132,000 Somali refugees into dozens of U.S. towns since 1983, according to U.S. State Department data, but the largest contingent has been sent to Minneapolis.

Judy Layer, seventy-six, one of the Linden Hills neighbors, was an eyewitness to the events of June 26–28, 2016. She is most infuriated by a group of commenters who swarmed a neighborhood website and tried to either downplay the incident as simply some obnoxious youngsters having summer fun or to say that it didn't happen at all.

"I'll just tell you what I saw, and it did happen. There are so many people who were saying it was all made up," Layer said. "I was walking my dog. I went around the block, came into my house, sat on my deck, and was reading on my iPad."

Her husband was still upstairs getting dressed. The couple has lived in Linden Hills for twenty-two years.

"I did see a pattern developing of about five cars coming in, turning around; then the kids would get out of the cars, be shadowboxing with each other. They were loud," Layer said. "Then I saw them all go into a cluster. They were speaking with [Sarah Penskey]. And I said to my husband, 'Come here. This looks like kind of a situation. She can't be too comfortable with this.' She was watering the lawn. So Jim called the police, and others did the same."

One young man came running down the hill in his dress shirt and took pictures of license plates, she said.

"I can understand why one police car would not want to come into this situation. I counted nineteen or twenty [refugees] at one time," she said. "But what I didn't like is that some people remarked on the [community's] website Nextdoor-LindenHills that, 'Oh, it's just a bunch of old people that like to call the police.' I don't sit around wanting to call the police."

LOCAL NEWSPAPER GOES DARK ON THE INCIDENT

The local newspaper, the Minneapolis *StarTribune*, ignored the incident. And only one TV station, KSTP Channel 5, has covered it.

"And so now it's being said that it's all being made up. It wasn't made up; this happened," Layer told me. "Why it was only being reported on Channel 5, I don't know."

Layer tried to capture the incident on video. "But I missed the part where all the cars were veering around, screaming," she said. "Had it been late at night, I think it would have been more dangerous. I wasn't trying to sensationalize it. But on the other hand, it did happen."

She went on to tell me that as the Somalis were harassing Penskey, they "named a practice" by which they could have four wives.

That would be sharia.

"DOGS ARE UNCLEAN"

After learning that Penskey's dog had been injured, Layer said this is not the first time Somalis using the adjacent beach have targeted dogs in her neighborhood. "There was an incident involving a girl . . . She had a dog and felt she was verbally accosted by this group," she said. "This girl at the lake made a police report. They think dogs are unclean."

Since hearing of that incident, Layer said she takes precautions when walking her own dog.

"I've got a dog, and I walk my dog, but I go a different path now. I just don't need that, so I'm happy to change my path," she said. "After that happened, yes, I changed my route. I thought, yeah, I'll just go down this alley and take my dog and come back. I'd rather do that than be confronted by something like that."

Penskey said she has also been maligned by online commenters who accuse her and others of making the situation worse by attempting to video the young Somali men.

"There are people online saying this never would have happened if not for the video. Do you think I'm stupid enough to walk out of my house and take video of them?" she asked. "Some neighbors were shooting video, but even the Somalis themselves took photos and video of what they were doing. But, no, I'm not stupid enough to stand in my yard and take video of nineteen or more twenty-year-old men."

Penskey and Layer both said Minnesotans are afraid to confront the issue of Somali terrorism and crime, even after six young Somalis were arrested in 2015 and charged with trying to join ISIS. They are among nearly forty who have been charged with trying to join foreign terror groups since 2007, and dozens of others have been convicted of providing material support to overseas terrorists.

"People are too afraid of the backlash, and that's why people are afraid to say something," Penskey said. "If you do, you'll either get a backlash or be called a bigot."

14

HOW SHOULD WE RESPOND?

America, every state is a terrorist breeding ground right now. They are in your backyards; they are in your schools; they are in your communities.

—ISIK ABLA

ON JANUARY 17, 2016, San Diego bishop Robert W. McElroy sat onstage with a Muslim Brotherhood operative and implored Catholics not to join their fellow Americans who engage in "the scourge of anti-Islamic prejudice." The bishop issued the challenge during an interfaith conference held at the University of San Diego's Joan B. Kroc Institute for Peace and Justice. The event was part of the first national Catholic-Muslim dialogue held at the Catholic university.

"We are witnessing in the United States a new nativism, which the American Catholic community must reject and label for the religious bigotry which it is," he said.

Had Bishop McElroy been dialoging with a representative of truly peaceful Muslims, we could agree with him. But he was sitting with Sayyid M. Syeed, national director of the Islamic Society of North America's (ISNA) Office for Interfaith and Community Alliances.[1]

ISNA, which represented U.S. Muslims at the conference, was created by the extremist Muslim Brotherhood, as documented in court records filed during the Holy Land Foundation terror-financing trial of 2007–08 in Dallas.[2]

IDENTIFYING "ENEMIES OF ALL FAITHS"

At the January 2016 conference, Syeed spoke glowingly of new bridges being built between Islam and the world's other major faith communities. He is the Brotherhood's point man for interfaith dialogue and as such plays a key role in the Brotherhood's strategy of nonviolent, civilization jihad. He speaks of peace and tranquility between all the world's religious communities even as the violent arm of his chief sponsor, the Muslim Brotherhood, is busy supporting Hamas, al-Qaeda, ISIS, and other violent jihadist elements around the world.

But as the Brotherhood's mouthpiece to the non-Muslim world, Syeed sounds almost like a Gandhi-type peacenik. Listen to his words as presented to the gullible Catholics gathered in San Diego:

> This is the shape of a new millennium of alliance-building for common values of mutual respect and recognition.
>
> All faiths are striving to promote those divine values enshrined in our sacred texts and scriptures, so that those who exploit them for reinforcing hate, extremism, violence and instability are identified as the enemies of all faiths.[3]

This is one of the leading voices of an extremist organization lecturing the world, Americans in particular, about the evils of extremism. It truly would be hard to make this stuff up.

And you have a prominent Catholic bishop, who not coincidentally is a member of the U.S. Conference of Catholic Bishops, which, as we have already discussed, is one of nine primary federal contractors who make millions of dollars every year off of the resettlement of Muslim refugees into American cities and towns, agreeing with the Islamist that it's "bigotry" to give honest criticism of Islam (remember our discussion of voluntary dhimmitude in earlier chapters?).

But it gets worse. Not only should we Christians not criticize Islam, but the good bishop says we should spread the lie that Islam is a religion of peace.

Bishop McElroy said U.S. Catholics should be repulsed by the "repeated falsehoods" that Islam is inherently violent, that many Muslims seek to supplant the U.S. Constitution with sharia law, and that Muslim immigration threatens "the cultural identity of the American people," reported the Catholic News Service.[4]

Now, I do not believe that every Muslim is "inherently violent." There are millions of peaceful Muslims throughout the world, but they are not typically the ones adhering to the tenets of sharia and following the violent instructions of their prophet, Muhammad, as laid out in the Quran and hadiths. Islam itself, as created by its Quranic texts, is most assuredly fraught with violent instructions, but that doesn't mean every Muslim will follow those instructions. In fact, when a nation becomes fully Islamized, those Muslims who refuse to comply with the sharia courts are persecuted just the same as non-Muslims.

But such claims, according to Bishop McElroy, smack of the anti-Catholic bigotry that was once prevalent in the United States.

The bishop's denunciation of bigotry "should not be seen as a denial of the reality of Islamic terrorism," according to the Catholic News Service.

"I want to underscore that it is not bigotry to fear or to combat the violence and terror which some Muslims in the world have unleashed in the name of faith," he explained, but then quickly added that some Christians are equally guilty of the same propensity toward violence.[5]

I don't know about the bishop, but I don't see daily attacks being carried out in the name of Jesus during the Easter or Christmas season the way we see jihadist attacks carried out during the Muslim holy month of Ramadan and throughout the year. Each year the death toll during Ramadan reaches into the hundreds even though the Western media publicize only the attacks that occur on Western soil. The attacks on hapless Christians and Jews in Israel, the Arab Middle East, Africa, Pakistan, the Philippines, Indonesia, and throughout Asia go largely unreported.

Even though you would have to go back a thousand years to the time of the Crusades to find an even close parallel of Christian violence, the

Left loves to draw moral equivalency between Islam and Christianity. But it doesn't hold up to historical scrutiny. Even though a case can be made that the Crusades started out as a legitimate defensive action against an aggressive Muslim enemy that had been mercilessly launching attacks on Eastern Christians for five hundred years, let's concede that these Western invasions were not the wisest response and that they ended up killing many innocents along with the Muslim aggressors. The obvious fact remains that violence in the name of Jesus Christ is completely outside the boundaries of Christ's teachings in the New Testament.

Generations of Christian leaders over the decades have apologized ad nauseam for the Crusades and continue to do so today. We see no similar mea culpa from Islamic leaders regarding the hundreds of jihads launched against non-Muslims throughout history. They make no apologies, and why should they? These jihads are fully in accordance with the teachings and the example of Muhammad. There is not a single act of jihad throughout history—whether carried out by the Ottoman Turks during the early twentieth century against Armenian Christians or by ISIS in the twenty-first century against Syrian Christians—that would not make Muhammad proud.

So Christians today should reject out of hand any comparison of their faith with that of Islam in terms of it being prone to violence.

Robert Spencer, an activist, researcher, and author of the blog *Jihad Watch*, responded to Bishop McElroy's comments about Islam:

> So apparently if you think that Islam is inherently violent, you're not only wrong, but you're a bigot. To avoid bigotry, you have to ignore or deny the readily demonstrable fact that the Quran exhorts believers to violence, and that all mainstream Islamic sects and schools of Islamic jurisprudence teach that the Muslim community has a responsibility to wage war against and subjugate unbelievers.
>
> You're also a bigot, in McElroy's view, of you believe that "Muslims seek to supplant the U.S. Constitution with sharia law." If you believe only some Muslims seek to do that, are you only a partial bigot? McElroy didn't say.[6]

As pointed out earlier, the Muslim Brotherhood is committed, according to its own internal documents, to "a kind of grand Jihad in eliminating and destroying the Western civilization from within and 'sabotaging' its miserable house by their hands and the hands of the believers so that it is eliminated and God's religion is made victorious over all other religions."[7]

So while decrying as bigotry the idea that Muslims are seeking to supplant the Constitution with sharia, Spencer noted that McElroy was "speaking alongside a representative of an organization linked to efforts to do exactly that."[8]

Ah, the wonderful ironies of "interfaith dialogue."

Bishop McElroy also said you're a bigot if you believe unfettered Muslim immigration threatens "the cultural identity of the American people." "He did not explain how the introduction into the country of massive numbers of people with no cultural or theological traditions of freedom of speech, freedom of conscience, and equality of rights for women could not end up threatening the cultural identity of the American people," Spencer responded. "He didn't have to explain: as far as he is concerned, these propositions are dogmas to be taken on faith, not assertions to be evaluated on the basis of evidence."[9]

Of course, McElroy is not out on a limb in speaking this way about Islam. His boss, the Holy Father himself, Pope Francis, has made unprecedented theological concessions to Islam since his ascension to the papacy. Francis in November 2014 said it was wrong for Christians to equate Islam with violence and called for an end to "Islamophobia," Reuters reported. He did call on Muslim leaders to "condemn terrorism" to help dispel the "stereotype," revealing a deep-seated ignorance about Islam's core teaching.

"You just can't say that [all Muslims are terrorists], just as you can't say that all Christians are fundamentalists. We have our share of them (fundamentalists). All religions have these little groups," he said.[10]

The pope, unfortunately, relies on the same false narrative pushed by the hard-core Left, a narrative that simply doesn't stand up to the facts.

The most "radical" fundamentalist Christians in America today might be those affiliated with the Westboro Baptist Church, which protests at the funerals of U.S. servicemen, holding signs with vile accusations about America and its tolerance of homosexuals. Yet, even this activity could be categorized at most as distasteful speech that even leftist courts have ruled falls well within the bounds of protected speech under the First Amendment. The Westboro goons, as unlikable and judgmental as they are, still don't go around killing unbelievers, as radical Islamists have done for centuries and continue to do today.

The pope went on to say that the Islamic State was committing a "profoundly grave sin against God" and called for interreligious dialogue and action against poverty to help end the conflicts in the region.[11] This meme of "poverty" being the root cause of Islamic violence is another proven falsehood and reminds us of the Obama State Department spokeswoman Marie Harf's comment in 2015 that the brutal jihadist violence being wrought on the Middle East by ISIS was nothing a good jobs program couldn't solve.[12]

Of course, this could not explain why almost all of the recent Islamic terror attacks have been carried out against the West by jihadists with at least some college education. Syed Farook, the San Bernardino killer, had a degree in environmental engineering; Muhammad Youssef Abdulazeez, the Chattanooga jihadist, had a degree in electrical engineering; and Jihadi John, the British Muslim who beheaded James Foley and other Westerners, also had an engineering degree.

Is the pope truly ignorant, unaware that the root of Islamic violence lies not in poverty or lack of job opportunities but in the Islamic texts, or is he being deceitful? I'll leave that up to you, but any honest reading of the Quran will make it clear that sharia-compliant Muslims do not see their own violence against the infidel as "terrorism." It is seen as a just act of war as laid out for them by the founder of their religion. Muhammad personally killed hundreds of men and boys in battle and took captured women as booty. How does this compare with the life of Jesus? I ask the pope.

Jesus always taught nonviolence, and when His disciples took any sort of action in a violent direction, He promptly corrected them and told them to put down their swords. "Those who live by the sword, die by the sword," he said in Matthew 26:52 (paraphrased).

On another occasion the pope said the Quran is a book of peace and Islam is a peaceful religion.[13] Perhaps he believes that if he just says it often enough and wishes hard enough, he can wish Islam's fanatical followers into a state of peace.

But Catholics are not the only ones who seem eager to compromise their faith in order to appease Islam. As you may recall from chapter 5, Anglican archbishop Justin Welby insists that Christians should "not [speak] about faith unless you are asked about faith."[14]

Really? Is that what Jesus taught? We'll attempt to answer that question in our closing comments, but for now we have more to report on the sincere yet misguided Christian apologists who water down the message of Christ in their efforts to convince Muslims that they are their friends.

I reported in the spring of 2016 that the Council on American-Islamic Relations, another Muslim Brotherhood front group, was making a major push to stamp out "Islamophobia" in America. In that article I quoted former Muslim imam and son of a Muslim Brotherhood operative Dr. Mark Christian.[15]

According to Christian, the term "Islamophobia" was an invention of the Brotherhood. The label is a way of creating fear among non-Muslims, essentially banning all speech criticizing Islam, which is one of the main tenets of sharia. Neither Muslims nor non-Muslims are allowed free speech under sharia when it comes to criticizing "the prophet" Muhammad or Islam in general.

Dr. Christian, who lives under a fatwa after leaving Islam in his native Egypt, said Christians should be taking the exact opposite approach to Islam. They should speak out about the Quran's encouragement of violence and its requirement that women be subjugated. And they should never, ever, hesitate to share the gospel with any Muslim.

As a young man in his twenties, Dr. Christian said he had already decided that he wanted to become a Christian but he could not find a Christian in Egypt who would give him a Bible and teach him about the sayings of Jesus. He even visited a Coptic monastery and asked for a Bible, begging to learn about Jesus, but the priests there told him to leave Egypt if he was sincerely seeking to learn about Christ. Why did they do that? Because under Islamic law they were operating as Christian leaders under dhimmitude, which, as shown in chapter 5, allows non-Muslims to practice their faith in a Muslim society as a protected class, but in return for this protection they must follow a strict set of rules. The most important rule is that a Christian "dhimmi" living under Islamic subjugation is not allowed to share his faith with any Muslim. To do so even in a moderate Muslim state like Egypt will bring severe punishment up to and including death.

The Coptic priest also warned Dr. Christian not to go to England, where many Christian leaders, like Archbishop Justin Welby, subscribe to a form of voluntary dhimmitude, reluctant to share the pure gospel with Muslims. They will not tell the truth about Islam and its propensity, grounded in Islamic texts, to subjugate non-Muslims whenever and wherever the opportunity exists.

One of the ways that Islamists begin to do this in a non-Muslim society is, as mentioned earlier, through nonviolent, civilization jihad. They accuse anyone who criticizes Islam in reaction to violent acts of jihad of being "Islamophobic."

The word *Islamophobia* itself is a reflection of a deep-seated Islamic intolerance and an absolute rejection of freedom of speech, Christian explained. Do we see Christian leaders scouring the United States, looking to shame and make examples of those who criticize their faith, labeling them "Christophobes"? No, we just accept that there are some who will never embrace our faith, and while we are uncomfortable with some of the harshest critics, the only time we see inflamed outrage is when the critics are funded by our own tax dollars! An example of this was the *Piss Christ* work of "art" that was funded in 1986 by the National Endowment for the Arts, which gave $15,000 to Andres Serrano for his photograph of a crucifix submerged in a glass filled with his own urine.[16]

Art galleries that presented *Piss Christ* received death threats,[17] but no actual killing or attempted killing ever took place. Supporters argued that the controversy over the photograph was an issue of artistic freedom and freedom of speech.

Contrast that with the reaction to Muhammad cartoon contests that have been held in Denmark and in the United States. The Muslims not only threaten to kill the cartoonists and their sponsors but have actually carried out attempts, some successful, on those they see as blaspheming the name of Islam's prophet. And keep in mind that these cartoon contests received no public funding. They were totally private endeavors. So who exactly are the intolerant bigots?

Omar Ahmad, one of the cofounders of CAIR, stated in 1998 that Islam's ultimate goal was to become the dominant religion in America, not to be one faith among many "equals." Ahmad tried to deny he ever made those comments, but the California newspaper that quoted him has stood by its story.[18]

Unless the Brotherhood's goal of banning speech deemed "anti-Islamic" or "Islamophobic" is reversed, America will end up in the same place as many European nations. They will be in a place of voluntary dhimmitude.

In Britain, for example, anti-sharia activists, such as Robert Spencer and Pamela Geller, are banned from entering the country. A petition to ban Donald Trump has gained more than half a million signatures in Britain.[19] Yet, Islamic preachers of jihad, such as Anjem Choudary, introduced in chapter 2, have been allowed for years to openly spread their message of hate across the UK. At the same time, Christian preachers who speak critically of Islam can be arrested and charged with hate crimes.

That's exactly what happened to Michael Overd, a Christian street preacher from Creech St. Michael, when he "made remarks over loudspeakers in Taunton, Somerset" that were labeled a "homophobic sermon," reported Robert Spencer on *Jihad Watch*.

"He was cleared of a second similar charge and another of causing 'racially-aggravated' harassment aimed at Muslims."

"What race is Islam again?" asks Spencer. "I keep forgetting."

According to the BBC article quoted by Spencer, Overd, fifty, "was fined £200 and ordered to pay compensation and costs totalling £1,200 at Bristol Crown Court." Sentencing judge Shamim Qureshi told Overd he "knew full well the power of words to hurt."

Overd initially refused to pay a court-mandated £250 to his victim, but he was threatened with a forty-five-day prison sentence if he did not. Similar cases are piling up across Europe.[20]

A Scottish man was arrested for a Facebook post disparaging Muslim refugees in Scotland.[21]

"A Dutch man was arrested for wearing a pig hat because it was deemed by police as being potentially insulting to Muslims (who were nowhere around)."[22]

In Germany the federal police conducted a pre-morning raid on sixty homes in July 2016, rounding up at least forty people and arresting them for posting anti-Islam comments on a private Facebook group. They were turned over to the police by Facebook.[23]

Even in America we are now seeing incidents of public shaming of those who speak out with truth about the differences between Christianity and Islam. We've covered cases of an Oregon pastor, a Washington state businessman, and a Minnesota billboard owner who were pressured in this way. It seems as though the harder Christians work to build bridges of "understanding" with their Muslim counterparts, the less tolerant the Muslims become, at least those Muslims affiliated with the Brotherhood.

HOW THEN SHOULD WE RESPOND?

So if interfaith dialogue is not the answer, what is?

We have covered a lot of ground to this point, explaining how the refugee resettlement program works, how it is profit-motivated while presenting itself as part of a false humanitarianism. We have shown how it leads to an inevitable decline in the national culture and national identity, and turns people in a community against each other in an ugly divisiveness that previously did not exist in these communities.

I urge patriotic Americans to become activists in their communities, to resist the secret planting of refugees that are hostile to America and are impossible to fully vet. Ask questions and seek information on how many are coming, from where, and what the costs will be. Use this information to hold your local leaders accountable at the state and local levels.

At the federal level, ask your U.S. senators and congressmen to support the Muslim Brotherhood Terrorist Designation Act. The Brotherhood is an extreme Islamist organization whose overarching goal is to create a global caliphate governed by sharia. It has chapters in eighty countries and has been banned by Russia, the United Arab Emirates, Saudi Arabia, and Egypt, where it was founded in 1928.[24] Israel and Jordan are also starting to crack down on this insidious organization. But in the United States it is not only tolerated but is embraced by scores of politicians in both major political parties. The bill to declare the Brotherhood a terrorist organization has so far been squelched by globalist Speaker of the House Paul Ryan and globalist House majority leader Mitch McConnell. This issue must be fought not only on the political level but also spiritually.

But what is the proper Christian response to Muslim migration into our communities? I've seen three different types of Christian responses, but only one of them is the correct and biblical response in my opinion.

From a public policy standpoint, I have stated my case for why our immigration system needs to be reined in and tightened up. Fewer people should be allowed in, and those who are welcomed to our country ought to be able to guarantee they will love this country, reject sharia, and assimilate into our communities. They should not be allowed to sponge off of the public dole. That means they should each have a private sponsor who is able to support them financially until they are able to support themselves.

American citizens who value freedom of speech, freedom of religion, and all of the other freedoms that make America great should also become activists at the local and state levels to fight back against the federal refugee program, which seeks to change our communities by secretly planting sharia-adherent Third Worlders who hate the very values of freedom we cherish, hate Israel, and see women as little more than chattel property. The globalists' plan, as we have explored earlier, is to change America by changing its people, making it less distinct and more like every other nation. And it's working. America, according to Pew Research Center's extensive demographic polling, is becoming more ethnically diverse and less Christian with a smaller middle class.[25]

Americans must understand that the best way to attack the refugee resettlement program is through its funding. While the program is administered by the president, Congress controls the purse strings. Don't let your member of Congress off the hook on this issue. Ask him or her to cut all funding for the resettlements until this program can undergo a complete audit. It's not only the refugees who need to be better vetted but the program itself, which to date has been carried out with little to no oversight by Congress.

Secondly, we must work at the local level to demand greater transparency from our city, state, and county officials. Ask them to provide the annual "abstract" which must be filed by the resettlement contractor for every resettlement community, detailing how many refugees will be coming to your town and from which countries, along with the services being provided to them. Once this information is obtained, the next step is to get it out to the public. Since we cannot count on our local newspapers and TV stations to publicize the information, we must do that through our own efforts, using social media, letters to the editor, speaking engagements and personal one-on-one sharing with our friends and family. When Americans of all political stripes are informed about the details of this program they almost universally will condemn it as misplaced charity.

Shouldn't this tax-funded aid be going to needy Americans?

But that still leaves a gap in our American response. How should we respond, not from a public-policy standpoint of seeking to protect our communities, but from a human and Christian point of view?

We have many options. We can join the "interfaith" movement where we attempt to "build bridges" of commonality between Christianity and Islam, where we don't share the gospel or try to evangelize our Muslim neighbors but we offer them food, clothing, and shelter while trying to "dialogue" with them in ways that won't "offend" their consciences.

Another option is to put up our guard and put down our collective foot in anger. We can show hatred toward the Muslim community, speak vile condemnations upon them, and try to scare them out of our communities, treating them as the "other" and hoping they will get a clue that they are not welcome in our midst.

I believe, however, that as we work as activists to reform and tighten up our immigration system, we also need to reach out in love to those Muslims who are already here. To confront them with hate only plays into the hands of the globalists who seek to destroy our national sovereignty through a divide-and-conquer strategy. Their goals are often to create divisions and foment violence, for it is out of chaos that they seek to create a new utopian order.

So I recommend a third route. Show them love, offering to feed, clothe, and shelter them where needed, but also not compromising our own Christian faith. We must boldly share with every Muslim the true, unadulterated gospel of Jesus Christ. We are like little John the Baptists. We give of ourselves selflessly, providing for material needs, but holding nothing back spiritually. We wear the cross of Jesus proudly; we quote the words of Jesus profusely, that He is the one and only Son of God, who died on a cross and rose from the dead and who alone holds the power of granting eternal life to us, to our Muslim friends, and to those of all backgrounds and nationalities.

In Matthew 28:18–20 we read, "Then Jesus . . . said, "All authority in heaven and on earth has been given to me. Therefore go and make disciples of all nations, baptizing them in the name of the Father and of the Son and of the Holy Spirit, and teaching them to obey everything I have commanded you. And surely I am with you always, to the very end of the age" (NIV). Notice He said to "go," which implies going out, often into difficult and dangerous places, to preach the gospel. He did not say to stay put and bring the world's lost and broken into your own nation.

While many of us may be locked into circumstances that make it difficult to "go" into these dark corners of the earth that have not heard the words of Jesus, our government, whether wisely or unwisely, seems intent on bringing the world to us. We can sit back and let Muslims' ways, their culture, and their religious practices transform our communities and perhaps even engulf our children or grandchildren into Islam. Or, we can take advantage of this historic opportunity as Christians to reach out with the gospel to those of not just Islamic backgrounds but also Hindus, Buddhists, Baha'i, and even pagan backgrounds.

Jesus also told His followers to expect persecution and to expect the Word of God to divide like a two-edged sword, to the point of dividing father against son and mother against daughter (see Hebrews 4:12; Matthew 10:35). Some will believe; others won't. If we share a gospel that is afraid to offend anyone, then we can be assured that this is not the true gospel of Jesus Christ. It is some other, watered-down, lukewarm version of Christianity, the likes of which Jesus said in Revelation that He would spit out of His mouth (see Revelation 3:16).

Many preachers teach that Jesus came to unite the world under a banner of peace. While that will happen one day, when He returns to rule and reign, we should not expect anything but division in the last days before He returns.

The globalist elites at the United Nations do have a plan for a counterfeit unity and a false peace, however, which attempts to deceive the world into thinking it is the true, lasting peace and unity promised by Jesus and other religious leaders down through the ages. Jesus warned us not to be deceived by these false teachers and false prophets who would seek to offer this false world unity and peace.

"Do you suppose that I came to grant peace on earth?" Jesus asked, then answered, "I tell you, no, but rather division; for from now on five members in one household will be divided, three against two and two against three. "They will be divided, father against son and son against father, mother against daughter and daughter against mother, mother-in-law against daughter-in-law and daughter-in-law against mother-in-law" (Luke 12:51–53 NASB).

What does this mean?

I believe Ann Naffziger, a Scripture instructor and spiritual director in the San Francisco Bay area, provides valuable insight on this passage:

> Upon first reading, Jesus' statement here does seem shocking, as does the prediction by the aged Simeon when Jesus was an infant that Jesus was "destined for the falling and the rising of many in Israel, and to be a sign that will be opposed . . ." (Luke 2:34). It appears in stark contrast to other promises that the Savior would bring peace. However, if we read this passage in the context of the prophetic tradition—which Luke draws on throughout his gospel—we realize that Jesus is challenging his listeners just like the prophets of old did before him. He denounces all manner of injustice and wrongdoing, calling for repentance and conversion. By calling his listeners to consciously and explicitly choose to walk in God's ways and turn from injustice, he points out the human reality that the peace will be disturbed because there are others who will not repent of their evil doings. When prophets issue challenges, they always disturb the peace. The division is not created by the prophets or by Jesus, it is a natural outcome of listeners making different decisions about whether to follow Jesus or not. Just so, Jesus declared 'Whoever is not with me is against me' (Luke 11:23).[26]

THE PRICE OF LUKEWARM CHRISTIANITY

If we don't do what Jesus said and preach the true gospel that causes some to push back in sometimes violent and divisive ways, there will be a terrible price to pay in terms of national judgment that is coming on our land. If we don't share the pure, authentic, unchanging gospel of Jesus Christ with those of other faiths, I believe God will use the Muslim migrants infused by our government into our communities to persecute and subjugate us. We may not feel it immediately or existentially, but we will be sentencing our children and grandchildren to an ominous future here in the "land of the free." They will increasingly find themselves living in a post-Christian society under principles of sharia, where freedom of speech, freedom of religious practice, and other bedrock American values are erased from their communities. Women will increasingly be treated like property, Christians and Jews will be persecuted, gun ownership will be forbidden, criticism of Islam will be met with death or imprisonment, and sharing one's Christian faith outside the four walls of a church will be strictly forbidden. This, my friends, is dhimmitude.

Whether voluntarily or whether by governmental edict, we are not to live like dhimmis, hiding our Christian light, our precious gospel message of freedom and liberty in Christ. We are never to hide this precious gift under any rock of darkness, whether that rock is placed upon us by Islam, by the radical left-wing secularists, or by any other anti-Christ power.

To save our children and grandchildren from this fate, we must first wake up to what is happening in our country and who is leading us to our own destruction. We can blame the Far Left and the Islamists, who have indeed made an unholy alliance against Christianity. But we also must look in the mirror and ask ourselves if we, individually and nationally, are truly living a God-ordained Christian life.

To make our testimony real, we must get our own spiritual houses in order. This is always the hardest part for any Christian, but it's what makes our sharing of the gospel authentic and believable to those standing outside of Christianity, waiting to get in. They are waiting for some Christian—you, perhaps—to share with them the truth of God. But they want to hear it from a credible source, a genuine Christian, not a fake or a showbiz Christian.

We are all imperfect vessels, to be sure, so we cannot expect any Christian to be fully Christlike, but we can expect that the more Christlike a person becomes, the more effective he or she can be as a witness for Christ. A person like this is infectious and inexorably successful at winning souls, whether they be Muslim or atheist, to the Savior.

One credible example of such a person, whom I will turn to for words of wisdom, is another former Muslim, a woman this time. Her name is Işik Abla.

Abla fled an abusive father in Turkey and an even more abusive husband while living in Europe, coming to America in 1996. In a message posted on YouTube in June 2016, she gives a dire warning to Americans. Radical Islam is invading the United States like a termite, Abla says.[27]

A termite's damage is not easily spotted in the early phases, but before long it will devastate any wooden structure.

The United States is not only in an undeclared war against Islamic terrorism; it is above all in a spiritual war with a demonic force. There is only one way to win such a war. "This is the time for everyone to wake up, stand up, and speak up," Abla says, while we still have the freedom to do so.

"People want to know the truth in America now. They have been fed lies for so long now. It is so wrong. And every American needs to know what kind of danger they are facing. And if you don't stand up, you are going to lose your children, and your grandchildren. . . . This is about your life; this is about your children's life. America is in danger because of radical Islam."

In the video, she talks about political jihad, educational jihad, and other types of nonviolent jihad that precede the full onslaught of violent jihad.

Abla says, rightly so, that there are ISIS sympathizers in every state, a claim that is backed up by FBI director James Comey, who testified before Congress in late 2015 saying his agency has more than nine hundred open ISIS investigations in all fifty states.[28]

"America, every state is a terrorist breeding ground right now. They are in your backyards; they are in your schools; they are in your communities," Abla said.

As for refugees, she also had a hard message of truth regarding them.

I went to refugee camps in the Middle East. I have so much heart for refugees. I sit down; I cried with refugees, but you know what? But it is not the best solution to bring Muslim refugees to the United States. . . .I know what I am talking about. I know Quran, and what Quran says about infidels. And when I say infidels, this is not only a threat to Christians. Every non-Muslim is under this threat. And I am warning you, please, please, give an ear. And start waking up, standing up, speaking up. Go on your knees and start fasting together. Start putting together prayer groups. America, this is a serious battle. America is at war, and America doesn't know that it is at war. Can you believe how stupid this is? How foolish this is. They are invading America like a termite in a building. They are invading your country, your land, like a termite. ISIS is persecuting all these people, trying to push them to the Western world, and not only America. England, Australia, Sweden, Denmark, France. All these countries are under distress. I am begging you, start changing your lifestyle. Start giving God more time in prayer. People are asking me, "What should we do?" I answer you back, "Why prayer sound so unattractive to you?" It's such a great tool, and you know what? There are times coming in America when every ground will be shaken. If you don't stand up for your country, if you don't start praying more and seeking God more, America will be shaken; the church will be shaken. Elijah times are coming: fire will come from heaven and consume you.

Abla said she found freedom in America and has great respect for military veterans who are fighting for our freedom, but America made a great mistake by bringing them back from Iraq, and the military alone cannot protect America. We need God.

She urges the church to repent and turn back to the roots of their faith.

Peaceful Muslims are also under threat of death, she said, because the Western world calls them "good Muslims," such as her own mother, who don't believe in radical Islam.

> You guys call them good Muslims, but they are hypocrites according to Quran, because Quran tells them, true Muslims to go, kill, and die, in jihad. Kill the infidel. And all this time, "Islam is a peaceful religion." What a big lie. If Islam is a religion of peace, do you see anywhere in the world a peaceful Islamic country, anywhere? I don't know. I am coming from a Muslim background and I don't know. I don't know a single Muslim who has a true peace of God in their lives. I grew up in a Muslim home. My mom still prays five times a day, during the month of Ramadan she's fasting every day. We Christians we don't fast. . . . They fast thirty days during the month of Ramadan. People [in America] don't even pray five minutes. And they pray five times a day. They have zeal for their God. And I am calling you today, if you don't have zeal, start praying. Say, "God, I need zeal." I am praying for you, America, "Please, God, give them zeal."

CONCLUSION

We can safely say that after years of assaults by secular humanists in and outside of government and a lack of vigilance on the part of Christians themselves in support of traditional biblical Christianity, the state of the American church is abysmal. It rests now, deep in a slumber, kept alive on life support. If things don't change, time is not on our side. The deep spiritual vacuum left by lukewarm apostate Christianity and advancing secularism is being filled by Islam, both religious Islam and political Islam. The far more awake and aggressive Muslims are filling this vacuum with the help of the Far Left, which control the media, the educational system, and most of the mainline institutional church. But these institutions are not the real church. That crown belongs to the remnant of Jesus-followers who still hold fast to the unchanging gospel "once delivered unto the saints," as it is described in the New Testament epistle of Jude (v. 3).

While political activism is necessary and encouraged as a form of resistance, the day may come when this form of pushback is no longer allowed. Let's be honest: even our greatest victories on the political level have only the effect of delaying the inevitable. The Bible clearly speaks of a time when the true followers of Christ will be mercilessly persecuted, and this is already happening in many countries throughout the world, with Islamic radicals the most frequent angels of death, all too eager to behead, burn, crucify, bomb, and shoot the Lord's people.

Once these Islamists gain control of a country, with the help of their leftist allies, the political game is over. It's too late at that point to push back with political activism, freedom of information requests, political campaigns, billboards, and letters to the editor. If we fight only on this level, it leaves us naked before God when those worldly options are taken away. We are left with a shallow, hollowed-out church lacking the Spirit of God, a shell of its former self, with houses of worship that look and sound more like mausoleums. Where prayer warriors and bold preachers once came to worship, we increasingly see prayerless purveyors of a milquetoast social gospel. Their messages may sound politically correct, but they lack the power to change lives.

So in the end the only real and lasting weapon, as Abla and others have stated, is to close the spiritual vacuum that the soldiers of Islam are rushing to fill. Beat them at their own game. Spend time reading the Bible, and learn what is in the Quran. Share your faith boldly with all who will listen. Display the cross and other Christian symbols at every opportunity. Muslims recognize the power of symbols, and we must also.

And last but not least, spend time on your knees, praying for America.

NOTES

PREFACE

1. http://www.wnd.com/2016/03/fbi-counter-terror-expert-sees-historic-islam-pivot/.
2. Jose Pagliery, "Sniper attack on California power grid may have been 'an insider,' DHS says," CNN Money, October 17, 2015, http://money.cnn.com/2015/10/16/technology/sniper-power-grid/.
3. Steve Visser, "Death Toll Rises to 85 in Bastille Day Attack in Nice," CNN, August 5, 2016, http://www.cnn.com/2016/08/05/europe/nice-france-attack-victim/index.html.
4. Melissa Eddy, "Afghan Teenager Spoke of Friend's Death Before Ax Attack in Germany," *New York Times*, July 19, 2016, http://www.nytimes.com/2016/07/20/world/europe/germany-train-ax-attack.html?_r=0.
5. John Hayward, "Hillary Clinton: Muslims Are 'Peaceful and Tolerant,' Have 'Nothing Whatsoever to Do with Terrorism,'" Breitbart, November 19, 2015, http://www.breitbart.com/big-government/2015/11/19/hillary-clinton-muslims-peaceful-tolerant-nothing-whatsoever-terrorism/.
6. See for example Ian Schwartz, "Obama: 'Islam Is A Religion That Preaches Peace'," RealClear Politics, September 28, 2014, http://www.realclearpolitics.com/video/2014/09/28/obama_islam_is_a_religion_that_preaches_peace.html and Obama address to the nation reported by CNN and posted to YouTube on September 10, 2014, https://www.youtube.com/watch?v=pwp8qKvE-0g.
7. Nicholas Kristof , "Obama: Man of the World," *New York Times*, March 6, 2007, http://www.nytimes.com/2007/03/06/opinion/06kristof.html?_r=0.
8. http://www.breitbart.com/big-government/2015/12/16/paul-ryan-betrays-america-1-1-trillion-2000-plus-page-omnibus-bill-funds-fundamental-transformation-america/.

CHAPTER 1: A TROJAN HORSE IN THE MAKING

1. Leo Hohmann, "DHS Caught Busing in Illegal Somalis from Mexican Border," WND, May 13, 2015, http://www.wnd.com/2015/05/dhs-caught-busing-in-illegal-somalis-from-mexican-border/.
2. Judicial Watch, "ISIS Camp a Few Miles from Texas, Mexican Authorities Confirm," *Corruption Chronicles* (blog), April 14, 2015, www.judicialwatch.org/blog/2015/04/isis-camp-a-few-miles-from-texas-mexican-authorities-confirm/.
3. "What A Downed Black Hawk In Somalia Taught America," NPR, October 5, 2013, http://www.npr.org/2013/10/05/229561805/what-a-downed-black-hawk-in-somalia-taught-america.
4. Caroline May, "Border Patrol Agent: 80 Percent of Illegals the Agency Apprehends Are Released into U.S.," Breitbart, May, 19 2016, http://www.breitbart.com/big-government/2016/05/19/border-patrol-agent-80-percent-illegals-agency-apprehends-released-u-s/.

5. See Yearbook of Immigration Statistics: 2013 Refugees and Asylees, Table 17, Department of Homeland Security website, https://www.dhs.gov/publication/yearbook-immigration-statistics-2013-refugees-and-asylees.

6. See Pew Research Center, "More Non-Mexicans than Mexicans Apprehended in 2014" (line graph) at http://www.wnd.com/files/2015/05/graphic-on-border-crossings.jpg.

7. Table 17, Individuals Granted Asylum Affirmatively by Region and Country of Nationality: Fiscal Years 2004 to 2013, *Yearbook of Immigration Statistics: 2013 Refugees and Asylees*, Department of Homeland Security, https://www.dhs.gov/publication/yearbook-immigration-statistics-2013-refugees-and-asylees.

8. Hollie McKay, "Iraqi Christians denied asylum in US, facing looming expulsion," Fox News, September 30, 2015, http://www.foxnews.com/us/2015/09/30/iraqi-christians-denied-asylum-in-us-facing-looming-expulsion.html.

9. Jeff Sessions, "SUBCOMMITTEE CHART: Obama Administration On Track To Issue Over 1 Million Green Cards To Migrants From Muslim-Majority Countries," News Release, June 17, 2016, http://www.sessions.senate.gov/public/index.cfm/2016/6/subcommittee-chart-chart-obama-administration-on-track-to-issue-over-1-million-green-cards-to-migrant-from-muslim-majority-countries.

10. Jeff Sessions, "SUBCOMMITTEE CHART: U.S. Issued 680,000 Green Cards To Migrants From Muslim Nations Over The Last Five Years," News Release, November, 25 2015, http://www.sessions.senate.gov/public/index.cfm/2015/11/subcommittee-chart-u-s-issued-680-000-green-cards-to-migrants-from-muslim-nations-over-the-last-five-years.

11. Karen Zeigler and Steven A. Camarota, "U.S. Immigrant Population Record 41.3 Million in 2013," Table 1, Center for Immigration Studies, September 2014, http://cis.org/immigrant-population-record-2013.

12. Ruth Igielnik, "Where refugees to the U.S. come from," Pew Research Center, June 17, 2016, http://www.pewresearch.org/fact-tank/2016/06/17/where-refugees-to-the-u-s-come-from/.

13. Phillip Connor, "Nearly half of refugees entering the U.S. this year are Muslim," Pew Research Center, August 16, 2016, http://www.pewresearch.org/fact-tank/2016/08/16/nearly-half-of-refugees-entering-the-u-s-this-year-are-muslim/.

14. *The Refugee Convention, 1951: The Travaux Preparatoires Analysed with a Commentary by Dr Paul Weis*, introduction, A(2), F., http://www.unhcr.org/4ca34be29.pdf.

15. Ibid.

16. Niraj Warikoo, "Muslims sue Sterling Heights after city rejected mosque," *Detroit Free Press*, August 11, 2016, http://www.freep.com/story/news/local/michigan/macomb/2016/08/10/muslims-sue-sterling-heights-mosque/88526616/.

17. U.S. Senate, Subcommittee on Immigration and Naturalization of the Committee on the Judiciary, Washington, D.C., February 10, 1965, pp. 1–3.

18. Ibid.

19. Ibid., 8.

20. FY 2017 Notice of Funding Opportunity for Reception and Placement Program, U.S. Department of State, March 21, 2016, http://www.state.gov/j/prm/funding/fy2017/254909.htm.

21. "Testimony to US State Department from author, activist James Simpson," Refugee Resettlement Watch, posted by Ann Corcoran May 19, 2016, https://refugeeresettlementwatch.wordpress.com/2016/05/19/testimony-to-us-state-department-from-author-activist-james-simpson/.

22. Ibid.

23. Julia Hahn, "Report: Obama's Plan to Import 10,000 Refugees Would Cost Taxpayers $6.5 Billion," Breitbart, September 11, 2015, http://www.breitbart.com/big-government/2015/09/11/report-obamas-plan-to-import-10000-refugees-would-cost-taxpayers-6-5-billion/.

24. Paul Bedard, "Sessions: Obama's Syrian refugee plan to cost $55 billion, demands it be killed," *Washington Examiner*, November 16, 2015, http://www.washingtonexaminer.com/sessions-obamas-syrian-refugee-plan-to-cost-55-billion-demands-it-be-killed/article/2576450.

25. Refugee Processing Center, Interactive Reporting, Admissions and Arrivals, http://www.wrapsnet.org/Reports/InteractiveReporting/tabid/393/EnumType/Report/Default.aspx?ItemPath=/rpt_WebArrivalsReports/MX%20-%20Arrivals%20by%20Destination%20and%20Nationality.

26. "President Ronald Reagan meets his Taliban friends in the White House," LiveLeak, posted by GUANTANAMOLANDOFREEDOM, July 18, 2003, http://www.liveleak.com/view?i=3d1_1374168674.

27. The conversation that follows is from a personal interview with Sister Hatune Dogan in Atlanta, Georgia, in December 2014.

28. Nick Gutteridge, "ISIS barbarity: How 100,000 Christians fled Mosul in ONE NIGHT," *Express*, October 20, 2015, http://www.express.co.uk/news/world/613149/ISIS-barbarity-100000-Christians-fled-Mosul-one-night.

29. Then shall the King say unto them on his right hand, Come, ye blessed of my Father, inherit the kingdom prepared for you from the foundation of the world: For I was an hungred, and ye gave me meat: I was thirsty, and ye gave me drink: I was a stranger, and ye took me in: naked, and ye clothed me: I was sick, and ye visited me: I was in prison, and ye came unto me. Then shall the righteous answer him, saying, Lord, when saw we thee an hungred, and fed thee? or thirsty, and gave thee drink? When saw we thee a stranger, and took thee in? or naked, and clothed thee? Or when saw we thee sick, or in prison, and came unto thee? And the King shall answer and say unto them, Verily I say unto you, Inasmuch as ye have done it unto one of the least of these my brethren, ye have done it unto me.

30. Leo Hohmann, "Nun pleads for Christians raped, sold, killed by ISIS," WND.com, December 23, 2014, http://www.wnd.com/2014/12/nun-pleads-for-christians-raped-sold-killed-by-isis/.

31. *Office of Refugee Resettlement Annual Report to Congress, FY 2014* (U.S. Department of Health and Human Services Administration for Children and Families Office of Refugee Resettlement, 2014), Table II-21: Public Assistance Utilization by Selected Refugee Groups, p. 107, http://www.acf.hhs.gov/sites/default/files/orr/orr_annual_report_to_congress_fy_2014_signed.pdf.32.
     The statements and statistics that follow are taken from "Subcommittee Chart: U.S. Issued 680,000 Green Cards to Migrants from Muslim Nations over the Last Five Years," press release, the website of Jeff Sessions, United States Senator for Alabama, November 25, 2015, http://www.sessions.senate.gov/public/index.cfm/news-releases?ID=A7F4D921-A030-4B69-84B7-EA26DBEE109A.

33. Jeff Sessions, "SUBCOMMITTEE CHART: Obama Administration On Track To Issue Over 1 Million Green Cards To Migrants From Muslim-Majority Countries," News Release, June 17, 2016, http://www.sessions.senate.gov/public/index.cfm?p=news-releases&id=32EBA988-9E36-4CC6-A8F3-ADEC5A705450.

34. Karen Zeigler, Steven A. Camarota "U.S. Immigrant Pop. Hit Record 42.4 Million in 2014," Center for Immigration Studies, September 2015, http://cis.org/us-immigrant-pop-hit-record-42-million-2014

35. Kate Trafecante and Craig Waxman, "Greek yogurt billionaire fills his plants with refugees," CNN Money, accessed September 13, 2016, http://money.cnn.com/video/news/2015/09/21/chobani-ceo-hamdi-ulukaya-fills-his-plants-with-refugees.cnnmoney/.

36. Kelly Riddell, "Feds' relocation of Somali refugees stresses Minn. welfare, raises terror fears," Washington Times, February 24, 2015, http://www.washingtontimes.com/news/2015/feb/24/islamist-terror-groups-target-minnesota-somali-ref/.

37. Ryan Gorman and AP, "Minnesota Has 'A Terror Recruiting Problem,'" Business Insider, April 20, 2015, http://www.businessinsider.com/minnesota-has-growing-terrorism-support-problem-2015-4.

38. Kristine Guerra, Jessica Contrera and Brian Murphy, "Minnesota stabbing survivor: 'He looked me dead in the eyes'," Washington Post, September 19, 2016, https://www.washingtonpost.com/news/post-nation/wp/2016/09/18/man-shot-dead-after-stabbing-8-people-in-a-minnesota-mall/?utm_term=.1d01325ee192.

39. "Officials hunt Afghan-born man in connection with New York, New Jersey bombings," Fox News, September 19, 2016, http://www.foxnews.com/us/2016/09/19/person-interest-to-named-in-nyc-bombing.html.

40. Laura Yuen, "U.S. Attorney, FBI to Answer Somali Community Questions Issues," MPR News, May 8, 2015, http://www.mprnews.org/story/2015/05/08/somali-community-questions.

41. Amy Forliti, "6 Minnesota Somali Organizations Receive Grants to Combat Terrorism," Twin Cities Pioneer Press, March 10, 2016, http://www.twincities.com/2016/03/10/6-minnesota-somali-organizations-receive-grants-to-combat-terrorism/.

42. Jeff Sessions, "SUBCOMMITTEE CHART: U.S. Issued 680,000 Green Cards To Migrants From Muslim Nations Over The Last Five Years," Press Release, November 25, 2015, http://www.sessions.senate.gov/public/index.cfm/2015/11/subcommittee-chart-u-s-issued-680-000-green-cards-to-migrants-from-muslim-nations-over-the-last-five-years.

43. "Office of Refugee Resettlement Annual Report to Congress," U.S. Department of Health and Human Services, FY 2014, https://www.acf.hhs.gov/sites/default/files/orr/orr_annual_report_to_congress_fy_2014_signed.pdf.

44. Center for Security Policy, "Poll of U.S. Muslims Reveals Ominous Levels of Support for Islamic Supremacists' Doctrine of Shariah, Jihad," press release, Center for Security Policy, June 23, 2015, http://www.centerforsecuritypolicy.org/2015/06/23/nationwide-poll-of-us-muslims-shows-thousands-support-shariah-jihad/.

45. The Polling Company, Inc./Woman Trend, Nationwide Online Survey of Muslims, the Center of Security Policy, June 2015, http://wizbangblog.com/wp-content/uploads/2015/06/Online-Survey-of-US_Muslims.pdf.

CHAPTER 2: A MASTER PLAN

1. See "The Peaceful Majority are IRRELEVANT. True Talk," YouTube video, 4:51, where Gabriel addresses the peaceful majority in response to an attendee's question, posted by "TheJourney000," July 18, 2014, https://www.youtube.com/watch?v=YnOF7y-KuHE.

2. See Leo Hohmann, "Poll: Most U.S. Muslims Would Trade Constitution for Shariah," WND, September 24, 2015, http://www.wnd.com/2015/09/poll-most-u-s-muslims-would-trade-constitution-for-shariah/.

3. Lorenzo Vidino, "Muslim Brotherhood Organizations in America: Goals, Ideologies, and Strategies, Foreign Policy Research Institute, December 3, 2011, http://www.fpri.org/article/2011/12/muslim-brotherhood-organizations-in-america-goals-ideologies-and-strategies/.

4. "The Muslim Brotherhood's 'General Strategic Goal' for North America," DiscoverTheNetworks.org, accessed August 16, 2016, http://www.discoverthenetworks.org/viewSubCategory.asp?id=1235.

5. Ibid., emphasis added.

6. Ibid.

7. "An Explanatory Memorandum on the General Strategic Goal for the Group in North America." You can view the entire document at http://www.investigativeproject.org/documents/misc/20.pdf (accessed August 16, 2016).

8. Proud Conservative, "25 Years Ago the Muslim Brotherhood Released Plan to Destroy America . . . Obama Refuses to Stop It,'" ProudCons.com, March 9, 2016, http://www.proudcons.com/muslim-brotherhood-released-plan-to-take-over/.

9. "An Explanatory Memorandum on the General Strategic Goal for the Group in North America."

10. Ryan Mauro, "Muslim Students Association (MSA)," Clarion Project, February 3, 2013, http://www.clarionproject.org/analysis/muslim-students-association#_ftnref16.

11. Brigitte Gabriel in a speech before the Family Research Council's Watchman on the Wall conference in July 2015, https://www.youtube.com/watch?v=TFxNPvns7nU.

12. Jonathan Clayton and Hereward Holland, "Over one million sea arrivals reach Europe in 2015," the UN Refugee Agency, December 30, 2015, http://www.unhcr.org/en-us/news/latest/2015/12/5683d0b56/million-sea-arrivals-reach-europe-2015.html.

13. Dr. Mark Christian in a personal interviews with the author on September 25, 2015 and later published in an article: Leo Hohmann, "U.S. in grip of 'Muhammad' baby boom," WND, January 6, 2016, http://www.wnd.com/2016/01/u-s-in-grip-of-muhammad-baby-boom/.

14. Ibid.

15. Ibid.

16. Ibid.

17. Ibid.

18. Ibid.

19. Leo Hohmann, "Poll: Most U.S. Muslims would trade Constitution for Shariah," WND.com, September 24, 2015, http://www.wnd.com/2015/09/poll-most-u-s-muslims-would-trade-constitution-for-shariah/.

20. Bob Unruh, "Muslim Brotherhood Front Slapped by Federal Judge," WND, June 4, 2015, http://www.wnd.com/2015/06/muslim-brotherhood-front-slapped-by-federal-judge/.

21. Art Moore, "Should Muslim Quran be USA's Top Authority?" WND, May 1, 2003, http://www.wnd.com/2003/05/18561/.

22. Art Moore, "Did CAIR founder Say Islam to Rule America?" WND, December 11, 2006, http://www.wnd.com/2006/12/39229/.

23. Lou Gelfand, "Reader Says Use of 'Fundamentalist' Hurting Muslims," *Minneapolis Star Tribune*, April 4, 1993, cached at http://www.anti-cair-net.org/HooperStarTrib.

24. Besheer Mohamed, "A new estimate of the U.S. Muslim population," Pew Research Center, January 6, 2016, www.pewresearch.org/fact-tank/2016/01/06/a-new-estimate-of-the-u-s-muslim-population/.

25. Center for Security Policy, "Poll of U.S. Muslims Reveals Ominous Levels of Support for Islamic Supremacists' Doctrine of Shariah, Jihad," press release, Center for Security Policy, June 23, 2015, http://www.centerforsecuritypolicy.org/2015/06/23/nationwide-poll-of-us-muslims-shows-thousands-support-shariah-jihad/.

26. Ibid.

27. Jonah Bennett, "New Europe Survey Finds 44% Of Muslims Believe In Islamic Fundamentalism," Daily Caller, May 27, 2016, http://dailycaller.com/2016/05/27/new-europe-survey-finds-44-of-muslims-believe-in-islamic-fundamentalism/.

28. Teaching Tolerance, "Sharia," accessed August 16, 2016, http://www.tolerance.org/publication/sharia. For the document itself, see Interfaith Alliance and the Religious Freedom Education Project of the First Amendment Center, *What Is the Truth about American Muslims? Questions and Answers*, http://www.tolerance.org/sites/default/files/general/What_is_the_Truth_About_American_Muslims.pdf. See questions 20 and 26.

29. *What Is the Truth about American Muslims?* See question 25.

30. Guy Adams, "Inside Britain's Sharia courts," *Daily Mail*, December 13, 2015, http://www.dailymail.co.uk/news/article-3358625/Inside-Britain-s-Sharia-courts-EIGHTY-FIVE-Islamic-courts-dispensing-justice-UK-special-investigation-really-goes-doors-shock-core.html.

31. Arsani William, "An Unjust Doctrine of Civil Arbitration: Sharia Courts in Canada and England," *Stanford Journal of International Relations* 11, no. 2 (Spring 2010): 42.

32. Ibid., 40.

33. "Florida Muslim Professor Defends ISIS Chopping off Hands!" YouTube video, 3:47, from an Islamophobia panel discussion hosted by the Muslim Student Association at Florida Atlantic University in May 2016, posted by "theunitedwest," May 24, 2016, https://www.youtube.com/watch?v=e43MSvIxb6k

34. Yusuf al-Qaradawi on Al-Jazeera Television (Qatar), January 24, 1999, http://www.aljazeera.net/programs/shareea/articles/2001/7/7-6-2.htm (no longer accessible), quoted in MEMRI SpecialDispatch Series, no. 447, December 6, 2002.

35. "British Islamist Anjem Choudary: They Give US Money, but We Attack Their System," YouTube video, 5:53, in a February 3, 2010, broadcast in which Choudary asserts that freedom and democracy are idols that must be destroyed and replaced with obedience to Allah, posted by "Schluss mit der Islamisierung," February 17, 2010, https://www.youtube.com/watch?v=Ne7z-_RXWeA.

36. See the article and video at: Anthony Furey, "Pro-Shariah Caliphate Lecture Held at Ontario College," *Toronto Sun*, upd. January 7, 2016, http://www.torontosun.com/2016/01/06/mohawk-college-distances-itself-from-refugee-crisis-speaker.

37. See https://www.youtube.com/channel/UCobIWczNQOtfeqg-Ay4tyVQ.

38. See Mazin AbdulAdhim on Facebook at https://www.facebook.com/mazin.abduladhim.

39. See "Jews tell the TRUTH about the 'Holocaust,'" YouTube video, 15:17, posted by "Black Serpent," September 13, 2013, https://www.youtube.com/watch?v=UxFEtbawPCk&feature=youtu.be.

40. Furey, "Pro-Shariah Caliphate Lecture Held at Ontario College."

41. William Wagner, "Islam, Shariah Law, and the American Constitution," Family Research Council, accessed August 17, 2016, http://www.frc.org/issueanalysis/islam-shariah-law-and-the-american-constitution.

42. John Guandolo, "Islamic Movement in U.S. Preparing for Battle," Understanding the Thread, September 13, 2016, https://www.understandingthethreat.com/islamic-movement-in-u-s-preparing-for-battle/.

43. Ibid.

44. See http://www.understandingthethreat.com/wp-content/uploads/2015/05/Underground_Movement_Plan1.pdf.

45. Guandolo, "Islamic Movement in U.S. Preparing for Battle."

46. Ashley Southall, "Muslim Officer Sues New York Police Dept. over No-Beard Policy," *New York Times*, June 22, 2016, http://www.nytimes.com/2016/06/23/nyregion/muslim-officer-sues-new-york-police-dept-over-no-beard-policy.html?_r=0.

47. Michael Daly, "Nidal Hasan's Murders Termed 'Workplace Violence' by U.S.," Daily Beast, August 6, 2013, http://www.thedailybeast.com/articles/2013/08/06/nidal-hasan-s-murders-termed-workplace-violence-by-u-s.html.

48. Pamela Geller, "FBI Director Comey: Investigation into Orlando Jihad Mass Murderer DROPPED after He Claimed His Co-Workers Were Islamophobic," Pamela Geller blog, June 13, 2016, http://pamelageller.com/2016/06/fbi-director-comey-investigation-into-orlando-jihad-mass-murderer-dropped-after-he-claimed-charges-were-islamophobic.html/.

49. Stephen F. Hayes, "Ignoring Reality," *Weekly Standard*, July 4, 2016, http://www.weeklystandard.com/ignoring-reality/article/2003013.

50. David K. Li, "Orlando massacre 911 tapes are revealed, scrubbed of references to Islam," *New York Post*, June 20, 2016, http://nypost.com/2016/06/20/i-did-the-shootings-orlando-gunman-911-recordings-revealed/.

51. Pamela Geller in an e-mail interview with the author, July 2015.

52. Manny Fernandez, Richard Pérez-Peña, and Fernanda Santos, "Gunman in Texas Shooting Was F.B.I. Suspect in Jihad Inquiry," *New York Times*, May 4, 2015, http://www.nytimes.com/2015/05/05/us/garland-texas-shooting-muhammad-cartoons.html.

53. Leo Hohmann, "Somali 'refugee' linked to San Bernardino terror attack," WND.com, December 6, 2015, http://www.wnd.com/2015/12/somali-refugee-linked-to-san-bernardino-terror-attack/.

54. Raymond Ibrahim, "Freedom Provocation and Targets: No Cartoons Required," Raymond Ibrahim's blog, May 11, 2015, http://www.raymondibrahim.com/2015/05/11/freedom-provocation-and-targets-no-cartoons-required/.

55. "Kenya attack: 147 dead in Garissa University assaul," BBC News, April 3, 2015, http://www.bbc.com/news/world-africa-32169080.

56. See Raymond Ibrahim, "Islamic State 'Sledgehammers' Christian Gravestones and Crosses in Mosul," Raymond Ibrahim blog, April 17, 2015, http://www.raymondibrahim.com/2015/04/17/islamic-state-sledgehammers-christian-gravestones-and-crosses-in-mosul/.

57. Ibrahim, "Freedom, Provocation, and Targets."

58. Ibid.

59. Ibid.

60. Pamela Geller, "Reverend Franklin Graham Calls for Sharia Law to be Banned in the USA," Pamela Geller blog, June 12, 2015, http://pamelageller.com/2015/06/reverend-franklin-graham-calls-for-sharia-law-to-be-banned-in-the-usa.html/.

61. CNN Staff, "ISIS Video Appears to Show Beheadings of Egyptian Coptic Christians in Libya," CNN, upd. February 16, 2015, http://www.cnn.com/2015/02/15/middleeast/isis-video-beheadings-christians/index.html.

CHAPTER 3: CULTURE CLASH

1. Aaron Klein, "Obama: America is 'no longer Christian'," WND, June 22, 2008, http://www.wnd.com/2008/06/67735/.

2. The information in this section is taken from Leo Hohmann, "Secret Weapon to Take Over America Revealed," WND, September 21, 2014, http://www.wnd.com/2014/09/secret-weapon-to-take-over-america-revealed/.

3. Dr. Christian's comments in this section are taken from Hohmann, "Secret Weapon to Take Over America Revealed."

4. See Aaron Klein, "Muslim Brotherhood Group to 'Connect all U.S. Schools,'" WND, January 23, 2013, http://www.wnd.com/2013/01/muslim-brotherhood-group-to-connect-all-u-s-schools/.

5. Victor Skinner, "PA School District Holds Staff Training, Joins Prayer Service at Islamic Mosque," EAGNews.org, June 9, 2015, http://eagnews.org/public-school-teachers-administrators-hold-staff-training-join-prayer-service-at-islamic-mosque/.

6. Edgar Sandoval and Ben Chapman, "New York City schools will close for Muslim Eid holidays," *New York Daily News*, March 4, 2015, http://www.nydailynews.com/new-york/education/nyc-schools-close-muslim-eid-holidays-article-1.2137025.

7. "Schools Accommodate Muslim Students," *Education Reporter*, Eagle Forum (blog), February 2008, http://www.eagleforum.org/educate/2008/feb08/muslim-students.html.

8. Tamar Lewin, "Some U.S. universities install foot baths for Muslim students," *New York Times*, August 7, 2007, http://www.nytimes.com/2007/08/07/world/americas/07iht-muslims.4.7022566.html?_r=0.

9. Maura Lerner, "At University of St. Thomas, Catholics and Muslims find common ground," *Star Tribune*, November 25, 2013, http://www.startribune.com/at-st-thomas-catholics-and-muslims-find-common-ground/233251591/.

10. "NJ Muslim Parents Militant About School Closure for Eid," Clarion Project, September 24, 2015, http://www.clarionproject.org/news/nj-muslim-parents-militant-about-school-closure-eid.

11. Todd Starnes, "Students Take Field Trip to Mosque, Receive Koran," FoxNews.com, September 17, 2013, http://radio.foxnews.com/toddstarnes/top-stories/students-take-field-trip-to-mosque-receive-koran.html.

12. Michael Lipka, "Muslims and Islam: Key findings in the U.S. and around the world," PewResearchCenter, July 22, 2016, http://www.pewresearch.org/fact-tank/2016/07/22/muslims-and-islam-key-findings-in-the-u-s-and-around-the-world/.

13. Holly Yan, ""The Truth about Muslims in America," CNN, upd. December 5, 2015, http://www.cnn.com/2015/12/08/us/muslims-in-america-shattering-misperception/index.html.

14. Gregor Aisch, et al., "What Investigators Know About the San Bernardino Shooting," *New York Times*, December 2015, http://www.nytimes.com/interactive/2015/12/02/us/california-mass-shooting-san-bernardino.html?_r=1.

15. Mark Krikorian, "It's Time for a Grown-Up Alternative to Trump's Crude Muslim-Immigration Proposal," National Review, December 8, 2015, http://www.nationalreview.com/donald-trump-muslim-immigration..

16. Besheer Mohamed, "A new estimate of the U.S. Muslim population," Pew Research Center, January 6, 2016, http://www.pewresearch.org/fact-tank/2016/01/06/a-new-estimate-of-the-u-s-muslim-population/.

17. "Distribution of Mosques in USA 2015," Islam Threat (blog), April 2015, http://islamthreat.com/distribution_of_mosques_in_usa_2015.html.

18. Ralph Sidway, "Muslim 'Breaking of the Crosses' in Syracuse, NY as Catholic Church Converted to Mosque," *Jihad Watch*, August 24, 2015, https://www.jihadwatch.org/2015/08/muslim-breaking-of-the-crosses-in-syracuse-ny-as-roman-catholic-church-converted-to-mosque.

19. bid.

20. John Guandolo, "Islamic Movement in U.S. Preparing for Battle," Understanding the Threat, September 13, 2016, https://www.understandingthethreat.com/islamic-movement-in-u-s-preparing-for-battle/.

21. Sidway, "Muslim 'Breaking of the Crosses' in Syracuse, NY as Catholic Church Converted to Mosque."

22. Ryan Mauro, "Al-Qaeda Declares 'We Must Eliminate the Cross'," Clarion Project, April 27, 2014, http://www.clarionproject.org/analysis/al-qaeda-declares-we-must-eliminate-cross.

23. Sidway, "Muslim 'Breaking of the Crosses' in Syracuse, NY as Catholic Church Converted to Mosque."

24. Pew Research Center, "The Future of World Religions: Population Growth Projections, 2010-2050," accessed August 29, 2016, http://www.pewforum.org/2015/04/02/religious-projections-2010-2050/.

25. Ibid.

26. Pew Research Center, Religious Landscape Study, "Muslim," Pew Forum, accessed August 17, 2016, http://www.pewforum.org/religious-landscape-study/religious-tradition/muslim/. See in particular the bar graphs "Belief in God among Muslims" and "Importance of religion in one's life among Muslims."

27. Pew Research Center, Religious Landscape Study, "Catholic," Pew Forum, accessed August 17, 2016, http://www.pewforum.org/religious-landscape-study/religious-tradition/catholic/, "Importance of religion in one's life among Catholics" (graph); Pew Research Center, Religious Landscape Study, "Mainline Protestants," Pew Forum, accessed August 17, 2016, http://www.pewforum.org/religious-landscape-study/religious-tradition/mainline-protestant/, "Importance of religion in one's life among Mainline Protestants" (graph)

28. Michael Lipka, "Muslims and Islam: Key findings in the U.S. and around the world," Pew Research Center, July 22, 2016, http://www.pewresearch.org/fact-tank/2016/07/22/muslims-and-islam-key-findings-in-the-u-s-and-around-the-world/.

29. The following statistics on FGM are taken from Lucy Westcott, "Female Genital Mutilation on the Rise in the U.S.," *Newsweek*, February 6, 2015, http://www.newsweek.com/fgm-rates-have-doubled-us-2004-304773.

30. Elizabeth Harrington, "Huge Increase in Girls Victimized by Genital Mutilation in U.S.," *Washington Free Beacon*, August 1, 2016, http://freebeacon.com/issues/huge-increase-girls-victimized-genital-mutilation-u-s/.

CHAPTER 4: OBAMA'S 'FORCED' WELCOMING PARTY

1. "Germany 'arson attack' destroys planned asylum shelter," BBC News, August 25, 2015, http://www.bbc.com/news/world-europe-34050393.

2. "Obama: 'Globalization Is Here to Stay'," NBC News, July 9, 2016, http://www.nbcnews.com/video/obama-globalization-is-here-to-stay-721921603992.

3. Pete Kasperowicz, "Kerry slams Trump's wall, tells grads to prepare for 'borderless world'," Washington Examiner, May 6, 2016, http://www.washingtonexaminer.com/kerry-slams-trumps-wall-tells-grads-to-prepare-for-borderless-world/article/2590596.

4. Unless otherwise noted, the remaining information in this section is taken from Leo Hohmann, "Obama Demands 'Welcoming' for Illegals," WND, April 17, 2015, http://www.wnd.com/2015/04/obama-demands-welcoming-for-illegals/.

5. "Strengthening Communities by Welcoming All Residents," White House Task Force on New Americans, April 2015, https://www.whitehouse.gov/sites/default/files/docs/final_tf_newamericans_report_4-14-15_clean.pdf.

6. See Leo Hohmann, "20 U.S. Cities 'Optimum Sanctuaries' for Migrants," WND, April 20, 2016, http://www.wnd.com/2016/04/20-u-s-cities-optimum-sanctuaries-for-migrants/.

7. Bryan Griffith and Jessica Vaughan, "Map: Sanctuary Cities, Counties, and States," Center for Immigration Studies, January 2016, http://cis.org/Sanctuary-Cities-Map.

8. See The White House Task Force on New Americans, *Strengthening Communities by Welcoming All Residents: A Federal Strategic Action Plan on Immigrant and Refugee Integration*, April 14, 2015, https://www.whitehouse.gov/sites/default/files/docs/final_tf_newamericans_report_4-14-15_clean.pdf.

9.   Leo Hohmann, "America's Newest 'Most-Wanted Terrorist' Was 'Refugee,'" WND, January 30, 2015, http://www.wnd.com/2015/01/americas-newest-most-wanted-terrorist-was-refugee/.

10.   "6 indicted in alleged plot to support ISIS, Al Qaeda," Fox News, February 7, 2015, http://www.foxnews.com/us/2015/02/07/6-indicted-in-alleged-plot-to-support-isis-al-qaeda.html.

11.   Cliff Pinckard, "Columbus man accused of supporting international terrorism," Cleveland.com, February 26, 2015, http://www.cleveland.com/nation/index.ssf/2015/02/columbus_man_accused_of_suppor.html.

12.   Judson Berger, "Anatomy of the terror threat: Files show hundreds of US plots, refugee connection," Fox News, June 22, 2016, www.foxnews.com/politics/2016/06/22/anatomy-terror-threat-files-shed-light-on-nature-extent-plots-in-us.html?intcmp=hpbt3.

13.   The White House Office of the Press Secretary, "Presidential Memorandum--Creating Welcoming Communities and Fully Integrating Immigrants and Refugees," November 21, 2014, https://www.whitehouse.gov/the-press-office/2014/11/21/presidential-memorandum-creating-welcoming-communities-and-fully-integra.

14.   Hohmann, "Obama Demands 'Welcoming' for Illegals."

15.   Ibid.

16.   Leo Hohmann, "Obama demands 'welcoming' for illegals," WND.com, April 17, 2015, http://www.wnd.com/2015/04/obama-demands-welcoming-for-illegals/.

17.   "Immigrant Contributions Uplifted as Communities Across the Country Celebrate National Welcoming Week," press release, Welcoming America, September 13, 2013, http://www.welcomingamerica.org/sites/default/files/wp-content/uploads/2013/09/Final-2013-National-Welcoming-Week-Press-Release.pdf.

18.   "National Welcoming Week kicks off on September 13th!" September 11, 2014, https://www.welcomingamerica.org/news/national-welcoming-week-kicks-september-13th.

19.   http://www.welcomingrefugees.org/blog.

20.   Alex Wagner, "Beyond Jan Brewer And Lou Dobbs: A Calm Center In The Immigration Debate," Huffington Post, June 14, 2011, http://www.huffingtonpost.com/2011/04/14/beyond-jan-brewer-and-lou_n_849128.html.

21.   Jamie McGee, "Obama honors immigrant rights leader David Lubell," Tennessean, December 9, 2014, www.tennessean.com/story/money/2014/12/09/obama-honors-immigrant-rights-leader-david-lubell/20156983/.

22.   J.M. Kaplan Fund website, http://www.jmkfund.org/funds/migrations/.

23.   See The J.M. Kaplan Fund 2013 Migration Grants, http://www.jmkfund.org/wp-content/uploads/2014/01/2013-Migration-Grants.pdf.

24.   New American Economy, "20 Communities Selected for "Gateways for Growth Challenge" to Welcome & Integrate New Americans," March 29, 2016, http://www.renewoureconomy.org/news/updates/twenty-communities-selected-for-gateways-for-growth-challenge-to-welcome-and-integrate-new-americans/.

25.   Ibid.

26.   Welcoming Interactive, Atlanta, Georgia, http://www.welcominginteractive.org/about/.

27.   "Office of Refugee Resettlement Annual Report to Congress," U.S. Department of Health and Human Services, FY 2014, https://www.acf.hhs.gov/sites/default/files/orr/orr_annual_report_to_congress_fy_2014_signed.pdf.

28.   See exhibit 7 in U.S. Department of Health and Human Services, ORR Indicators for Refugee Resettlement Stakeholders (Office of Refugee Resettlement, June 2015), p. 11, https://www.acf.hhs.gov/sites/default/files/orr/508_compliant_fy_2016_orr_indicators_for_refugee_resettlement.pdf.

29. Lenny Bernstein and Joel Achenbach, "A group of middle-aged whites in the U.S. is dying at a startling rate," *Washington Post*, November 2, 2015, https://www.washingtonpost.com/national/health-science/a-group-of-middle-aged-american-whites-is-dying-at-a-startling-rate/2015/11/02/47a63098-8172-11e5-8ba6-cec48b74b2a7_story.html.

30. Todd Spangler, "New poll shows Clinton and Trump nearly tied in Michigan," *Detroit Free Press*, September 16, 2016, http://www.freep.com/story/news/politics/2016/09/15/donald-trump-hillary-clinton-michigan-poll/90381296/.

31. Cities for Action, "Actions," accessed August 18, 2016, http://www.citiesforaction.us/actions.

32. See Division for Sustainable Development, UN-DESA, "Transforming Our World: the 2030 Agenda for Sustainable Development," Sustainable Development Knowledge Platform, accessed August 18, 2016, https://sustainabledevelopment.un.org/post2015/transformingourworld.

33. Patrick Wood, "Sustainable Development, Migration and the Multi-Cultural Destruction of the Nation State," *Technocracy* (blog), April 5, 2015, https://www.technocracy.news/index.php/2016/04/05/sustainable-development-multi-cultural-destruction-nation-state/.

34. Ellen Wulfhorst, "UN Lectures World: Let 'Refugees' In And Stop Xenophobia And Racism," Technocracy, May 12, 2016, https://www.technocracy.news/index.php/2016/05/12/un-lectures-world-let-refugees-stop-xenophobia-racism/.

35. Division for Sustainable Development, UN-DESA, "Transforming Our World."

36. Ibid.

37. Ibid.

38. United Nations, *The Road to Dignity by 2030: Ending Poverty, Transforming All Lives and Protecting the Planet: Synthesis Report of the Secretary-General On the Post–2015 Agenda* (New York: December 2014), http://www.un.org/disabilities/documents/reports/SG_Synthesis_Report_Road_to_Dignity_by_2030.pdf.

39. Ibid., 3 (1.4).

40. United Nations, *The Road to Dignity by 2030*, 13

41. Ibid., 14 (2.1.48).

42. Ibid., 3 (1.3).

43. '2030 Agenda will be crucial for the economic empowerment of all migrants' ' Lakshmi Puri," Big News Network, March 25, 2016, http://www.bignewsnetwork.com/news/242515851/2030-agenda-will-be-crucial-for-the-economic-empowerment-of-all-migrants--lakshmi-puri.

44. "The World's Billionaires," Forbes, http://www.forbes.com/profile/david-rockefeller-sr/.

45. David Rockefeller, *Memoirs* (New York: Random House, 2002), 405.

46. David Rockefeller, speaking at the UN Ambassadors Dinner of the UN Business Council, September 23, 1994. The C-Span video of this speech can be see at "The world according to Rockefeller," YouTube video, 7:37, posted by "iching64," November 15, 2007, https://www.youtube.com/watch?v=MM8NpjmXD00. This comment at 4:27.

47. Henry Kissinger in an address to the Bilderberger meeting at Evian, France, May 21, 1992.

48. https://www.youtube.com/watch?v=4x__looLj9c)

49. See "Henry Kissinger: 'Obama will create a New World Order," YouTube video, 0:59, Kissinger on the Economy, as broadcast on CNBC, posted by Patriot News Organization, September 21, 2012, https://www.youtube.com/watch?v=q1r-3q9PXoM.

50. Henry Kissinger, as quoted in the *New York Times*, October 28, 1973; and "The world according to Henry Kissinger," *Telegraph* (UK), May 21, 2011, http://www.telegraph.co.uk/news/worldnews/us-politics/8528270/The-world-according-to-Henry-Kissinger.html.

51. David Hughes and Kate Ferguson, "National borders are 'the worst invention ever', says EC chief Jean-Claude Juncker," Independent, August 22, 2016, http://www.independent.co.uk/news/world/europe/national-borders-are-the-worst-invention-ever-says-ec-chief-jean-claude-juncker-a7204006.html.

52. George Soros, *The Crisis of Global Capitalism: Open Society Endangered* (New York: PublicAffairs, 1998), xxix.

53. George Soros, *The Age of Fallibility: Consequences of the War on Terror* (New York: PublicAffairs, 2006), xvi.

54. http://www.discoverthenetworks.org/individualProfile.asp?indid=977.

55. Ibid.

56. Unless otherwise noted, the rest of the material in this section is taken from David Galland and Stephen McBride, "How George Soros Singlehandedly Created the European Refugee Crisis—and Why," *The Passing Parade*, July 8, 2016, http://www.garretgalland.com/passing-parade/how-george-soros-singlehandedly-created-the-european-refugee-crisisand-why/.

57. "George Soros," A Guide to the Political Left, Discoverthenetworks.org, http://www.discoverthenetworks.org/individualProfile.asp?indid=977.

58. Caroline B. Glick, "Our World: Soros's campaign of global chaos," Jerusalem Post Opinion, August 22, 2016, http://www.jpost.com/Opinion/Our-World-Soross-campaign-of-global-chaos-464770.

59. Ibid.

60. Matthew Boyle, "National Immigration Forum Funded by Soros and the Left," Breitbart, June 2, 2013, http://www.breitbart.com/big-government/2013/06/02/national-immigration-forum-lead-evangelical-jim-wallis-funded-by-george-soros-other-bastions-of-institutional-left/.

61. Ibid.

62. Lynette Wilson, "Refugee women, children rebuild lives in Arizona," Episcopal News Service, March 2, 2015, episcopaldigitalnetwork.com/ens/2015/03/02/refugee-women-children-rebuild-lives-in-arizona/; emphasis added.

CHAPTER 5: UNHOLY ALLIANCE

1. David Boroff, "Michigan city of Hamtramck, once 90 percent Polish, is first Muslim-majority city in U.S.," *New York Daily News*, November 24, 2015, http://www.nydailynews.com/news/national/residents-nervous-majority-muslim-michigan-city-article-1.2445093.

2. Jeremy Stahl, "Mike Pence Called a Central Premise of Trump's Campaign 'Offensive and Unconstitutional'," *Slate*, July 14, 2016, http://www.slate.com/blogs/the_slatest/2016/07/14/mike_pence_called_key_donald_trump_plan_offensive_and_unconstitutional.html.

3. The following facts on the founding fathers and the history of Islam's spread are taken from "Founding Fathers Rip Obama's Muslim 'Fabric,'" WND, August 3, 2014, http://www.wnd.com/2014/08/founding-fathers-refute-obamas-muslim-fabric/.

4. Casey Ross, "Newt Gingrich correctly states Hillary Clinton wants to increase Syrian refugees by 500 percent: RNC 2016 Fact Check," July 20, 2016, Cleveland.com, http://www.cleveland.com/rnc-2016/index.ssf/2016/07/newt_gingrich_correctly_states.html.

5. Stephen Mayer, "Messages on church reader board stir controversy," Komo News, May 14, 2016, http://komonews.com/news/nation-world/messages-on-church-reader-board-stir-controversy.

6. Leo Hohmann, "Tiny Christian church in holy war with Islam," WND, June 7, 2016, http://www.wnd.com/2016/06/tiny-christian-church-in-holy-war-with-islam/.

7. Stephen Mayer, "Messages on church reader board stir controversy," Komo News, May 14, 2016, http://komonews.com/news/nation-world/messages-on-church-reader-board-stir-controversy.

8. Hohmann, "Tiny Christian church in holy war with Islam,"
9. The following details about Belmont Drive church are taken from Hohmann, "Tiny Christian Church in Holy War with Islam."
10. Interview with Shahram Hadian on July 18, 2016.
11. The following story is taken from http://www.wnd.com/2016/06/muslim-immigrant-attacks-flag-waving-american-family/.
12. Leo Hohmann, "Feds clear Muslim flag attacker of hate crime," WND, June 20, 2016, http://www.wnd.com/2016/06/fbi-decides-whether-muslim-flag-attack-was-hate-crime/.
13. "Police: Woman attacks homeowner with American Flag," AP June 2, 2016, http://bigstory.ap.org/article/0942a3abfbe44fffaa531a9339d2071b/police-woman-attacks-homeowner-american-flag.
14. Ibid.
15. "An Explanatory Memorandum on the General Strategic Goal for the Group in North America: 5/22/1991," page 7 of 18, http://www.investigativeproject.org/documents/20-an-explanatory-memorandum-on-the-general.pdf, emphasis added.
16. Laura Mowat, "Christians ordered to keep faith quiet... by the Archbishop of Canterbury," *Express*, May 21, 2016, http://www.express.co.uk/news/uk/672579/Archbishop-of-Canterbury-orders-Christians-keep-faith-quiet.
17. Jon Stone, "David Cameron promised to take in 20,000 Syrian refugees. What have the Tories actually delivered?" *Independent*, September 1, 2016, http://www.independent.co.uk/news/uk/politics/syrian-refugee-crisis-refugees-british-government-20000-4000-progress-how-many-migrants-immigration-a7219971.html.
18. Ibid.
19. Leo Hohmann, "Christian Leader: Don't Share Faith with Muslims," WND, May 25, 2016, http://www.wnd.com/2016/05/christian-leader-dont-share-faith-with-muslims/
20. Ibid.
21. Nanette de Visser, "Why Are So Many Muslim Refugees in Europe Suddenly Finding Jesus?" *Daily Beast*, May 25, 2016, http://www.thedailybeast.com/articles/2016/05/25/why-are-so-many-muslim-refugees-in-europe-suddenly-finding-jesus.html.
22. "Caring for Refugees: A Declaration of Evangelical Response," *Christianity Today*, December 17, 2015, http://www.christianitytoday.com/ct/2015/december-web-only/caring-for-refugees-declaration-evangelical-gc2summit.html.

CHAPTER 6: EUROPE UNDER ASSAULT

1. Thomas D. Williams, "Pope Francis: 'Migrants Are Not a Danger, They Are in Danger,'" Breitbart, May 29, 2016, http://www.breitbart.com/london/2016/05/29/pope-francis-migrants-not-danger-danger/.
2. "'Migrants not dangerous but in danger' Pope Francis tells children in Vatican meeting," Reuters, May 28, 2016, http://www.abc.net.au/news/2016-05-29/pope-francis-meets-with-children-amid-italys-migrant-crisis/7456828.
3. Williams, "Pope Francis."
4. Virginia Hale, "Christians Told to 'Pray in Silence . . . Don't Disturb The Migrants,'" Breitbart, June 6, 2016, http://www.breitbart.com/london/2016/06/06/parishioners-told-pray-silence-migrants/.
5. Caritas Europa, "Protection of Refugees," accessed August 29, 2016, http://www.caritas.eu/functions/policy-advocacy/protection-of-refugees.
6. Hale, "Christians Told to 'Pray in Silence.'"

7. Da Mario Guglielmi, "Ventimiglia, 400 migranti in città. Ioculano: 'Situazione insostenibile, fermateli!'," Riviera Press, March, 6, 2016, http://rivierapress.it/2016/06/03/ventimiglia-400-migranti-citta-ioculano-situazione-insostenibile-fermateli/.

8. Oliver JJ Lane, "Parish Church Strips Out Crosses, Pulpit, Pews For The Comfort of Migrants," Breitbart, November 1, 2015, http://www.breitbart.com/london/2015/11/01/parish-church-strips-crosses-pulpit-pews-comfort-migrants/.

9. "Dhimmitude in Europe: Christians Told To 'Pray In Silence… Don't Disturb The Migrants' ," Facing Islam Blog, June 9, 2016, http://facingislam.blogspot.com/2016/06/dhimmitude-in-europe-christians-told-to.html?utm_source=feedburner&utm_medium=email&utm_campaign=Feed%3A+FacingIslam+%28Facing+Islam%29.

10. Robert Spencer, "Germany: Church holds Muslim funeral for slain Islamic State jihadi," *Jihad Watch*, June 4, 2016, https://www.jihadwatch.org/2016/06/germany-church-holds-muslim-funeral-for-slain-islamic-state-jihadi.

11. See https://www.jihadwatch.org/2016/04/video-muslim-migrants-riot-throw-stones-at-police-and-tear-down-greek-border-fence or http://www.bbc.com/news/world-europe-34180378.

12. http://www.independent.co.uk/news/world/europe/aylan-kurdi-s-story-how-a-small-syrian-child-came-to-be-washed-up-on-a-beach-in-turkey-10484588.html.

13. Adam Withnall, "If these extraordinarily powerful images of a dead Syrian child washed up on a beach don't change Europe's attitude to refugees, what will?" Independent, September 2, 2015, http://www.independent.co.uk/news/world/europe/if-these-extraordinarily-powerful-images-of-a-dead-syrian-child-washed-up-on-a-beach-don-t-change-10482757.html.

14. Saif Hameed, Stephen Kalin, Anna Willard, "Syrian toddler Aylan's father drove capsized boat, other passengers say," Reuters, September 11, 2015, Saif Hameed; Writing by Stephen Kalin; editing by Anna Willard.

15. Daniel Meers and Ben McClellan, "Aylan Kurdi: Drowned boy's father accused of being people smuggler in charge of boat that crashed denies claims," *Daily Telegraph*, September 11, 2015, http://www.dailytelegraph.com.au/news/aylan-kurdi-drowned-boys-father-accused-of-being-people-smuggler-in-charge-of-boat-that-crashed/news-story/1987ed0bc6a5d65a34ca4762d2c15d7f.

16. https://www.facebook.com/EuropeSaysOXI/posts/1708942532659556:0.

17. "Germany 'arson attack' destroys planned asylum shelter," BBC News, August 25, 2015, http://www.bbc.com/news/world-europe-34050393.

18. "Fertility rate, total (births per woman)," the World Bank http://data.worldbank.org/indicator/SP.DYN.TFRT.IN.

19. Ibid.

20. Adrian Edwards, "Global forced displacement hits record high," UN Refugee Agency, June 20, 2016, http://www.unhcr.org/en-us/news/latest/2016/6/5763b65a4/global-forced-displacement-hits-record-high.html.

21. Robert Spencer, "The Hijrah Into Europe," *Frontpage Magazine*, September 4, 2015, http://www.frontpagemag.com/fpm/260019/hijrah-europe-robert-spencer.

22. Leo Cendrowicz, "Refugee crisis: EU faultlines revealed as Hungary's PM warns of risk to 'Christian' culture," Independent, September 3, 2015, http://www.independent.co.uk/news/world/europe/refugee-crisis-eu-faultlines-revealed-as-hungarys-pm-warns-of-risk-to-christian-culture-10485403.html.

23. Clare Lopez in an interview with the author on September 4, 2015, http://www.wnd.com/2015/09/isis-smuggler-we-will-use-refugee-crisis-to-infiltrate-west/.

24. See graph on 'demographics' of refugees: http://data.unhcr.org/mediterranean/regional.html.

25. Much of the material in the remainder of this section is taken from Pat Buchanan, "Islam's Conquest of Europe," September 7, 2015, http://www.wnd.com/2015/09/islams-conquest-of-europe/.

26. Rachel Stoltzfoos, "German Welcome Inspires Second Wave Of Migrants," Daily Caller, September 8, 2015, http://dailycaller.com/2015/09/08/german-welcome-inspires-second-wave-of-migrants/.

27. Buchanan, "Islam's Conquest of Europe."

28. Ibid.

29. Soeren Kern, "Germany's Migrant Rape Crisis Spirals out of Control," Gatestone Institute, August 9, 2016, https://www.gatestoneinstitute.org/8663/germany-migrants-rape.

30. The remainder of the material in this section is taken from Leo Hohmann, "Disturbing Reality: Muslim 'Sex-Grooming Gangs,'" WND, April 24, 2016, http://www.wnd.com/2016/04/disturbing-reality-muslim-sex-grooming-gangs/.

31. http://www.express.co.uk/news/uk/695066/Police-arrest-900-Syrians-in-England-and-Wales-for-rape-death-threats-and-child-abuse.

32. You can read these verses at https://quran.com/4.

33. "Nearly 163,000 people sought asylum in Sweden in 2015," Migrationsverket, January 12, 2016, http://www.migrationsverket.se/English/About-the-Migration-Agency/News-archive/News-archive-2016/2016-01-12-Nearly-163000-people-sought-asylum-in-Sweden-in-2015.html.

34. Richard Orange, "Swedish music festivals hit by reports of rapes by 'migrants'," *Telegraph*, July 4, 2016, http://www.telegraph.co.uk/news/2016/07/04/swedish-music-festivals-hit-by-reports-of-rapes-by-migrants/.

35. Selina Sykes, "Blood-smeared floors where Swedish social worker was stabbed to death in 'frenzied attack'," *Express*, May 24, 2016, http://www.express.co.uk/news/world/673261/Swedish-social-worker-murdered-migrant-child-asylum-seeker.

36. Rachel Stewart, "The Men with Many Wives: the British Muslims who practise polygamy," *Telegraph*, September 24, 2014, http://www.telegraph.co.uk/culture/tvandradio/11108763/The-Men-with-Many-Wives-the-British-Muslims-who-practise-polygamy.html.

37. "Having a Second Wife in Western Countries," Islam Awareness blog, http://www.islamawareness.net/Polygamy/fatwa001.html.

38. Donna Rachel Edmunds, "Students Publicly Humiliated by School Because Parents Refused Permission for Mosque Visit," Breitbart, April 29, 2015, http://www.breitbart.com/london/2015/04/29/students-publicly-humiliated-by-school-because-parents-refused-permission-for-mosque-visit/.

39. http://europe.newsweek.com/access-jihadi-book-turns-prisons-islamic-extremism-incubators-322271.

40. Aaron Brown, "'Just wait...' Islamic State reveals it has smuggled THOUSANDS of extremists into Europe," Express, November 18, 2015, http://www.express.co.uk/news/world/555434/Islamic-State-ISIS-Smuggler-THOUSANDS-Extremists-into-Europe-Refugees.

41. Laura Colby, "How Tree Germans and a Venture Capitalist Hope to Integrate Europe's Refugees," Bloomberg, July 20, 2016, http://www.bloomberg.com/news/articles/2016-07-20/preparing-syria-s-future-leaders-one-college-course-at-a-time.

42. "German intelligence chief warns radical Islamists may try to recruit young refugees arriving in the country," Reuters, September 22, 2015, http://www.independent.co.uk/news/world/europe/german-intelligence-chief-warns-radical-islamists-may-try-to-recruit-young-refugees-arriving-in-the-10512475.html.

43. Anthony Faiola, "Germany is trying to teach refugees the right way to have sex," *Washington Post*, May 13, 2016, https://www.washingtonpost.com/news/worldviews/wp/2016/05/13/germany-is-trying-to-teach-refugees-the-right-way-to-have-sex/?tid=a_inl.

44. The following quotes from the pope are taken from Guillaume Goubert and Sébastien Maillard, "Interview: Pope Francis," translated into English by Stefan Gigacz for *La Croix*, May 17, 2016, http://www.la-croix.com/Religion/Pape/INTERVIEW-Pope-Francis-2016-05-17-1200760633.

45. Jim Hoft, "Unbelievable! Pope Francis Compares Jesus' Disciples to ISIS Killers," *Gateway Pundit*, May 20, 2016, http://www.thegatewaypundit.com/2016/05/good-lord-pope-francis-compares-jesus-disciples-isis/.

46. Barney Henderson, "Austrian cardinal tipped to be the next pope warns of an 'Islamic conquest of Europe' ," *Telegraph*, September 14, 2016, http://www.telegraph.co.uk/news/2016/09/13/austrian-cardinal-tipped-to-be-the-next-pope-warns-of-an-islamic/.

47. "International Rescue Committee: US commitment to accept up to 8,000 Syrians not enough," International Rescue Committee Press Release, September 2, 2015, https://www.rescue.org/press-release/international-rescue-committee-us-commitment-accept-8000-syrians-not-enough.

48. Sebastian Shakespeare, "SEBASTIAN SHAKESPEARE: Revealed - David Miliband is paid a staggering £425,000 as boss of New York-based refugee charity," Daily Mail, December 30, 2015, http://www.dailymail.co.uk/news/article-3379572/SEBASTIAN-SHAKESPEARE-Revealed-David-Miliband-paid-staggering-425-000-boss-New-York-based-refugee-charity.html.

49, Ibid.

50, "Dear, Loss and grief, pain and shock, anger and helplessness," Lutheran Immigration and Refugee Service blog, http://my.lirs.org/site/MessageViewer?em_id=4261.0&dlv_id=7321#.V8TbVbUzNrF.

51. Ishaan Tharoor, "The Arab world's wealthiest nations are doing next to nothing for Syria's refugees" *Washington Post*, September 4, 2015, https://www.washingtonpost.com/news/worldviews/wp/2015/09/04/the-arab-worlds-wealthiest-nations-are-doing-next-to-nothing-for-syrias-refugees/.

52. Brown, "'Just Wait . . .'"

53. Stephanie Nebehay, "Up to 3,000 refugees, migrants expected a day in Macedonia: UNHCR," Reuters, August 25, 2015, http://www.reuters.com/article/us-europe-migrants-un-idUSKCN0QU12M20150825.

54. Michael E. Miller, "In Sweden's Ikea attack, two migrants, two slayings and rampant fear of refugees," Washington Post, September 29, 2015, https://www.washingtonpost.com/news/morning-mix/wp/2015/09/29/in-swedens-ikea-attack-two-migrants-two-murders-and-rampant-fear-of-refugees/.

CHAPTER 7: "BUILDING COALITIONS"

1. Pam Key, "Farrakhan: We Must Rise Up and Kill Those Who Kill Us; Stalk Them and Kill Them," Breitbart, August 4, 2015, http://www.breitbart.com/video/2015/08/04/farrakhan-we-must-rise-up-and-kill-those-who-kill-us-stalk-them-and-kill-them/.

2. Meridith McGraw, "Department of Justice Will Go After Anti-Muslim Hate Speech," ABC News, December 4, 2015, http://abcnews.go.com/US/department-justice-anti-muslim-hate-speech/story?id=35585946.

3. Josh Gerstein, "Lynch recalibrates message on hateful speech," *Politico*, December 7, 2015, http://www.politico.com/blogs/under-the-radar/2015/12/lynch-recalibrates-message-on-hateful-speech-216488.

4. Ian Schwartz, "Obama: This 'Medieval Interpretation Of Islam' Is Rejected By '99.9%" Of Muslims, Not A "Religious War'," RealClear Politics, February 1, 2015, http://www.realclearpolitics.com/video/2015/02/01/obama_this_medieval_interpretation_of_islam_is_rejected_by_999_of_muslims_not_a_religious_war.html.

5. "The World's Muslims: Religion, Politics and Society," Pew Research Center, April 30, 2013, http://www.pewforum.org/2013/04/30/the-worlds-muslims-religion-politics-society-overview/.

6. Cynthia Yacowar-Sweeney, "Honor Killing Entrenched in Islam," December 14, 2011, http://canadafreepress.com/article/honour-killing-entrenched-in-islam.

7. Alyssa Canobbio, "Kerry: Air conditioners as big a threat as ISIS," *Washington Free Beacon*, July 23, 2016, http://www.foxnews.com/politics/2016/07/23/kerry-air-conditioners-as-big-threat-as-isis.html.

8. John Hayward, "Hillary Clinton: Muslims Are 'Peaceful and Tolerant,' Have 'Nothing Whatsoever to Do With Terrorism'," Breitbart, November 19, 2015, http://www.breitbart.com/big-government/2015/11/19/hillary-clinton-muslims-peaceful-tolerant-nothing-whatsoever-terrorism/.

9. "Launch of Strong Cities Network to Strengthen Community Resilience Against Violent Extremism," Department of Justice, Justice News, September 28, 2015, https://www.justice.gov/opa/pr/launch-strong-cities-network-strengthen-community-resilience-against-violent-extremism.

10. National Law Enforcement Officers Memorial Fund, "2016 Mid-Year Law Enforcement Officer Fatalities Report," July 26, 2016, http://www.nleomf.org/facts/research-bulletins/?referrer=http://www.foxnews.com/us/2016/07/27/shooting-deaths-law-enforcement-spike-in-2016-report-reveals.html.

11. Mary Chastain, "Counter Jihad: Islamic Revolution in America," Breitbart, March 17, 2016, http://www.breitbart.com/big-government/2016/03/17/counter-jihad-islamic-revolution-in-america/.

12. "The Muslim Brotherhood's 'General Strategic Goal' for North America," DiscoverTheNetworks.org, accessed August 16, 2016, http://www.discoverthenetworks.org/viewSubCategory.asp?id=1235.

13. Leo Hohmann, "FBI Counter-Terror Expert Sees Historic Islam Pivot," WND, March 24, 2016, http://www.wnd.com/2016/03/fbi-counter-terror-expert-sees-historic-islam-http://www.wnd.com/2016/03/fbi-counter-terror-expert-sees-historic-islam-pivot/#!.

14. http://www.crisismagazine.com/2016/islam-revolution-black-lives-matter.

15. Hohmann, "FBI Counter-Terror Expert Sees Historic Islam Pivot."

16. Daniel Greenfield, "Turn Your Islamic Centers, Mosques into Registration Centers for Voters," Counter Jihad Report, January 27, 2016, https://counterjihadreport.com/2016/01/27/turn-your-islamic-centers-mosques-into-registration-centers-for-voters/.

17. Hohmann, "FBI Counter-Terror Expert Sees Historic Islam Pivot."

CHAPTER 8: TRANSFORMING SMALL TOWN AMERICA

1. Jackie Crosby, "Fired Muslim workers claim discrimination at plant in Owatonna," *Star Tribune*, April 27, 2016, http://www.startribune.com/fired-muslim-workers-claim-discrimination-at-plant-in-owatonna/377295741/.

2. Vicki Ikeogu, "Dayton: Minnesotans who can't accept immigrants 'should find another state'," *St. Cloud Times*, October 14, 2015, http://www.duluthnewstribune.com/news/3860965-dayton-minnesotans-who-cant-accept-immigrants-should-find-another-state.

3. Pamela Geller, "Town of 4,000 finds out it will receive 3,000 migrants: "If you don't like hosting refugees in your town, you can leave the country"," Freedom Outpost, October 16, 2015, http://freedomoutpost.com/town-of-4000-finds-out-it-will-receive-3000-migrants-if-you-dont-like-hosting-refugees-in-your-town-you-can-leave-the-country/.

4. Andrew M. Luger, "U.S. Attorney Andrew Luger: Minnesota must face Islamophobia head-on," Star Tribune, November 2, 2015, http://www.startribune.com/u-s-attorney-andrew-luger-minnesota-must-islamophobia-head-on/339642831/.

5. "Are Massachusetts, Michigan, and Minnesota Surrendering to the Jihadis?," Understanding the Threat blog, November 9, 2015, https://www.understandingthethreat.com/are-massachusetts-michigan-and-minnesota-surrendering-to-the-jihadis/.

6. Jackie Crosby, "Fired Muslim workers claim discrimination at plant in Owatonna," *Star Tribune*, April 27, 2016, http://www.startribune.com/fired-muslim-workers-claim-discrimination-at-plant-in-owatonna/377295741/.

7. Bruce Parker, "Lone alderman in on refugee secret 'stunned' at speed of decision," Vermont Watchdog, July 26, 2016, http://watchdog.org/271513/alderman-stunned-by-speed-of-refugee-resettlement-decision/.

8. Brian MacQuarrie, "Syrian refugees face pushback in Vt.," *Boston Globe*, July 13, 2016, https://www.bostonglobe.com/metro/2016/07/13/setback-for-plan-resettle-syrian-refugees-vermont/6GUlFdRVphaSMT9iQE8AvO/story.html.

CHAPTER 9: ROLLING OVER FOR ISLAM

1. Leo Hohmann, "U.S. city rolls over for radical mosque," WND, July 26, 2016, http://www.wnd.com/2016/07/u-s-city-rolls-over-for-radical-mosque/.

2. Ibid.

3. Ibid.

4. Nora Warikoo, "Muslims sue Sterling Heights after city rejected mosque," *Detroit Free Press*, August 11, 2016, http://www.freep.com/story/news/local/michigan/macomb/2016/08/10/muslims-sue-sterling-heights-mosque/88526616/.

5. Gus Burns, "Gov. Snyder taking note of Hamtramck's growing Bangladeshi immigrant population," M Live, November 5, 2015, http://www.mlive.com/news/detroit/index.ssf/2015/11/gov_snyder_taking_note_of_hamt.html.

6. "ISNA ACTION ALERT: Contact Michigan Governor Over His Remarks at ISNA Convention," Islamic Society of North America, September 2, 2014, http://www.isna.net/isna-action-alert-contact-michigan-governor-over-his-remarks-at-convention.html.

7. See http://refugeeresettlementmonitormichigan.org/.

8. See http://pamelageller.com/2015/11/german-teachers-union-warns-girls-to-stay-away-from-muslim-migrants.html/.

9. In an interview with the author on June 1, 2016.

10. Benjamin Weiser, "U.S. Unfairly Tying Imam to Terror Suspect, Lawyer Says," *New York Times*, March 6, 1999, http://www.nytimes.com/1999/03/06/nyregion/us-unfairly-tying-imam-to-terror-suspect-lawyer-says.html?_r=0.

11. Ibid.

12. Tresa Baldas, "Feds sue Pittsfield Twp. for shunning Islamic school plan," *Detroit Free Press*, October 26, 2015, http://www.freep.com/story/news/local/michigan/2015/10/26/feds-sue-pittsfield-twp-shunning-islamic-school-plan/74644268/.

13. See: http://www.wnd.com/2016/10/city-agrees-to-pay-mosque-1-7m-for-discriminatory-zoning-regs/.

CHAPTER 10: PIERCING THE SILENCE IN RURAL GEORGIA

1. Quotes in this section from a phone interview with Dami Arno on July 7, 2016.

2. Leo Hohmann, "Feds clear Muslim flag attacker of hate crime," WND, June 20, 2016, http://www.wnd.com/2016/06/fbi-decides-whether-muslim-flag-attack-was-hate-crime/.

3. Ibid.

CHAPTER 11: TRAGEDY AND COVER-UP IN IDAHO

1. The following story is taken from: Leo Hohmann, "Cops, Media Hide Idaho Girl's Sex Assault by Muslim Migrants," WND, June 20, 2016, http://www.wnd.com/2016/06/muslim-migrant-boys-accused-of-assaulting-idaho-girl-5/; Leo Hohmann, "Mom of Idaho Rape Victim: 'We're Being Treated as Criminals,'" WND, July 11, 2016, http://www.wnd.com/2016/07/mom-of-idaho-rape-victim-were-being-treated-as-criminals/; and from a phone interview with the victim's mother,

2. Hohmann, "Cops, Media Hide Idaho Girl's Sex Assault by Muslim Migrants."

3. Leo Hohmann, "5-year-old Idaho girl 'afraid to go out of her house' after sex assault," WND, June 28, 2016, http://www.wnd.com/2016/06/5-year-old-idaho-girl-afraid-to-go-out-of-her-house-after-sex-assault/.

4. Eugene Volokh, "Chief Idaho federal prosecutor warns: 'The spread of false information or inflammatory or threatening statements … may violate federal law'," Washington Post opinion, June 26, 2016, https://www.washingtonpost.com/news/volokh-conspiracy/wp/2016/06/26/chief-idaho-federal-prosecutor-warns-the-spread-of-false-information-or-inflammatory-or-threatening-statements-may-violate-federal-law/?utm_term=.f62b8c9e3c5e.

5. Meridith McGraw, "Department of Justice Will Go After Anti-Muslim Hate Speech," ABC News, December 4, 2015, http://abcnews.go.com/US/department-justice-anti-muslim-hate-speech/story?id=35585946.

6. "Feds won't prosecute matters of free speech in Twin Falls case," Idaho Statesman, June 28, 2016, http://www.idahostatesman.com/news/state/idaho/article86438952.html.

7. U.S. Department of Justice, "U.S. Attorney Wendy J. Olson Issues Statement on Building Resilient Communities," News Release, July 10, 2015, http://media.spokesman.com/documents/2015/07/olson-statement.pdf.

8. Ibid.

9. Ibid.

10. "Idaho jury convicts Uzbek refugee Fazliddin Kurbanov on terror charges," Associated Press, August 12, 2015, www.nydailynews.com/news/crime/idaho-jury-convicts-uzbek-refugee-terror-charges-article-1.2323902.

11. Kelly Riddell, "Feds' relocation of Somali refugees stresses Minn. welfare, raises terror fears," Washington Times, February 24, 2015, http://www.washingtontimes.com/news/2015/feb/24/islamist-terror-groups-target-minnesota-somali-ref/.

12. James Gordon Meek, Cindy Galli, and Brian Ross, "Exclusive: US May Have Let 'Dozens' of Terrorists Into Country As Refugees," ABC News, November 20, 2013, http://abcnews.go.com/Blotter/al-qaeda-kentucky-us-dozens-terrorists-country-refugees/story?id=20931131.

13. Judson Berger, "Anatomy of the terror threat: Files show hundreds of US plots, refugee connection," Fox News, June 22, 2016, http://www.foxnews.com/politics/2016/06/22/anatomy-terror-threat-files-shed-light-on-nature-extent-plots-in-us.html?intcmp=hpbt3.

14. Hohmann, "Cops, Media Hide Idaho Girl's Sex Assault by Muslim Migrants."

15. Leo Hohmann, "Syrian refugee assaults girl, 13, at Boston pool," WND, July 9, 2016, http://www.wnd.com/2016/07/syrian-refugee-assaults-girl-13-at-boston-pool/.

16. Ann Corcoran, "Phoenix: Four Liberian refugee boys ages 9-14 rape 8-year-old," Refugee Resettlement Watch, July 24, 2009, https://refugeeresettlementwatch.wordpress.com/2009/07/24/phoenix-four-liberian-refugee-boys-ages-9-14-rape-8-year-old/.

17. Kristin M. Kraemer, "Kennewick rape suspect flies to Dubai days before trial," Tri-City Harald, July 26, 2016, http://www.tri-cityherald.com/news/local/crime/article92031977.html.

18. Betsy Z. Russell, "False story on social media charges Syrian refugees raped Idaho girl," *Spokesman-Review*, June 20, 2016, http://www.spokesman.com/stories/2016/jun/20/false-story-on-social-media-charges-syrian-refugee/.

19. Nathan Brown, "Public Criticizes Council for Handling of Assault Allegations," Magic Valley, June 21, 2016, http://magicvalley.com/news/local/govt-and-politics/public-criticizes-council-for-handling-of-assault-allegations/article_2f3f9f76-a983-568f-896e-a90d8a74ea80.html.

20. Phone interview with the author on July 27, 2016.

CHAPTER 12: AMARILLO, TEXAS: A BRAVE MAYOR PUSHES BACK

1. Except as noted, the material in this section is taken from Leo Hohmann, "Texas City Where Cops Shot Walmart Hostage-Taker Flooded with Refugees," WND, June 15, 2016, http://www.wnd.com/2016/06/u-s-city-where-cops-shot-walmart-hostage-taker-flooded-with-refugees/.

2. Garrett Zamora, "What we know: Mohammad Moghaddam," CBS News Channel 10, June 15, 2016, http://www.newschannel10.com/story/32231913/what-we-know-mohammad-moghaddam.

3. Steven Graves, "Amarillo Mayor takes refugee concerns to state level," ABC News 7, April 27, 2016, http://abc7amarillo.com/news/local/amarillo-mayor-takes-refugee-concerns-to-state-level.

4. Ann Corcoran, "Breaking news! Spartanburg, SC Christians have run out of "vulnerable" Americans in need of help!" Refugee Resettlement Watch, May 25, 2016, https://refugeeresettlementwatch.wordpress.com/2016/05/25/breaking-news-spartanburg-sc-christians-have-run-out-of-vulnerable-americans-in-need-of-help/.

CHAPTER 14: HOW SHOULD WE RESPOND?

1. Denis Grasska, "Bishop Challenges Catholics to Combat Anti-Islamic Bigotry," AmericanCatholic.org, February 22, 2016, http://www.americancatholic.org/news/report.aspx?id=31702.

2. See http://www.investigativeproject.org/case/65/us-v-holy-land-foundation.

3. Grasska, "Bishop Challenges Catholics to Combat Anti-Islamic Bigotry."

4. Ibid.

5. Ibid.

6. Robert Spencer, "Bishop of San Diego challenges Catholics to combat 'anti-Islamic bigotry'," *Jihad Watch*, February 23, 2016, https://www.jihadwatch.org/2016/02/bishop-of-san-diego-challenges-catholics-to-combat-anti-islamic-bigotry.

7. See http://www.investigativeproject.org/document/20-an-explanatory-memorandum-on-the-general.

8. Robert Spencer, "Bishop of San Diego challenges Catholics to combat 'anti-Islamic bigotry'," *Jihad Watch*, February 23, 2016, https://www.jihadwatch.org/2016/02/bishop-of-san-diego-challenges-catholics-to-combat-anti-islamic-bigotry.

9. bid.

10. Philip Pullella, "Pope says it is wrong to equate Islam with violence," Reuters, November 30, 2014, http://www.reuters.com/article/us-pope-turkey-mideast-idUSKCN0JE0AD20141130.

11. Ibid.

12. "State Department spokeswoman floats jobs as answer to ISIS," Fox News, February 17, 2015, http://www.foxnews.com/politics/2015/02/17/state-department-spokeswoman-floats-jobs-as-answer-to-isis.html.

13. "Pope says Koran is a book of peace and Islam is a peaceful religion," *Daily Mail* video, http://www.dailymail.co.uk/video/news/video-1140549/Pope-says-Koran-book-peace-Islam-peaceful-religion.html.

14. Laura Mowat, "Christians ordered to keep faith quiet... by the Archbishop of Canterbury," *Express*, May 21, 2016, http://www.express.co.uk/news/uk/672579/Archbishop-of-Canterbury-orders-Christians-keep-faith-quiet.

15. Leo Hohmann, "Muslim group rallies Americans against 'Islamophobia'," WND, February 22, 2016, http://www.wnd.com/2016/02/muslim-group-rallies-americans-against-islamophobia/.

16. See *NEA Annual Report 1986*, p. 170, https://www.arts.gov/sites/default/files/NEA-Annual-Report-1986.pdf.

17. Coco Fusco, "Shooting the Klan: An Interview with Andres Serrano," *High Performance Magazine*, Fall 1991, archived at Community Arts Network Reading Room, https://web.archive.org/web/20090913054209/http://www.communityarts.net:80/readingroom/archivefiles/2002/09/shooting_the_kl.php.

18. Art Moore, "Did CAIR founder say Islam to rule America?" WND, December 11, 2006, http://www.wnd.com/2006/12/39229/.

19. "Block Donald J Trump from UK entry," Petitions UK Government and Parliament, https://petition.parliament.uk/petitions/114003.

20. Robert Spencer, "UK: Muslim judge convicts Christian preacher of hate speech," *Jihad Watch*, March 30, 2015, https://www.jihadwatch.org/2015/03/uk-muslim-judge-convicts-christian-preacher-of-hate-speech.

21. Libby Brooks, "Man arrested for Facebook posts about Syrian refugees in Scotland," *Guardian*, February 16, 2016, https://www.theguardian.com/uk-news/2016/feb/16/man-arrested-facebook-posts-syrian-refugees-scotland.

22. John Guandolo, "Islamic Law of Slander the Continued Destruction of Free Speech," Counter Jihad Report, February 24, 2016, https://counterjihadreport.com/2016/02/24/islamic-law-of-slander-the-continued-destruction-of-free-speech/.

23. Leo Hohmann, "Facebook helping Germany crack down on anti-Islam speech," WND, July 14, 2016, http://www.wnd.com/2016/07/facebook-helping-germany-crack-down-on-anti-islam-speech/.

24. "Muslim Brotherhood," Discover the Networks.org, http://www.discoverthenetworks.org/groupProfile.asp?grpid=6386.

25. D'vera Cohn and Andrea Caumont, "10 demographic trends that are shaping the U.S. and the world, Pew Research Center, March 31, 2016, http://www.pewresearch.org/fact-tank/2016/03/31/10-demographic-trends-that-are-shaping-the-u-s-and-the-world/.

26. Ann Naffzinger, "Why Does Jesus Say He Came to Divide?" September 4, 2013, http://bustedhalo.com/questionbox/why-does-jesus-talk-about-coming-to-divide-the-world.

27. "ISIS in America! Shocking! SEE the TRUTH!" https://www.youtube.com/watch?v=gQ96KHoYt6s.

28. https://counterjihadreport.com/tag/james-comey/.

INDEX